WOMEN'S PROPERTY RIGHTS IN INDIA

WOMEN'S PROPERTY RIGHTS IN INDIA

(With Latest Amendment and Cases)

Dr. Urusa Mohsin

KALPAZ

Women's Property Rights in India

Rs. 750

ISBN: 978-81-7835-790-4

Published in 2010 in India by
Kalpaz Publications
C-30, Satyawati Nagar,
Delhi-110052
E-mail: kalpaz@hotmail.com
Phone : 9212729499

Lasser Type Setting by: Quick Media, Delhi
Printed at : Gian Ridhi Offset Printers, Delhi

Dedicated
to my
beloved
brothers

Contents

Preface

Deprived, destitute, desolated, discriminated, despaired and deserted etc. are the other names of a woman. On one front she is loved, respected, even worshipped and placed at the highest social status but on the other she is humiliated, illtreated, brutalized and put to contempt. The reason for all these torture is monetary dependence and economic inequality.

Man and woman are supposed to be the two halves of the society and neither can reach its highest creative excellence without the cooperation of other. Even then blatant injustice is being perpetrated on them since ages. Though we have stepped in the new millenium, the status of woman has not improved due to the traditional biases and prejudices towards that segment of the society, which were segregated from main stream for no fault of their own.

The discrimination stems not from legislative in sufficiency but from the attitudinal biases of the society. Time to time material and substantial modifications have been done in laws, which brought radical changes including recent enactments that spell about woman's dignity and equality as a global norm. Inspite of all these, the discrimination in respect of property rights along with many others still continues and till now the women possess only one percent of immovable property in their own name.

Today women are storming most male bastions and proving themselves equal in every walk of life. Though she might be found wanting when it comes to using brute force of the savage kind. She is better endowed with the gift of civilization. There is no reason why a woman should be dominated simply for being a woman.

I would like to utilize this opportunity while writing the preface of this work that substantial and fundamental changes have been brought in the Hindu Succession Act 1956 after the completion of this work. It seems that my thoughts have been caught by the wisdom of the legislature and translated in the body of the Hindu Succession (Amendment) Act 2005. Sub Section (2) of section 4 of the Act has been deleted. Section 6 has been substituted by new provisions. The right of daughter as a coparcener has been recognized. Section 23 and 24 of the Principal Act has also been omitted. Section 30 of the Act has been amended by including females within the section with full rights of testamentary disposition of property capable of being disposed off. The schedule has been amended by bringing in certain specified heirs in class I. The changes affected fundamentals and the old law stood abrogated and substantially altered. A diligent effort has been made to incorporate the provisions of the amending Act and its effect at appropriate place in this work, with new cases upto 2009.

It is solely and exclusively due to the showering mercy of Almighty Allah (SWT) who is most benevolent, merciful, omnipotent, omnipresent and omniscient that I have been able to complete this work.

I owe my heartiest gratitude to Prof. Akhlaq Ahmad, Dean and Chairman, Department of Law, A.M.U. Aligarh for his inspiring attitude and constant encouragement to complete this study.

It is not difficult but impossible to give expression in the words to the feelings of respect, sense of gratitude, indebtness devotion and admiration towards a teacher. Despite of his busy schedule he has given ample time to evaluate critically the whole work and made it possible to complete the work in time. Yet it gives me immense pleasure to express my profound gratitude and sincere thanks to my learned teacher and supervisor Prof. (Dr.) Iqbal Ali Khan for his unparallel guidance, inspiring attitude and constant encouragement throughout the course of study.

I navigate my deep sense of gratitude towards Prof. Saleem Akhtar, Prof. Mohammad Shabbir, Prof. Nazeer Hasan Khan, Prof. Faizan Mustafa and all my learned teachers of the Department of Law, A.M.U. Aligarh and L.U. Lucknow for their guidance, co-operation, motivation and constructive advice to concentrate on quality and originality of research work.

I salute and venerate to my (late) parents. I extend my sense of elevation to all my kith and kin specially my brothers and sister whose love and benediction fill the vaccum of parental love.

I am proud of having very sincere and devoted friends, seniors and juniors who have co-operated me at every stage to complete this work. From the kernal of my heart, I am thankful to my hostel mates also.

I am also beholden to the staff members of the Law seminar and office bearers of A.M.U. Aligarh, L.U. Lucknow and the staff of the Nadwatul Ulema for their assistance and help rendered to me.

My pleasant duty has made to express my sense of gratitude to all those who have directly and indirectly inspired and prompted me to undertake this difficult task. I extend my sense of elation to all those who have contributed in my elevation to the status of writing this book.

Last but not least, my special thanks to my typist Mr. Mohd Yaseen Khan for typing my book with care, devotion and diligence.

Urusa Mohsin

Abbreviations

- AA — All India Reporter Allahabad
- AB — All India Reporter Bombay
- AC — All India Reporter Calcutta
- AD — Appellate Division (South Africa)
- AFC — All India Reporter Federal Court
- AJ&K — All India Reporter Jammu & Kashmir
- AIR — All India Reporter
- All — Allahabad (Indian Law Report) Series
- All LJ — Allahabad Law Journal
- ALJ — Aligarh Law Journal
- IAHC — All India High Court
- An. WR — Andhra Pradesh Weekly Reporter
- AC — Appeal Cases
- AP LJ — Andhra Pradesh Law Journal
- APC — All India Reporter, Privy Council
- ASC — All India Reporter Supreme Court
- ALR — American Law Reporter
- BLR — Bengal Law Reporter
- Bom LR — Bombay Law Reporter
- BC — Before Christ
- BHCR — Bombay High Court Reports
- C — Consanguine
- Cal — Calcutta
- Cal LJ — Calcutta Law Journal
- Cl — Clause

- ChD Chancery Division
- CED Convention on Elimination of All Forms of Discrimination Against Women
- CLJ Cambridge Law Journal
- CIT Commissioner of Income Tax
- CriLJ Criminal Law Journal
- Cal WN Calcutta Weekly Notes
- CLT Cuttack Law Times
- D Daughter
- DK Distant Kindred
- Dec, December
- ed. Edition
- eg. Exempli gratia
- etc. Etcetera
- F Father
- FF Father's father
- FFF Father's father's father
- FM Father's mother
- FAD Female Agnatic descendants
- FN Footnote
- FFM Father's father's mother
- FCR Federal Court Report
- FB Full Bench
- Guj Gujrat
- GPF General Provident Fund
- GM General Manager
- Gau Gauhati
- Gen General
- HC High Court
- HL Hindu Law
- HLC Hindu Law Court

- HSA Hindu Succession Act
- HP Himachal Pradesh
- HT Hindustan Times
- H Husband
- HHS How High Soever
- HLS How Low Soever
- H Hijri
- HL House of Lords
- IA Indian Appeals
- IC Indian Cases
- Illus Illustration
- IMLJ Indian Muslim Law Journal
- ILJ Indian Law Journal
- ILR Indian Law Report
- ISA Indian Succession Act
- Jhar Jharkhand
- J & K Jammu and Kashmir
- Karn Karnataka
- Ker Kerala
- Ker LT Kerala Law Times
- Ker LJ Kerala Law Journal
- KB King Bench
- Ltd Limited
- LR Law Reporter
- LJ Law Journal
- Lah Lahore
- Luck Lucknow
- LW Law Weekly
- M Mother
- Mad Madras
- Md Mohammad

- Mohd Mohammad
- MLJ Muslim Law Journal
- MP Madhya Pradesh
- Mys Mysore
- MPL Muslim Personal Law
- Mad LW Madras Law Weekly
- Mah LJ Maharashtra Law Journal
- MM Mother's Mother
- MAD Male Agnatic Descendants
- MA Male Agnate
- MMM Mother's mother's mother
- MMF Mother's mother's father
- MFM Mother's father's mother
- Moo IA Moore's Indian Appeal
- MIA Moore's Indian Appeal
- MHC Madras High Court
- MLJ Madras Law Journal
- Nag Nagpur
- No Number
- NOC Notes on Cases
- Ori Orrissa
- P Page
- PC Privy Council
- Pesh Peshawar
- Punj Punjab
- Pat Patna
- Pvt Private Limited
- P & H Punjab and Haryana
- Pubh Peace be upon him
- PUBH Peace Be Upon him
- Pat. LJ Patna Law Journal

- PLR Punjab Law Report
- PD Probade Division
- Res Residuary
- Raj LW Rajasthan Law Weekly
- Rang Indian Law Reports Rangoon Series
- Raj Rajasthan
- Re In the matter of
- RA Rahmatullah Alaih
- Rang Rangoon
- Supra Above
- SCR Supreme Court Report
- SCWR Supreme Court Weekly Report
- SAW Sallullaho Alaih Wassallam
- S Son
- S'S Son's son
- S'S'S Son's son's son
- S'D Son's Daughter
- SCC Supreme Court Cases
- SC Supreme Court
- Sec Section
- SWT Subhanaho Wa Tala
- Trav C Indian Law Report, Travancore Cochin Series
- Tr GM True Grand Mother
- Tr GF True Grand Father
- UP Uttar Pradesh
- U Utcrinc
- US Uterine Sister
- UB Uterine Brother
- Vol Volume
- V Verses
- WR Weekly Report

Table of Cases

193. Land Board v Cyriac Thomas AIR (2000) SC 3161 — 269
194. Laxmappa v Batawa K.T. Chavdi AIR (1996) SC 3439 — 251
195. Laxmi Kantha v Vijay Laxmi AIR (2004) Ker 295 — 128
196. Laxmi N. Judu v Basti Mahajan AIR (2004) Jhar 121 — 99
197. Lechho Devi v Balbhadra RA (1998) AIHC 3696 — 252
198. M. Khazir Bhatv Ahmad Dar AIR (1960) J&K 57 — 84
199. M/S Piyare Lal Adishwar v Income Tax Commissioner AIR (1968) SC 678 — 67
200. Ma Bi v Ma Khatun AIR (1930) Rang 72 — 84
201. Ma Khun v Ma Ahma 12 Rang 184 — 158,164
202. Madhu Kishwar v State of Bihar (1999) 5SCC125 — 255
203. Maharashtra v Narayan Rao AIR(1985)SC716 — 112
204. Mahesh Kumar Patil v Mahesh Kumar Vyas (2000) AIHC 485 — 134
205. Maimuna Bibi v A. Khawaja Mohiuddin (1970) IMLJ 266, AIR (1970) Mad 201 — 83,256
206. Manjamma v State of Karnataka (1999) AIHC 2003 Kar — 115
207. Mallapa v Shivappa (1962) Mys 140 — 132
208. Mancherji v Mithibai 1 Bom 349 — 271
209. Mangal Singh v Smt. Ratno AIR (1967) SC 178 — 125,247
210. Manjunath Gowda v CED(1977)1 OSCC684 — 109
211. Mannikyamma v Venkta Subba Rao (1978) 2 ANWR 18 — 130
212. Maqsood Begum v Shanawaz Khan AIR (1991) J&K 8 — 240
213. Mary Roy v State of Kerala (1986) 2 SCC 209 — 269
214. Masilamani Mudaliar v Idol of Sri Swaminathsswami, AIR (1996) SC 1697 — 251
215. Mathew Jacob v Selestine Jacobs AIR (1998) Del 370 — 268
216. Mazirannessa Bibi v Khondakar Golam Kibria AIR (1970) Cal 387 — 248
217. Md. Abdul Rahim v Abdul Hakim AIR (1921) Cal 653 — 84
218. Md. Hussain v Krishwa Nadan 64,1-A, 250 — 66
219. Md. Lbrahim v Shaik lbrahim AIR (1922) PC 59 — 233
220. Md. Jafar Bindaneem v Kulsoom Bibi 24 IA 196 — 230
221. Md. Kaden v Ludden ILR 14 Cal 276-286-7 — 230

1

Introduction

An Overview

Gender bias discrimination is a global phenomenon. Today the greatest challenge, before the world, is that of gender justice. There is not a single gender just society neither in advanced Western World nor in traditional Asian and African societies. At present we stand at he remnant of the 21st Century but we are still unable to boast of, a society where there is total gender equality.

Woman, the most disadvantaged group of human species, is a architect of civilization, a nucleus of the family, a protector of the house, an inspiration and strength of man on every front, who shaped the destiny of human race. She has proved that she is not frail, fragile and delicate, though physically weak yet spiritually strong who raised Prophet and Pharoah. It is the woman to whom the Creator has empowered to transform the man into the desired mould through the influence of her motherhood. A powerful generation is impossible without the powerful women. It is a stigma and a stain for the entire human race if woman is compelled to remind society for her rights. Social democracy, for its full strength, requires the women empowerment, social and economic both. The discriminatory status of woman is constantly lamentable and produces unsatisfactory results. No development is possible unless and until the woman's rights are protected.

Prof. Harold. J. Laski observed, "Rights are those conditions of social life without which no man can seek in general, to be himself at his best."

For the emancipation of women, the economic independence is of a reverence importance. If misfotune strikes the women are most vulnerable. It also makes prominent gender gaps. If the female headed families suffer with the lack of sufficient means to afford the education of both the daughter and sons, it is the daughter who has to sacrifice her studies, that makes her limping to the chance of employment outside the agriculture and cripple her to access the land in rural areas especially. Sometimes she is prevented to inherit the property in the name of customs, family honor, welfare and social prestige. She is given only 20% of share in her husband and parents property. Alongwith economic independence the total development of women is needed special consideration by making equilibrium between their rights and responsibilities. The secret polygamy, utter illiteracy, occupational disproportion and economic denigration are the ground realities of today. Domestic injustice and body violence are escalating day by day. The nuptial thread is also no longer as strong as it was till the recent past and the rate of divorce is increasing.

When the woman is desolated, despaired, desperate and deserted, the first question which comes in the mind of destitute female, is that—what option left for her? There is luminous literature available on the offences against women, the law relating to dowry and other matrimonial disputes but very little attention is given towards the property rights of women. At ancient time the woman was devoid of any property right in any legal system except in Islam. In Hindu legal system some property rights, subject to certain restrictions, had been given to her in the name of Stridhana. In West there was no concept of property right of females. The rights, which were attributed to females, were also very discriminatory. With the heralding of new millennium, the problem of women's property right stands as one of the most important challenge.

The discrimination is the fate of women since the incipient of civilization to the present day, all over the world. The women, who constitute the world's half population, are the subject of male chauvinism and treated as a second-class citizen. From cradle to grave they are meek to the unfair social custom and gender prejudices. The basic cause of this degraded status of female is chiefly attributed to the factors shaping the traditional society.

Freedom, for which nations clashed, wars were waged, peace was sought and forsaken, is men's inner urge and call. It is the life and blood of society. The freedom, especially when it relates to women, is the given freedom from the imposed instructions of men. From the dawn of civilization the women suffer from submissiveness and the fight for equality and freedom, continue-till the date. Despite her lofty role in the world affairs, her status changed little with changing times and claims. Her misuse continues at every place and at every time. Chinese believed that :

> *"Eighteen goddess like daughters are not equal to one son with a hump."*[1]

> Jews daily prayer is, *"blessed, art thou Lord that thou has not made me a woman."*[2]

The Christian philosopher Malleus Maleficarum in the Holy Book termed woman as, *"imperfect animal, naturally fickle deceivers who in the lust of flesh, were easily led by the devil in becoming witches."*[3] Bible too is the product of patriarchal society which states, *"wives submit yourselves onto your husband* as *unto the Lord."*[4] Sir Bernard Shaw called her face *'the burning wind'*, and her voice *'the hissing of snakes.'* The Hindu scholar Chanakya says, *"telling* a *lie, acting without thinking and foolishness are the defects lies in woman, you can learn manners from princess, politeness from scholars, falsehood from gambler and wickedness from woman."* Islam, which is considered as the torchbearer in such darkness also, placed the husband next to God. She was always as an evil temptress.

However, these old adages appear to be losing its significance and the above scenario are being changed though slowly and not absolutely. Steps are being taken to promote education among female and also for the empowerment of women socially and politically. It is a welcome gesture. But it will take time for the male dominated society to submit to the female mutiny.

The feminist movement started from the first United Nation's World Conference on Women held in Mexico in 1975. Harold Coffin said, *"remember when feminist movement were something, men gathered on street corners to admire the girls strolled by."* The international recognition of the women's problems all over the world resulted as the women's decade from 1975-1985. The publication of the report of the National Committee, on the status of women in 1975, stressed that despite constitutional guarantees—roles, rights and participations of women in almost all spheres of life, were limited. In fact the various conferences and seminars were indicative of the growing awareness of the plight of women all over the world. The International women decade came to an end in 1985, with the birth of witnessing a series of conferences, seminars, actions, programmes, emergence of women's organizations and women's movements against atrocities meted out to them in all stages and areas of their life. A wide spread awareness about women's life, conditions, problems and issues faced by them has been noticed recently in almost all corners of the globe. The Beijing Conference held in China in 1995, also high-lighted the problems with special reference to domestic violence and gender injustices.

Among all these international instruments the CEDAW acquired importance in the Indian sub-continent along with many other countries. It is considered as the Magna Carta for the rights of women. The discrimination is defined in this convention as :

> "...any *distinction, exclusion or restriction made on the basis of* sex *which has the effect or purpose of impairing or nullifying the ecognition, enjoyment or exercise by women, irrespective of their marital status, on a basis of equality of men and women, of human rights and fundamental freedom in the political, economic, social, cultural, civil or any other field."*

This convention provides the basis to undertake effective measures to equalize men and women in every walk of life by giving equal opportunities in, economic, political and public life. By abolishing all discriminatory laws, all forms of traffic in women and exploitation of women, this convention affirms the reproductive rights of women and targets culture and tradition as influential forces, which shaped gender roles and family relation.

The Convention, on Elimination of all forms of Discrimination Against Women (CEDAW), 1979, is the main foundation of the rights of women, which recognized the discrimination against them, which in turn hampers economic growth and affects the society at large.

Countries that have ratified or acceded to the convention are legally bound to put its provisions into practice. The signatory countries are consigned to present national reports at every four years, about the steps they have taken to comply with their treaty obligations. India is also among them.

The large part of the world society present woman as the weaker sex. On the lack of equal opportunities in every field, the possibilities of women competing on an equal stage with men are naturally bleak. According to one report of United Nations Organization, 1980, *"Women contribute 2/3 of total working hours, still they earn only 1/10 of the world's income and possess only 1% of immovable property in their name."*[5]

Gender inequality exists in different form but the most harmful one is in the field of property rights. The women, in every religion and legal system, are now discriminated to inherit the property only on the basis of sex.

There is no such difference as visualized by the society between the male and female. They all are human beings. It is only a recognition or division of the work and role. No one is superior over the other.

The difference is only genetic, ethical and physical as two brothers are not identical. The difference and discrimination are not synonymous. Difference is a natural phenomenon but discrimination is a conduct, which is done intentionally or unintentionally. To do discrimination between two human beings is a sin. The women suffered a lot of discrimination from the time of sex determination to the Sati leap. Some time she is worshipped as '*Devi*' and some time she is treated as '*Dasi*' but never be considered as a human being.

About the feminist movement Justice Krishna Iyer rightly, pointed out *"the fight is not for women's status but for human worth. The claim is not to end inequality of women but to restore universal justice."*

Umesh C Benerji J said, *"Manifest injustice is curable in nature rather than incurable."*[6]

To ensure the dignity of human being, envisaged in the contemporary world to the other half or better half, it is necessary to bring qualitative changes in their situation. Their personal dignity is trivialized. The question of women's dignity and rights has to include wider issues.

In ancient time the women were not having any property right in any part of the world except in Islam. These economic rights were non-existent and their fate was wholly depended upon the sweet will of their husband, father and guardian. Because of the financial security, man thought that they could subject her to abject humiliation. Property always plays a vital role in the life of individual, community and country. The protagonists of social contract theory of State, Hobbes, Locke and Rousseau also admired the importance of property. The practical significance of the property lies in the fact, that it enables us to solve the problem of poverty and to give at least the necessaries of the life, if not the means of comfort.

There is a glut of International Conventions, starting with the Declaration of Human Rights in, 1945, followed by the United Nations Declaration, 1948, Rome Convention for Protection of Human Rights and Fundamental Freedoms 1950 and it's protocol in, 1952. European Social Charter, 1961, American Convention on Human Rights, 1969, International Convention on Civil, Political and Economic Rights, 1976. The Convention on Elimination of all Forms of Discrimination Against Women, 1979, African Charter on Human and Peoples Rights 1981 and Vienna Declaration and Programme of Action 1993, all contain yardsticks of gender equality. These resolutions, declarations and platform of action to wipe out the in justice and inhibitions of a misogynic malignancy remained dormant because of the absence of enforcing agencies for these International laws. Indeed every statutory remedy enacted or executive policy proclaimed, remains a remedy that aggravates the malady. It is also that law cannot go in alone, courts cannot cure or correct by heavy punishment and profound pronouncement the masculine culpability. The feminist movement cannot be successful unless the men themselves come forward to join hands with them. Participation, of both men and women, is equally important to make the society a better place.

The property rights of the females are still discriminatory, inspite of the plethora of International Conventions and Declaration in support of property rights of women. The UNO stands at the apex seat, in its commitment to protect the women's property right world over. The females of Muslims,

Hindus, Christians and Parsis all are the victims of this discrimination of property right in some or the other form. In ancient time there was no concept of women's inheritance, she was not considered as an heir and competent to inherit the property. Islam is, perhaps, the first religion, which entitles females to inherit the property whether she is a mother, sister, daughter, grand-mother, or widow.

The law of inheritance is an important subject to be considered not only because it ensures the future security of woman both married and spinster but also because it may lead to social tragedies in accordance to system adopted. It is also, more or less, a subject of controversy on the point that the woman has been devoid of her equal rights with man in the matter of inheritance. Although such conflicts at present are between the traditionalist and reformers and rather than technical and legal.

Indian Scenario

Before the annexation of British regime the major laws of inheritance in India had either their roots in their respective religion or were deeply influenced by personal laws, owing their allegiance to religion. The religious based distinction of the personal laws is evident and accepted fact. These laws are zealously guarded, fiercely protected and justified by various religious communities. The notable feature of these laws was that they were unanimous in relegating women to background with respect to inheritance. There was uniformity in their general preference of agnates over cognates and in conferment of superior rights to males in comparison to their female peers. Under the grab of religious injunctions and customs, the custodians of these laws, many times denied them the inheritance rights totally where they indeed had some rights.

The discrimination against women and consequently the inferior status conferred on them and a tendentious attitudes of the superiority of males, are some of the factors that stand out even after a bare reading.

The contact of Islamic law with India is almost a millennium old. It started with the Arab conquest of the Sindh in the beginning of the 18th Century. Both Hinduism & Islam represent two varieties of traditional worldviews. The pattern of cultural syncretism between Hinduism and Islam are significant social movement. The process, of the development of the Islam in India, has been evolved through three stages. These stages were set by the historical forces and greatly influenced the structure of its tradition. The first stage relates to the duration of the Islamic law in India, second stage was initiated after the establishment of the British domination and finally the third stage was marked at the beginning of the Indian freedom movement, leading to the countries political independence. Islamic law, which is a body of rules, gives practical expression to the religious faith and aspiration of the Muslim. It does not leave the world to the whim and caprice of an individual or the group of persons neither in economic nor in any other field of culture. Islamic law has brought many sound changes in socio-economic status of males and females, providing standard of behaviour for the believers in every field of life. Islam enforced its followers to remove pain, destitution, social and economic disabilities from the lives of the woman by granting them a status equal to men in their respective spheres.

The edifice of a splendid legal system of Islam is based on the injunctions of the Holy Quran and the urges of the Prophet (PBUH). It provides minute details of the rights, duties and privileges of human being. It has awarded a graceful image to the woman and placed them at high platform at the time when the females of the world had no identity of their own. From the historical point of view there is an interesting phenomenon of growth of Islamic law.

Islamic law of inheritance is a misunderstood subject all over the world though it is supposed to be one of the most perfect laws obtainable in the juristic era. It is portrayed globally as a means of persuasion, torture, abnegation and oppression in the hand of callous, egoistical, tyrannical and often uneducated Muslim males, especially the matters related to females. It is visualized that Muslim women is the most miserable creature of the world. This caricature of the Islam has polluted the mind of even the right thinking people of the society.

Actually there is a great deal of diversity in the manner in which Islam is practiced and perceived. Many times these practices go against the basic tenets or grains of Islam. The Islamic law relating to women has passed through different channels of development. Law, culture, traditions, attitudes and government policies are the determining factors of the status of women in society. The status of Indian women has also undergone various transformations under the various foreign colonizers who brought their institutions and legislations to India. Before the Britishers came in India, the Indian females were enjoying high social standard.

In regard to the status of women in England, which could be true to the other countries in the West, Mrs. Ray Strachey said, *"this favourite was denied every civil right, was shut out from education and from all but lowest form of wage earner and has to surrender her property and herself to her husband."*[7]

The trend of giving preference to the anti-women customs and usages was started from British period and continued till today, even after the 58 years of independence. The most shameful thing is that they got the seal of judiciary over it, inspite of the fact that all these are very much repugnant to the principles of Islam. Even in Muslim dominated states these anti-woman customs still exist such as *pisare-e-parwarda,' 'khana-e-damad'* and *'dukhtar-e-khana nashin',* etc. in Jammu and Kashmir. Time and again voices were raised by different women's organizations and right thinking people of different communities against these unjust, illogical and anti-women policies of the Government. As a result the British Government took different legislative actions and so many territorial enactments were passed such as Coach Behars Muhammadan Inheritance Act, 1897, the Moplah Succession and Wills Act 1918-1928, the Cutchi Memon Succession Acts of 1928 -1938 and the Shariat Application Act, 1935. But the peoples were not satisfied. A movement *'Ghasab-ul-Mirath'* was launched all over India, which was resulted in the formulation of the Muslim Personal Law Shariat Application Act 1937. Under section (2) of this Act, certain provisions were made governing the law of inheritance.

Section (2) of the Act, 1937, talks about the special property of females. It includes all the property inherited or obtained under contract or gift or any other provision of personal law. In Islamic law there is no concept of different kinds of property.

The Act, of 1937 has been excluded from its application the succession of an agricultural land, because that is the subject of the state laws. Different state's laws[8] excluded the females from inheriting the agricultural land as section 171 of the Uttar Pradesh Zamindari Abolition and Land Reform Act, 1950 leaned towards the male agnates. Tamil Nadu, Andhra Pradesh and Kerala had made an amendment in the Shariat Act, 1937 after independece and made the agricultural land also the subject of Shariat Act, 1937. But in other States it still prevails which keeps the women away from the landed property.

Application of the Shariat Act, 1937, on the inheritance and Wills to the Muslims in suppression of the anti-women's customary practices and usages, had been a major legal issue in India since the days of British regime. Much hue and cry was made. Instead, in Malabar after the enactment of Shariat Act, 1937, law was enacted to protect the custom of matriarchal succession among certain sections of Moplah Muslims and the validity has been affirmed in some judicial pronouncement after the Independence, though for Hindus it was abolished in 1975, in Kerala.

The ceiling laws, generally, treat husband and wife as a single entity, which is against the Islamic law. Under Islamic law the girl on marriage does not merge her personality in that of husband, instead she retains her personality individually with full proprietary rights. To avoid, the Government Escheat of excess land under Ceiling Laws Acts Muslim women claimed some fake divorces.[9]

In 1939, the Dissolution of Muslim Marriage Act, 1939, gave absolute proprietary rights to Muslim women, which were already possessed by a Muslim female in the Austinian sense from the advent of Islam. On the other hand it has gone a step ahead in favoring the female, which was contrary to Islamic law that the husband interference in the proprietary right of wife be a ground for the obtaining of divorce.[10]

The local legal culture had also not spared even the tribal woman. In every tribal society the women are generally looked up with great respect but they do not have the right to inherit the property. Only form of security that was assured in traditional tribal society was that the village council used to take care of them at the point of distress.

The Hindu law is as old as the Indian civilization and traces the rules, which are found in the Vedic literature of about 1500 BC. The fundamental rules of law and their spiritual supports are available in texts, which are usually dated between 500 BC and AD 200. Exact chronology is defied by the traditional materials, which had so long a working life.[11]

In the field of property right, as the Indian culture developed because of the patriarchal system, only male agnates have the right to hold and to inherit the property. The concept of women's property existed only in the form of Stridhana which was very complicated and subject to certain restrictions.

The Hindu Law of Inheritance was based on the patrilineal system. The instrument of patriarchy has been, the denial of property rights to woman. The gradual growth of property law continued to be complex and discriminatory against women. The earliest Act, which is the first step in connection, was the Married Women's Right to Property Act, 1856, that gave some relief to married women to earn and to hold property. But the benefit of this Act was not fruitful for the Hindu and Muslim female because of the non-interference policy of the Britishers. Some other Acts which gave some relief to the females were the Caste Disabilities Removal Act, 1850, Hindu Widows Remarriage Act, 1856, Hindu Law of Inheritance Act, 1928, its Amendment Act, 1929, Hindu Women's Right to Property Act, 1937, and most vigourous step was taken in 1956, by the passing of the Hindu Succession Act, 1956. Recently, an amendment has been made (The Hindu Succession Amendment Act, 2005) which has, to a great extent, ameliorated the economic position of daughters by making them a coparcener.

It seems that the nineteenth century, in the Hindu Women's World is a piecemeal, in which many reforms were brought not only in economic sphere but also in improving their social status that removed certain deep rooted evils such as Sati Pratha, temple prostitution, child marriage, polygamy, polyandry, lack of inheritance, remarriage of widows and female infanticide etc. So many legislative steps have been taken to do away these evils.

No doubt Hindu Succession Act, 1956, was the most revolutionary effort but the latest step taken by the legislature in 2005, seems to be more effective attempt for women empowerment which removed almost all the defects and drawbacks of the previous Act of 1956 and equalize the females to the male heirs in every respect.

In England the married women had no right to own and to appropriate the property independently and was subject to the restriction of her husband. The law was very discriminatory and the married women were economically dependent to their husband. In 1882 the Married Women's Right to Property Law was passed which enabled the married women to own and to inherit the property. The Act was passed because of the pressure, which was made upon the British Parliament to remove the injustice after the famous case of Caroline Norton.

Practical Significance of Different Acts

There is always a gap between policies, ideologies and its implementation. The sanctifying role of the judiciary is crucial in the process of the upliftment of the social, economic and legal status of women since time immemorial. The best laws can be rendered meaningless by an ineffective implementation of the justice delivery system.

It seems that Indian legislature is fully committed to ameliorate the status of women and conscious about the need to protect the interest of women and to give them equal status to their counterpart men. The Indian women do not suffer from legal disparities but they suffer from practical disparities because the enforcement of the legislative policies generally remains neglected.

The Hindu women in the country despite the revolutionary provisions of the Hindu Succession Act of 1956 remain generally deprived of property right. In reality it has been a mere legislative showpiece. Though the Act brought revolutionary changes which have been more often ignored by the family members in actual practice because the provisions goes against the established Hindu social ethos.

Generally, there is no proof that a woman actually inherits. The court's function ends with the definition and interpretations of the rights in the estate under the relevant laws. Mostly the matter of succession is settled out of the court and without woman inheriting at all. To prevent the family property, within the control of family, females are generally persuaded not to claim their share. The system of kinship relations in traditional society is so vital to the protection and security of women that they are willing to renounce property right for its sake[12]. Some time the women transfer their share in the estate by sale deed without consideration, or gifted out of natural love to brothers, or other male member of the family. The unmarried girl who lived with her brothers and was supported by them renounced her share in favour of her germane brothers. In many cases the females are pressurized to make a will in favour of male relatives to avoid the family's considerable fortune being fragmented by intestate succession.

The statutory laws on women's property rights are of course intact and enforce, but the actual practice in the society, however presents a different picture. Before 2005, several legislative steps had been taken such as Hindu Succession Act and Dowry Prohibition Act with all their successive amendments, but these Acts remain paper tiger with no teeth. These Acts are better known through their blatant violations rather than for a faithful complicance with their provisions.

Another Legislative Step (The Amendment Act 2005)

After fifty-eight years of independence, the 5th September 2005 will be remembered as a red-letter day in the era of Hindu women's world. The recent initiative in amending the Hindu Succession (Amendment) Act, 2005 is a landmark event for the cause of women's equality, a lucid Act which has brought a light in the darkness and erodes all the discriminatory provisions of the Act of 1956, such as sections 6, 23, 24, and 30. It gives absolute and equal rights of inheritance to females. The Act of 2005 covers, inequalities on ancestral property, dwelling house, widows rights and also protect the interest of some new heirs by inserting them in the list of I Class heirs.

It is a step further to the cause of social justice for women. The Act is passed on the recommendations of the 174th report of the Law Commission on, *"Property Rights of Women Proposed Reform Under the Hindu Law"*. It really gives a deathblow to the old Hindu Law where females were made devoid of any property rights. This Act is welcomed by the Hindu women's world. Now the Hindu daughter of Mitakshara joint family will also born with a silver spoon in her mouth. She will possess all the rights, which her male counterpart has. But simultaneously she is also burdened with same liabilities as a male in respect of coparcenary property. Under the provisions of an Amendment Act, 2005 she is entitled to claim partition in the dwelling house. The bar, which disentitled the widow to inherit the property of her husband on remarriage, has also been abolished.

These amendments will have far reaching consequences for the emancipation of Hindu females if got practical significance. By making women coparcener in the joint family property the Act has given them great importance in the family. Now the women become the 'Karta' of the family and will got same importance as the males have. Unfortunately if divorce, took place the girl can return to their home by right.

How much temptous and alluring this Act seems to be but the time will say how it really proved in eradication of discrimination. In reality, there is a visible gap between the law as it stands and the law as it operates. It is regularly impaired by incidents of overwhelming discrimination. All these are theoretically, very laudable efforts but the difficulty lies not in recognition of the women's property rights but trying to enforce them. On the scale of socialistic approach, the actual practice shall face many problems in the context of people's orthodoxness and ancient cultural attitude. As the conceptualization of the law is grounded in society so let act the lofty guarantees in our constitution or the generous endowments in our enactments deceive us for a moment or detract from the reality that we are in society which has institutionalized acceptance of social hierarchy, where men have control over women, where woman have internalized lower gender status as personal failure, where violence against women is considered to be a personal harm rather than a social injury.[13]

The women's emancipation is still a distant dream. Nothing is fair when it comes to the talk of fairer sex. On the whole though law of inheritance is gradually changing yet women are not at much comfort.

Hypothesis

The prime object, of the present study, is to critically evaluate the statutory and customary laws relating to women's property under different religio-legal systems and brings out certain controversial problems on the surface. The horrendous problem facing the society is regarding the discriminatory share of females in the matters of inheritance.

The other object of this study is to see the reasons of non implementation of the statutory laws mend for the upliftment of the women. The object can be achieved to a large extent if the state has a will to implement the statutes in their right earnest.

The other problem to see, is whether the shares allotted to Muslim females in Holy Quran under different capacities are justified, keeping in view the liabilities discharged by them in the family?

The above problems have prompted me to undertake a research study on the above subject. So a modest attempt has been made by the researcher in the work to suggest certain measures to enable the females to get just shares in the property of their ancestors. Some useful suggestion have also been given which may go a long way not only to improve the socio-economic position of women but to impart Justice with the class that has been suppressed, oppressed, discriminated and avoided for long.

There is a lot of scope for further research on the topic such as the impact and outcome of the new Amending Act of 2005 on the females. Though on the face of the Act, it seems that equal shares shall be given to females but the thing to be seen is how the courts will see it and get the provisions of this Act implemented? Another thing is how does the society perceive and accept this amending Act?

Scheme of Work

The present work consists of six chapters. The first chapter is the introductory part of the thesis in which a brief introduction about the subject of the research has been made. The researcher has tried in this chapter to highlight various discriminatory customs, practices and laws. An endeavour has also been made to surface the plight of females in the society. The aims and objectives also find place in this chapter.

The concept of the women's property under various religio-legal system of the contemporary world is dealt with in the second chapter. Gender based discrimination meted out to a woman in regard to the evolution of property has also been prominated.

In third chapter an effort has been made to identify and ascertain the share of females under different system of laws. A critical evolution of the relevant provisions relating to inheritance has been made.

The fourth chapter is devoted to formulate the comparative charts of the shares of females under different capacities under different religions. By this, an effort has been made to domestify the complicated law of inheritance, which will help the members of a given society to know the shares of females at a glance.

As a critique the long journey of the judicial decisions of the apex courts and different high courts have been discussed at full length and corrective measures have been submitted at appropriate places.

Holding the entire study in retrospect, the recapitulation is made in the six chapter and a meager but honest attempt has been made to suggest certain measures for women's empowerment, emancipation of women from gender bias system and equality of rights in matter of inheritance.

Research Methodology

The research methodology, adopted by the present researcher in completing the research work, is purely doctrinal. An exhaustive and critical study has been made of all available relevant statutes, acts and case laws on inheritance. An attempt to prepare exhaustive comparative chart of the shares of females under Muslim, Hindu, Christian and Parsi laws, has been made.

The research materials, for the present thesis, consist of various books on the subject, relevant case laws from various reports, different articles published in various journals, encyclopaedias, various commissions' reports on the subject and relevant statutes. Published articles in National Dailies, magazines, and periodicals have also been consulted and incorporated in the thesis at appropriate place. The relevant verses of Holy Quran, Hadith, Dharamshastras, Vedas and the saying of prominent scholars have also been incorporated wherever these are needed.

References

1. Whitehead R.N. and Booth G.V. : The Sexes Changing Relationship in a Pluralistic Society, Toranto Gage Publishing Ltd. 1986. pp. 5-6, cited by Munawar A. Anees in his Article "Survival of the Sexiest" Islamic Culture An English Quarterly Vol. LXVIII, No. 3, July, 1994.
2. *Ibid.*
3. Hummudah, Abd-Al-Ali, Family Structure in Islam, Indianapolis, American Trust Publication (1977), p. 185 (cited by Munawar A. Anees) *op. cit.*
4. Gonsalves Lina : Women and Human Rights, p. 34.
5. Agarwal B.D. : Inheritance Injustices, Law Teller, p. 518.
6. Rupa Ashok Hurra v Ashok Hurra (2002) 4 SCC 388 para 2.
7. Hammetor J.A. : Universal History of World, London n.d. Vol. 1, p. 378 (Cited by Ali Nadwi; Status of Women, p. 11).
8. a. Section, 26 of Bombay Regulation Act of 1827.

   b. Section, 5 & 6 of Punjab Laws Act, 1872.

   c. Section, 5 & 6 of Central Province Laws Act 1875.

   d. Section 3 of Oudh Laws Act 1876.

   e. Section, 16 of Madras Civil Court Acts, 1883.
9. The famous Oudh Divorce Case.
10. Clause (d) of sub-section (viii) of section 2.
11. See Nickman N.A. and Macheon R : The Edicts of Ashoka, (Chicago) London Phonex 1966.
12. Ahron Layish : Women and Islamic Law in Non-Muslim States, p. 303.
13. Jaising Indira : Domestic Violence and Law Report Collegium on Justice for Women, Empowerment through Law (Lawyer's Collective Women's Rights Initiative, Butter Worth India, New Delhi.

2

Concept of Women's Property under Different Legal System

An Overview

In early stages, the word *'property'* was not understood in its modern sense. With the passage of time and the development of the industrialized world, the notion of *'property'* has become complicated. As an object of legal right, the property means a thing or group of things owned by an individual in the context where it is found. With the globalization of the world, the word property became the technicality of law. It includes so many interests and rights concerning the objects. Its area is going to be very wide.

It is difficult to understand the real nature of any thing unless we know when and how it was born. The true nature of things really lies in their genesis, *'it is'* says, Vico, "*nothing but their birth in certain times and in certain forms.*"[1] The history of property indeed lies in the analysis of the history of human nature itself.

The Concept of Property

The English word, *'property'* derives its origin, either directly or through French *'propriete'* or from Latin *'proprietas'*, which means the peculiar nature or quality of a thing and (in post Augustian writing;) *'ownership'*. The Latin word, *'proprietas'* is derived from *'proprius,'* which means *'pecular'* or *'own'*. The origin of the word *'proprius'* is uncertain it may be originated from the Latin- *'pro'*, *'prae'* and *'prop'*, Greek 'pro' and *'prin'* and Sanskrit - *'pra'* which may stand for *'in front of'*, *'before'*, *choose, to'* and *'on behalf of'*.[2]

Generally, property is defined as the rights of a person with respect to a thing. Thing may be tangible or intangible. Jurist used the term property in more than one application. The diversity, of the property system of societies, suggests that any concept of property depends, upon the culture in which it is found. Lord Porter said, that *'property'* is not a term of art but takes its meaning from the context in which it is found.[3]

The essence of property is, in its relations among men arising out of their relations to things. By *'property'* means an exclusive right to control an economic good. By *'private property'* means the exclusive right of a private person to control an economic good. By *'public property'* means the exclusive right of political unit (city, state, nation etc.) to control an economic good.[4]

According to Charmer, *'general property is a synonymous for ownership where as special property refers to lesser interest."*[5]

Holland stated, *"the sum total of man's fortune, including not only the objects of which he is owner but also the value of any claims which he may have against other persons, after deducting the amount of any claim, which might be made good against himself, is described as his property and he is said to own it."*[6]

Homes described, *"property denotes the consequences and cannotes the facts...there are always two things to be asked, firstly, what are the facts which make up the group in question and then, secondly, what are the consequences attached by the law of that group."*[7]

Bentham said, *"property is nothing but a basis of expectation, the expectation of deriving certain advantages from a thing which we are said to possess, in consequences of the relation, in which we stand towards it. There is no image, no painting, no visible trait, which can express the relation that constitutes property. It is not material, it is metaphysical, it is a mere conception of mind. To have a thing in our hands, to keep it, to make it to sell it, to work it up into some thing else, to use it, none of these physical circumstances, nor all united, convey the idea of property. The idea of property consists in an established expectation; in the persuasion of being able to draw such an advantage from the things possessed according to the nature of the case."*[8]

At another place Bentham said,[9] *"property is fictitious entity seeming to have some connections with possession and possession itself proves to be a fictitious entity."* According to him, in speaking of a property there are four things, to be considered.

First: The nature of the thing is whether corporeal or incorporeal.

Second: The person who is said to possess the property or to whom the property is said to belong, who is styled as the proprietor and whose property, the thing is said to be.

Third: The nature of the relation or proprietorship which subsists between that person and the things and in virtue of, where the person is said to be the object of the property or the possession of the thing, briefly the property or the possession of that person.

Fourth: The facts in which the exercise of the property consists.

Some jurists use the term 'property' to denote ownership or the subject of ownership or valuable things. In the first of these applications, ownership is not frequently considered, as the aggregate of the rights of an owner, who has absolute control over the thing, whose interest is unlimited as to duration, and who has absolute power to dispose of it. But this is taking too limited, a view of significance of the word. It seldom happens that all the rights over a thing are centered in the same person. The distribution of rights, says Sir William Marks- by, *'detached from ownership which we actually find in use, is very extensive and yet it is the holder of the residuary right in a thing' or subject of ownership, whom we in common parlance, always consider as the owner of the thing and distinguishes the holder of the detached rights as owner of a particular right.'* In all above these applications, the word *'property'* and the idea of a right to exclude all others from the enjoyment of the subject of ownership are predominant. In the case of public property although no one has the right to exclusive enjoyment, and none can rightfully prevent another from enjoying it."[10]

Salmond points out in his book. *'On Jurisprudence'* that the word 'property' is used in four different senses.[11]

First: In the widest sense *'property'* includes all person's legal rights of whatever description. A man's property is all that is his in law.

Second: In the narrow sense property includes not all rights of a person but only rights in respect of things and not in respect of persons, the former constitutes his status or personal condition. In this sense a man's land, chattels, shares and debts due to him or his rights in action, are his property but not his life or liberty or reputation.

Third: The property includes not even all proprietary rights, but only those which are both proprietary and real, in other words a man's right in things in rem and not a man's right in things in personum. In this sense free hold or lease hold estate in land or a patent or copy right is property but a debt or the benefit of a contract, is not.

Fourth: Finally, in the narrowest use of the term property includes nothing more than corporeal property that is to say that the right of ownership in a material object or that object itself identified with the right by way of metonymy.

The relation between religion and wealth changes from one type of society to another, so we have to look the socio-religious traditions, which have affected the different economic conditions of the primitive, archaic or prehistoric societies. A new tapestry of myth emerged about the concept of wealth and property due to the influence of religion. The theological based societies changed from hunting to agriculture. With the advent of cities, settled agriculture, writing and the historic religions like Hinduism, Christianity, and Islam, the relation between religion and wealth changed from Africa to the Far East. Ancestral spirits were worshipped in order to bring wealth and prosperity to the family. The religion sanctioned the family ownership of wealth.[12]

Under Different Legal System

The concept of property is changed according to the society, culture and legal system, in which it is founded. Ehrilich says that, *"the center of gravity of legal development lies not in legislation, nor in juristic science, nor in judicial decision but in society itself."*[13] Religion played a very important role in the development of legal ideas in primitive days, according to their own tenets and philosophies. Max Weber writes, *"When we are concerned with law, legal order and rule of law, we must strictly observe the distinction between a juristic and a sociological point of view. Jurisprudence asks for the ideally valid legal norms. Sociology investigates what is actually happening in the society because there is a certain chance that its members believe in the validity of an order and adopt their behaviour to this order."*[14] Now we have a look upon the different legal system to ascertain in what sense the term property is used or understood there, such as in Islam, Christianity and Hinduism.

Islamic Legal System

In Islam the concept of property is very simple. It includes wealth, estate attribute and what is one's own. *'The word property under Islamic legal system is applicable only to the objects which have a perceptible assistance in the out side world that is, to say, to things corporeal and tangible,*[13] says Abdur Rahim. This definition of Abdur Rahim does not cover all the modern concept of property, which is recognized at present by cause Islamic luminaries and jurists. It is a very narrow one and does not cover many rights such as intangible and incorporeal, as intellectual property right or copyright etc. Actually in the Islamic legal system there is no classification of different kinds of properties, as real or personal property, legal or equitable estates and ancestral or self-acquired property.[16]

Generally, the world '*mal*' is used for the property in Islamic law which is defined as that can be hoarded or secured for use and enjoyment, can be made at the time of need or that to which a man's desires incline and which can be given away to others and excluding others there form.[17] The word *'mal'* has much narrower meaning than the word *'property'* and it cannot be said that the *'mal'* is the true reflector of Islamic concept of property. In Islamic legal system the word property is used in much more wider sense than any other legal system because there is no concept of limited estate and ownership without possession. It recognizes absolute ownership. Islamic law does not recognize the concept of community or joint family property. Proprietorship is individual. Islamic law does not recognize the joint Muslim family or tenancy in common.[18]

When the members of a Muslim family live in commensality they do not form a joint family in the sense in which the expression is used under Hindu Law.[19] In *Shahid Ahmad vs Sultan,*[20] the recognition has not been given to a joint family as a legal entity under Islamic law. Under Islam there is no concept of matrimonial property or common property resulting from marriage as in Western Law. There does not exist, any thing like Stridhana, Woman's limited estate or hold property in lieu of maintenance as under Hindu Law. Islamic law does not divide or make any distinction between male or female's property. Under Islam, female got absolute right to hold and dispose of the property like males.

Privy Council in the case of Nawazish Ali Khan discusses the distinguishing features of Islamic laws at length.[21] About the concept of property there is not much difference among the different schools of Islamic law. According to Abu Yousuf and Abu Mohammad, *'the waste land are' as sort of common goods and become the property of cultivator by virtue of his being the first possessor in the same manner as in the case of seizing game or gathering fire wood'*[22]

In the light of the given definitions of property, it is deduced that property has two different meanings one is narrow, which includes person's rights in respect of a thing. On the other hand, property in its wider sense includes all the person's legal rights of whatever description they may be. Under Islamic law the word property is understood in such a wider sense that it covers all the conceptions of property, which is understood in the modern society.

In Encyclopaedia of Islam the word *'mal'* which is used as the property in Islamic law, stand for the possession. Property referring among the Bedouin was particularly to camels but also to estates, money and in any case to concrete things.

The word is originated from the word *'ma'* and *'le'* means property or any thing, which belong to any one.[23]

In Islam the wealth and property is regarded as a part of creation since Allah (SWT) is the owner of the world, so absolute property rights are impossible. Religious traditions established limitations on the possession of land and slaves. The ownership vests in Allah (SWT) and the individual is only a trustee. *"Islamic economics"* is often based on the welfare state and religious antinationalistic idealism but rejected the Western hedonism.[24]

The *'mal,' 'property'* or *'estate',* which is the subject of inheritance, is called *'tarka'*. The word *'tarka'* is derived from the word 'tark' which means property left. In relation to inheritance, *'Tarka'* means, the property left behind by the deceased. *'Tarka'* in AI-Bahr-al-Ra'iq has been defined as :

> *"Tarka means that property, which the deceased leaves behind him and there is no right of another particular person attached with that property."*[25] It means that a property, with which the right of another person is attached, shall not form part of the estate of the deceased, until the facility on that property paid off.

Honafi School

According to Hanafi School, *"only that property is the estate of the deceased over which there was no right of a stranger"* Hence, the property over which there exists a right of stranger as mortgagee etc. shall not be included in the estate until the mortgage money is paid or it has been released from the property itself.[26]

Maliki School

According to Malikis, the right of some other person in the

estate of the deceased attached to the property itself shall be considered as having excluded the said property from the definition of the estate.[27]

Shafi-i-School

Shafi-i as jurists said, that every thing which belongs to man in his life and what he leaves behind after his death whether it be the properties or rights, shall be called his estate, but if stranger's right is attached with the estate that property will not be considered deceased property, till it is not paid off.[28]

Hanbali School

Hanbali jurist also considered same as Hanafis. To them the estate is that property or proprietary right which the deceased leaves behind him.[29]

Shia School

According to Shia jurists, the property left by the deceased, should be considered to be his estate, but if it is submerged under debt it shall be the property of the ancestor merely in law. Being submerged under debt, it shall not devolve upon the heirs. If it is not so submerged, it shall be divided among the heirs, after payment of debts.[30]

In fact there is not much dispute so far as the question for the property of inheritance is concerned but the only difference is about the rights. Whether rights also included within the meaning of property or not? Maliki, Hanbali and Shafii all considered that the property or estate includes both properties and rights (except right in perosnum). Hanafis hesitate to include rights in estate.

Hindu Legal System

The ancient or earlier hymns are claimed to show, that the people were nomadic herdsmen having no fixed habitation, wandering about from place to place with their cattle – being their only property, with the agricultural development they settled down to permanent habitation.[31] So long as men knew of no means of subsistence but the chase pasturage or agriculture, his patrimony was a share in the soil a part of the all mend[32]

Coulanges said about the property, *"the land belongs to the man who first cleared it as the deer belongs to the man who first wounds it"*[33]

Rig Veda speaks about, *"the individual's proprietorship of a log of wood."* (x: 155,3)

The idea of property begins with the development of the civilization. Traditional societies were based on a zero sum economy; greed was roundly condemned in scripture, myth and folk-lore. As time passed by, more specific guidance was offered. In India Kautilya Arthshastra described, an economy based on agriculture, guilds, family ownership and a bureaucratically centralized state. Most interesting thing was, that this text elevates the pursuit of wealth and power *(artha).* In contrast the law of Manu reverses the relationship between artha and dharma and idealizes more or less static economy based on caste duties *(varna dharma)*.[34]

Artha is defined in the Kamsutra (1:20) as education, land, gold, cattle, corn, domestic utensils and friends and augmenting of what is acquired.[35]

The idea of property refers to the ownership of the whole complex of the mass of rights in rem and in personam, as man's property. The word property cannot be confined to the material object e.g. a person may have certain rights as lease holder or mortgagee., over the property of another. In this way the word property is much more comprehensive and things in action and obligation both are included in the definition of the term property. Under Roman law the right to the performance of an act by another was considered as property though an incorporeal one.[36] In the Conveyancing Act 1882 (Sec.11), property was defined as including any debt and anything in action and any other right or interest.

The two words *'swa'* and *'swami'* are co-relative. The idea underlying both is the same and they are the two aspects of the same question *'swa'* means what belong to a person *i.e.* property, swami means master or owner for the idea of ownership.[37] It means both these are interdependent. These two represents the relation between the person and the thing but property is more than mere ownership.

Classification of Property

Property is generally divided by most Smrities into two kinds *'stharva'* immovable such as land and houses and *gangama*—movable such as cattles etc.[38] Some other Smrities divided property into three kinds *'bhu'* (land including houses),' *'nibandha'* (inaccurately rendered as corrdy) and *'dravya'* (gold, silver and other movable). sometimes, however the word *'dravya'* is employed in the sense of all property whether movable or immovable as –

'dravya pitamahopatto gangma stharva tatha."

Under ancient Hindu law the property is divided into two kinds—joint family property and separate property. Joint family property is either ancestral property, or property acquired with or without the aid of ancestral property, or property acquired separately but thrown into the common stock[39]. This contains the doctrine of merger of estate by blending.[40] The very nature of joint family pre-supposes a continuing preference for a sharing of gains and losses.[41]

Derrett said, *"In keeping with what I have said there is no presumption that a joint family has any property, it is, in its property aspects a reservoir into which property flows from various quarters and out of which rivulets flow feeding the numerous categories of members and dependants. It is primarily a psychological set up and secondarily a legal entity.* The word *'ancestral property'* has a technical sense it belongs to is *'pitamah'* *i.e.* paternal grandfather or great grandfather. In *Md. Hussain,*[43] case it was made clear. The Orissa High Court held, that there could be no presumption that the family because it is joint, possesses joint property. Even a member in a joint family may possess separate property which would exclusively belong to him and no other member of the coparcenary not even his male issue, acquires any interest in it by birth.[44]

Self acquired property or separate property is also called the *'svaarjit'* property. It is earned by the skill and labour of the earner and it is absolutely one's own. Sometimes the difficulty arises when the manager or the coparcener of a joint family earned money on the basis of his personal qualities without using the joint family assests, and the question has to be decided whether it is his separate property or joint family assests. In an old case *M/s Piyare Lal Adishwar Lal vs I.T. Commissioner,*[45] Supreme Court held, that earnings made by the manager was his separate property. The argument was made that the manager earned the salary, which he could not have earned if a large part of family's capital was not deposited as security. But Supreme Court held, that the earnings were the rewards of the earner's skill and labour and not the fruit of family investment. In another case,[46] the plaintiff was a teacher drawing good salary and there were documents which revealed that he had drawn substantial amounts of loan from (GPF) account, the property in dispute was purchased by him in the same year in which he had withdrawn the loan. The properties were consequently held to be self-acquired and not joint family property.

The word '*daya*' has been used even in the oldest period of the Vedic literature '*Sarvasya dayam Vibhajantey ebhyah*'[47]

It means a share or a reward. *Daya*' stands for '*dhana*' follows from another passage of Tai. S (11. S, 2, 7) which simply means wealth that is to be divided. The V. Mayukha defines '*daya*' as that wealth, which is to be divided and which is not the wealth of re-united member. The word '*daya*' though derived from the word '*da*' means to give, does not apply to heritable wealth in the literal sense of gift.[48] Mit divide[49] '*daya*' into two varieties – '*apratibandha*' (unobstructible) and '*sapratibandha*' (obstructible). All '*daya*' is sapritibandha and the ownership arises in another only on death of the previous owner. Dayabhaga's doctrine is '*uparamasvatvavada*' ownership arising on death. On the other hand the Mitakshara hold the view of '*ganamsvatavada*' means the ownership arises by birth. Dayabhaga does not recognize that the son, grand son or great grand son acquire by birth any interest or right of ownership in the ancestral property held by father or their ancestor. But Mitakshara recognizes it.

Thus, we see that there is vast difference between the concept of the property and its ownership between the two schools of Hindu law.

Stridhanam

Stridhanam is the most controversial term of Hindu Jurisprudence. There is great difference of opinions about the Stridhana among Smrities, Vedas and Shastras. The germs of the Stridhana can be traced back to the Vedic literature. As Derrett says,[50] that Indian jurists have been proud rightly, that at least in theory their indigeneous jurisprudence allowed women (Stridhanam) assets at their disposal or atleast generally available for their enjoyment and for their security at a time when in the west wives were unable to own property, separately from their husbands except as beneficiaries under some trust or settlement. Though Muslim women have traditionally enjoyed the absolute right to own and to dispose of or to manage the property in whatever manner they like. It is a novel feature of Hindu jurisprudence because Stridhana is women's absolute property with all rights to dispose of at her own pleasure though not in all cases, as during covertures or widowhood. Sir Guroodas Banerjee remarks,[51] nowhere proprietary rights of women recognized so easily as in India, and in very few ancient system of law have these rights been so largely conceded as in our own.

Great diversity of views prevail on the topic that what constitute the Stridhana. As Jimutvahana says, in the Dayabhaga after finishing his discourse on Stridhana, *"thus, has been explained the most difficult subject of succession to a childless woman"*.[52]

By parsing of the term of Stridhana, it clearly shows that the starting of the term '*Stri*' – means woman and '*dhana*' stand for wealth. It means, Stridhana signifies the woman's wealth or property. The term Stridhana is referred by different names – as '*manjal kani*' in south, bangdicholi in Bombay, '*Kalnam*' in Andhra Pradesh and '*Patribhagam*' in Madras.[53] In an ancient Smiriti work the literal meaning of the Stridhana was restricted to certain kinds of property given to woman on certain occasions or at different stages of her life.

Kautilya defines, "*Stridhana as means of subsistence and what could be tied up on the body* (*i.e.* ornaments or jewellary) *constitute Stridhana.*[54]

Manu defines, *"what was given before the nuptial fire, what was given on the bridal procession, what was given in token of love, what was received from her brother, mother and father, that is called the six fold woman's property."*[55]

Katyana defines the stridhana in most comprehensive way, *'what was given to women at the time of marriage before the nuptial fire is declared by the wise to be 'adhyagni'. "Stridhana, what was obtained at the time of procession from her father's house is declared to be 'adhyvahmika"* Stridhana, what was given to a woman through affection by her father or mother in law at the time of doing obeisance at the feet, is said to be *'pritidatta'* Stridhana, what was given to her as the price of house hold utensils, of beasts, of milch cattle, ornaments and slaves is declared to be *'sulka'*, what was given to her after marriage from the family of her husband and also from the family of her kinsmen is declared to be *'anvadheya'*, Katyana's definition have been accepted by all digests. At another place Katyana restricts the literal sense of the Stridhana over that wealth that is obtained by a woman by mechanical arts or from a stranger through affection.

'Samdayika' is a synonymous of Stridhana in the technical sense. The Stridhana is also defined by Yajnavalkya, Narada and Vishnu. But all these definitions only says about the kinds of Stridhana, which means what constitute the Stridhana. From the analysis of the above definitions it seems that only those properties or wealth are Stridhana over which the woman have absolute authority to donate, sell or enjoy, independently of her husband's control. To ascertain whether the particular thing is Stridhana or not? Three test are laid down by jurists and commentators are as follows:

- from which source the property is acquired?
- when the property is acquired what is the status of the woman, whether she is maiden, coverture or widow?
- the last test is to which school the woman belongs?

If the property held by a Hindu female is not a Stridhana then, what it be called. Actually the property held by Hindu woman is of two types - women estate and Stridhana. Hindu female property is either some form of entitlement of maintenance of a Hindu woman from the joint family which is called the women's estate, or it is women's absolute property for which the term Stridhana (women's wealth) has been known since classical times.[56] V. Mayukha divides,[57] Stridhana into two kinds— *'Paribhashika'* (technical) and *'apribhashika'* (non-technical), which has been already discussed in the passing paragraph.

Women Estate

The property, which is not Stridhana, is Women's estate over which she possesses very different rights. She is the owner of that property as long as she lives. She has exclusive right of enjoyment and management of it but her ownership is restricted. She cannot dispose of neither she can sell it, except in some special circumstances. On her death the property does not pass to her heirs, but to the next person from whom she has inherited it.[58] The property obtained in lieu of maintenance would be divided amongst the other sharer, as it would have been if she has never taken it. Any interest devolving on a Hindu widow shall be limited interest known as a Hindu women's estate, provided however that she shall have the same right of claiming partition as a male owner. The Apex court in *Kalawati Bai v Soiryabai*,[59] held that under the provision of the Act of 1956, the limited ownership of Hindu widow would be converted into absolute ownership, existed when the Act came into force or there after. The intention of the legislature is clear that in fact a female Hindu originally had a limited right and later acquired the full right does not in any way alter the rules of succession given in sub. section (2) of section 15 of the Act of 1956.[60] The topic of Women's estate will be discussed at length at another place. Now come to the continuing topic of Stridhana.

Under the Hindu Law in operation prior to the coming into force of the Hindu Succession Act, 1956, a woman's ownership of property was limited. Great diversity of opinions prevail over the issue of Stridhana and woman's property in regard the absolute power of alienation. In this connection the main thing, which was considered, is the source from which the property is acquired and the status of woman as maiden, married or widow. No doubt it is true to say that the complexity of the shastric laws relating to Stridhana argues that it was never a wholly settled system.[61]

In *Prahadoeswara Mudaliar* v *Rajgopal Pillai*[62] an interesting question came before the court that, whether the property of a dancing girl can be treated as Stridhana. It was held that the property of a dancing girl is her Stridhana and will devolve upon her female issue in preference to her male issue.

The verses of Katyayana and Narada,[63] which governed the rules of the rights of a female over Stridhana depend on three things the sources, the status and the school of women.

"The wealth, which is earned by mechanical arts or which is received through affection from a stranger, is subject to her husbands dominion." Katyayana.[64]

The property, which she has received from her husband, father or brother, or gifts from kindered, are technically, considered her Stridhana over which she has absolute ownership. The property given to her, by her husband if movable, after his death, she may dispose of it at her own pleasure.

A very crucial question came before the court in the case of *Rashmi Kumar v Mahesh Kumar Bhada,*[65] whether the Stridhana property was exclusive property of the wife or was a joint property owned and held by both the spouses? All the three judges concurred on the point, that the Stridhana is the exclusive property of the wife. Fazal Ali J said, that the possession over Stridhana of a Hindu married female is clear and unambiguous. Stridhana is not a joint property of the wife and husband. By merely living in matrimonial home the Stridhana does not becomes joint property of the spouses. It is also not a partnership property of the spouses. Though the husband in extreme distress can utilize it. Yajnavalkya[66] says *"that the husband is not liable to return to the wife her stridhana taken by him in a famine, for religious acts, in distress or when imprisoned."*

Status of the female also plays an important role in deciding the woman's right over Stridhana. In maidenhood a Hindu woman could dispose of her Stridhana property of every description at her pleasure. During the maiden-hood what the female earned, by her own labour is her absolute property, over which she has all the right to dispose of and to alienate it, minor can not dispose of her property. Married woman have absolute right over the property, which is called Saudayika or Stridhana in technical term. In *Brij Inder* v *Janki Koer*[67] held that a Hindu widow has absolute power over every kind of property.

Dayabhaga School allows the women to claim as Stridhana only the movable property that is not inherited, but given to her by her husband. The immovable property is excluded from the preview of Stridhana. Under Mitakashara school very little property is treated as Stridhana.

Christian Legal System

Christianity is defined by Friedrich Schiermacher (1768-1834) as a *"monotheistic faith. ...Essentially distinguished from others. Such faith by the fact that in it, every thing is related to the redemption accomplished by Jesus of Nazareth.*[68]

Magnificent (Luke 1:52) stated that *"God has put down the mighty from thrones and exalted those of low degree"*. The early church father rarely addressed the issue of economic justice but later on the leaders began to soften the hard saying of Jesus about riches. In scholastic period, the distribution of wealth was treated from a point of view that combined signature and the writings of the church fathers with the works of Aristotle and Islamic thinkers.[69]

In England a notion of property in land emerged at the end of 12th century from a mass of partly discretionary, partly customary, feudal rights and obligation.[70] Property according to Pufendrof, is founded in the physcial power manifested in seizing in the object of property (occupation)[71] Bentham viewed, *'property is nothing but an expectation of protection created by the legislator and by settled practice.'* John Stuart Mill associated property with liberty and suggested, that security of property is essential for man to maximize his potential for liberty. The communist Manifesto (1847) of Karl Marx and Friedrich Engle's held, *property is nothing but a device in the social warfare between the capitalist and proletarian classes the means by which the capitalist expropriates the labour of the proletarian and keeps him in slavery*[72]

Now in the civil law system the term *'property'* applies to those tangible things that can conveyed inter vivos and to a very few, if any intangible. It includes every thing that is the object of the law of succession.

Anglo American law distinguishes between real and personal property. The real property is land and every thing attached to it as iimovable property and all other property - as moveable is termed as personal property. There are also two sets of laws to be adopted to these real and personal property.[73]

The roots of American property law are in the feudal land law of England. Accordingly, it distinguishes real and personal property. Real property is historically consisted, chiefly of feudally important estate in land, personal property includes such intangible as contract right including bank deposits, corporate stocks, industrial property including patents and copy rights. They are consisted of others assets like corporeal and incorporeal. In U.S. the rules of intestate succession are now largely the same for real and personal property.[74] In the feudal age practical ownership consists of a life interest inalienable in most cases and of a reversion or remainder which again when vested, is simply another life interest.[75]

In later part of the 18th century the Napolean code was framed on individualistic principles and the right of ownership to be absolute exclusive and perpetual, was recognized.[76] The concept of family property is accepted in France and rules were made for the protection of this property for the benefit of future family member. The assets of family are considered as family property. Till then the concept of family property is unknown to English law.[77]

In classical Roman Law the sum of rights, privileges and powers which a person could have in a thing, was called dominium, ownership or has frequently proprietors. In the English Bankruptcy Act 1914, Property is defined in section 167 as-

"Property includes, money, goods, things in action, land and every description of estate, interest and profit present, past and future, vested or contingent arising out of or incident to property as above defined.[78]"

In *Jones* v *Skinner*,[79] Landale M.R. has described the word 'property' as being the most comprehensive of all terms which

can be used in as much as it is indicative and descriptive of every possible interest which the party can have. But Bentham consider as metaphorical and improper the extension of the term to includes other rights than those which relate to material thing.[80]

The Concept of Matrimonial Property

Traditionally under English law the married woman was subject to a variety of legal disabilities, which grew out of the view that husband and wife were one person. The legal personality of a female merged in that of her husband after the marriage. The husband was regarded as the quasi guardian of her wife. All of the woman's personal property and real property vest to the husband on marriage. This property is called the marital property over which the wife has no power.[81] The woman was cursed economically and made wholly to depend on man. She had no control even on her own earnings as those were all seized by the husband with full proprietory rights, though she would regain all the property if she became widow.

Many writers commented on the concept of Stridhana in Hindu law and the concept of marital property in English law. In marital property the personality of wife is merged in that of husband and what ever the property she possess goes to husband, disadvantaging...women in terms of property rights.[82] Though the concept of Stridhana and marital property are different but also resemble up to some extent. In regards to Stridhana the wife has absolute right subject to some exceptions and not so handicapped as under the concept of marital property of English Law.

As long as Western law remained under the sway of Christian priest woman remained without rights in those land.[83]

In some countries and under some religious set ups though the situation is different, as Muslim woman owned and managed their own property and have absolute right to property. In Russia the wife is permitted to own and manage her property. In relation to property the Roman wife also enjoyed independence.[84]

In the later part of the 19th century some radical reform were made in the laws related to marital property. As the consent of both the spouses were made necessary for disposal of property. The Federal Republic of Germany in 1950 introduced legal equality in the matter of finance and property of the male and female. In 1965 the French Civil Code, in 1969 Qubec Civil Code and in 1950 China made comprehensive changes in the laws related to property for women in terms of property rights. These reforms effected the other countries also and tremendous changes were brought in the position and power of women.

Parsi Law

Under Parsi, law there is no difference between movable and immovable real and personal, self-acquired and ancestral property. It means there is no different set of rules like Christian law or Hindu Law to govern these properties. Though before the amendment the laws governing the succession of agricultural land of a Parsi intestate was the subject of the Act of 1865 in which the son's share was four times more than the daughter and widow's share was double of daughter but the Orissa High Court held that succession to agricultural land would be same as any other property.

Recapitulation

At last it can be said that the word property has different meaning in different times under different legal systems in different circumstances and even in different mythologies. Sometime it is treated as fictitious entity, on the other hand some one has understood the word property in terms of possession and ownership. Whatever the meaning is ascribed to the property its relation with human being is never denied. It is some thing, which is related to a human being, though under Muslim Law the property is related to Allah (SWT) who is considered under Islamic law the absolute owner of the world. Every thing in this world belongs to Allah (SWT) and man is only an agent or trustee.

References

1. Pal Radhabinod: The History of Hindu Law (1958) p. 6.
2. The New Encyclopaedia Britanica-Vol. 26, 15 ed. 1993. p. 181.
3. Nokes v Donester Amalgamated Collieries Ltd. (1940) A.C. 1014, 051 (The Cambridge Law Journal) (1997) CLJ part. 1, Vol. 56, p. 577.

4. Ely : Property and Contract in their Relation, to the Distribution of Wealth, Vol. 1, Book 1, (quoted by Cohem and Donester, Reading in Jurisprudence and Legal Philosophy, p. 7)
5. Cf. Sewell v Burdick (1884) 10 APP cases 74, 92, 93.
6. Holland : On Jurisprudence, 10th ed. P. 202.
7. Homes, note 29 at p. 215 (Cambridge Law Journal) (1997) CLJ part II, Vol. p. 577.
8. Morris R. Cohen and Felixs Cohen: Reading in Jurisprudence and Legal Philosophy (New York) Prentice Hall Inc. (151) p. 8.
9. Bentham Jermy: The Limits of Jurisprudence Defined, (Charles Warren Everrett) Columbia University Press, New York, Morning side Heights Mem, Lv 1945, p. 35.
10. Mitra Ram Charan: The Law of Joint Property and Partition in British India, Tagore Law Lecture II ed. P.N. 3.
11. Salmond : On Jurisprudence 9th ed, p. 578-580.
12. Encyclopaedia of Religion Vol. 15, p. 362.
13. Prof. Eagen Ehrilich: Fundamental Principles of the Sociology of Law (foreword).
14. Webber Max: Essays in Sociology, (translated and edited by H.H. Gerth and C.W. Wills), New York (1946), p. 226.
15. Abdur Rahim: The Principles of Mohammaden Jurisprudence, p. 249.
16. Ram Abidi v Mirza Ahmad AIR (1925) Oudh.
17. *Ibid.*
18. Abdul Rashid v Sirajuddin (1933) 145 (C, 641).
19. Krishnajiram v Md. Mashiuddin Mandal AIR, (1921) Cal. 653; see also Hakim Khan v Cool Khan (1882) 8 Cal. 826.
20. (47) A. Mad. 287; Sukrullah v Zakira Bibi AIR (1932) ALL 512.
21. AIR (35) 1948 p.c. 134 (from Oudh; 30 AIR (1943) Oudh 243).
22. Hamilton: Hedaya, Book IXLV para 3 (Gardy's ed.) 610.
23. Encyclopedia of Islam-New ed. 2000 (glossary and Index of terms Vol. I-IX) p. 238.
24. Encyclopaedia of Religion, Vol. 15, p. 364.
25. Ibn Nujaym Zaynuddin Ahmad b. Ibrahim (d. 970 A.H.): Al Bahr-al-Rai'q. Dar-al-Kutub-al-Kubra Cairo 1334 A.H., Vol. VIII, p. 489
26. Dr. Rehman, Tanzilur-A Code of Muslim Personal Law, Vol. II, Islamic Publishers, D-73/J North Nizamabad, Karachi 33 Pakistan, p. 408.

27. Al-Abdul Sami 'Jawahar-al-Aklil Matba Mustafa-al-Babi, Cairo 1366 A.H., Vol. II, p. 327.
28. Al-Sharbini Mohd-al-Katib: Mughni-al-Muhtaj Matba Mustafa-al-Bibi. Cairo 1377 A.H., Vol. III, p. 2.
29. Yousuf Musa (Dr.) Al-Zarkaho-wal-Mirath, Daral Kutub-al-Arbi, Cario 1960, p. 72.
30. Al Hilli, Najamuddin (d. 474 A.H.) Beirut pt. Iv, P.N. 183.
31. Pal Radhabinod: *op cit.,* p. 39.
32. *Ibid.,* p. 312.
33. Coulanges F. De: Origin of the Private Property, p. 131.
34. The Encyclopaedia of Religion, Vol. 15, p. 362.
35. Vide, Hindu Dharamshastra Vol. II, Part I, p. 9, note 22 (quoted by V. Kane-History of Dharamshastra).
36. See Code Civil Art. 529.
37. See Salmond *op. cit.*, Chap. XII, pp. 339-40, 9th ed. of 1937.
38. Yajnavalakya: 11, 121.
39. Manu-IX 204, Quoted by V. Kane p. 576.
40. See Shibaprasad v Priya Kumari, L.R. 59, A, 331: 34 Bom. L.R.
41. Derrett: A critique of Modern Hindu Law, p. 587.
42. Derrett, *op. cit.,* p. 61.
43. Md. Husain v Krishwa Nandan 64, 1-A, 250.
44. Harihar Seethi v Ladu Kishore Sethi, (Annual, Survey of Indian Law (2002), Vol. XXXCIII, p. 401.
45. AIR (1968), SC 678.
46. Supra note 44,
47. Rig. II, 32, 4, p. 388.
48. Kane V. : History of Dharmashastra IIIrd ed, 1946, p. 546.
49. *Ibid*, p. 547.
50. Derrett J.D.M., *op. cit.,* p. 195.
51. Sir Guroodas Benerjee: Marriage and Stridhana 5th ed. of 1923, p. 370.
52. Mulla Dinshaw: Principles of Hindu Jurisprudence, p. 168.
53. AIR (2004), p. 151.
54. 111.2, p.152.
55. Dharamshatra-IX, 194.

56. Werner F. Menski: Hindu Law Beyond Tradition and Modernity, Oxford University Press, p. 486.
57. V. Mayukha, p. 160.
58. Vide Sheo Shankar v Debi Sahai L.R. 301, A.202, Debi Mangal Prasad v Mahadev Prasad L.R. 39, I.A 121, 131-32.
59. AIR (1991) SC 1581.
60. Bhagat Ram v Teja Singh (2002) 1 SCC 210.
61. Goorodas Bannerji: *op cit.*
62. AIR (34) 1947, Mad. 71 (C.N.30).
63. Verses 905-907, 911.
64. Dayabhaga, Chap. 4 section 1, para 19, cited by Mulla (*op. cit.*).
65. (1997) 2 SCC 397.
66. Verses 11, 147.
67. (1877) 1 Cal.
68. Encyclopaedia of Religion, Vol. 3, p. 348.
69. *Ibid.,* p. 363.
70. The Origin of the Western Idea of Property are examined by Barry Nicholas in "An Introduction to Roman Law" (1962) reprinted 1987.
71. Encyclopaedia Britanica; Vol. 26, p. 184.
72. *Ibid.*
73. Walsh W.F., Outlines of the History of English and American Law; (1626), pp. 41-42.
74. Powell An Introduction to the Legal System of United States, p. 126.
75. Smith S. : The Development of European Law, p. 172.
76. Alarez A: The Progress of Continental Law in the 19th Century (1819), p. 1-3.
77. "Financial Obligation with in the Family," The Cambridge Law Journal Vol. 60 (2001) part 1.
78. Cited in Bans Gopal Case (1949) AIR (36) All 433.
79. 1835-42 R.R. 274 at p. 176 (5 L.J.N.S) Ch. 87.
80. Bentham : Principles of Legislation p. 231 see Salmond Jurisprudence 9th ed. pp. 578-80.
81. Werner : American Family Laws (1331-38) p.133.
82. Werner : *op cit.,* p. 486.
83. Encyclopaedia Britanica, Vol. 19, p. 80.
84. Kidwai M.H. 'Woman Under different Social and Religious Laws, p. 26.

3

Shares of Females under Different Legal System

An Overview

Inheritance or succession means the devolution of property on an heir or heirs upon the death of the propositus. Every society has some kind of system, for dealing with the things or property that are in the control of the member who has died. It is quite complicated in every society. The laws and regulations which deal with the property to be distributed among the heirs differ according to the set ups, norms and values of each society.

The law of inheritance is a body of principles and regulations governing the means by which assets and liabilities may be transferred, after the death, to the heirs. The concept of inheritance depends upon a common acceptance of the notion of private ownership of goods and property. In early societies a dead man's relics were buried with him as a ritual practice or apportioned to relations and other tribesman. The rules, governing the succession universally, depend upon the view of the deceased and the kinship as a primary consideration. Before going into detail about the law of inheritance we will have a look, how the law of inheritance has developed.

Development of Family System

The English word 'family' is derived from the Latin word '*familia*,' which means '*house hold.*' The organizations of household or families are varied from place to place. With the development of the political institutions, the family become a private place and characterized by humanity, intimacy and support. In ancient Greek cities or states four level of towns grouping could be traced out, which are–

- the phratry *(phratra)*
- the aristocratic clan (*genos*)
- the kindred *(anchisties)* and
- the house hold *(oikos)*.

The *"phratries"* were large tribal sub-divisions, consisting of families claiming to common kin relation. At the apex of each *"phratry"*, there were aristocratic clans that had certain hereditary rights such as the right to hold priest offices. The kindred consisted of a set of relatives who can claim the inheritance. The patrilineal kin groups were called the *'gens"*. Each 'gens' had one or more recognized chiefs. Property was inherited with in the gents.[1]

The Romans distinguished two kinds of blood relatives, agnates and cognates. Agnates were relatives through male line and reckoned to be close because they have the right to inherit the property and the marriage has forbidden between them. The cognates were any other blood relatives.

The ideals of Christianity, dominance of church and emergence of feudalism played an important role in shaping the medieval and post medieval families. With the spread of Christianity the close kin's marriages were forbidden and the inherited property was dispersed, which lessened the influence of kins based group. In the Middle Ages the women and children got rights in their own capacity independent of the head of household.

The family is considered the basic unit of the society. Islam had provided an elaborate scheme for the establishment of a systematic and mutual family life.

After the very brief history of the family system and the development of the law of inheritance, we will discuss elaborately the rules governing the law of succession in different religio-legal system.

Laws of Inheritance in Different Religio-Legal System

Like all other laws, the rules governing the estate of a deceased also differs from place to place. Every system has its own rules and regulations to govern the succession suited to its socio-economic conditions.

From the opening paragraph of the Sirajiyah—

"Learn the laws of Inheritance and teach them to the people, for they are one half of the useful knowledge."[3]

"It is (inheritance) the most difficult subject of Hindu jurisprudence."

Colbrook said, "no *branch of jurisprudence is more important than the law of succession and inheritance as it constitutes that part of any national system of laws which is the most peculiar and distinct and which is of most frequent use and extensive application."*[4]

Fitz-Gerald's opinion is that, "in all system of law the doctrine of succession is, the touch stone of the lawyers, the legal mind delights in its suitable intricacies, the layman in repelled."[5]

"All laws of inheritance are made up of the debris of the various forms which the family has assumed."[6]

Like all other laws the rules governing the estate of a deceased also differs from place to place. Every system has their own rules and regulations to govern the succession suited to their socio-economic conditions.

By these saying of legal luminaries it is evident that the law of succession is the most important part of any legal system as it affect the interest of all description of people and deserve special notice.

Under Islamic Law

Great tribute is paid to the Islamic Law of Inheritance not only by Muslims but by the Western world also. As Coulson says, *"Jurisdically the law of succession is a solid technical achievement and Muslim Scholars takes a justifiable pride in the mathematical precision with which the right of various heirs in any given, situation can be calculated."*

William Jones *"I am strongly disposed to believe that no possible question could occur on the Muslim Law of Succession which might not be rapidly and correctly answered."*

Al Sirajiyah, *"Islamic Law of Inheritance in its present form is a fixed scientific and beautiful harmonious system,."*

The eminent writers and jurist because of its completeness, perfectness and elaborate provisions always admire the Islamic law of interifance. Islamic law of Inheritance brought many reforms in the existing system of succession in pre-Islamic world. In pre-Islamic days the notions of kinship were based on blood feud, which was comradeship in arms. On this basis, women and children who were unable to bear arms, disqualified in regard to inheritance.[7] Holy Quran laid down that nothing could furnish so strong a claim to inheritance as blood relation. This provision generally strengthens the family tie.[8]

'And they who believed and left their homes afterwards and have striven along with you, these are also of you; but those who are united by ties blood are nearer to each other, by Book of God."[9]

By these Quranic injunctions, it is proved that Islam has brought a revolutionary change in the law of inheritance and gave importance to the family and relationship.

To govern the Islamic law of inheritance there is a whole Surah (*Surah Nisan*) in which some injunctions are given. The Islamic Law introduced some changes in the pre-Islamic rules of inheritance. As by Islam the husband, wife and cognates were made entitled to inherit. There is no need to discuss the whole Islamic law of inheritance and succession with its minute details but to understand the women's property right it is necessary to give a brief draft of Islamic law of Inheritance.

Salient Features of Islamic Law of Inheritance

"Nemo est heirs viventis,"

Right of inheritance arises only after the death of propositus, no person is the heir of a living Muslim,[10] the person whose property is to be distributed unless he is dead.[11] The estate vests immediately in each heir at the moment of the death, in proportion to the share prescribed by Holy Quran.[12]

Dual Basis of Islamic Law of Inheritance

The whole Islamic law of inheritance is based on two bases with the exception of Shia Law. First - Holy Quran, second - pre-lslamic customs and usages. The pre-lslamic customs and usages have an important place in the law of inheritance. The customs, which were not expressly abrogated by the Holy Quran, continued to prevail. The Holy Quran did not away all the existing laws of succession of pre-lslamic world.[13]

The Nearer in Degree Excludes the Remoter

The preference will be decided by the nearness of the consanguinity[14]

Rule of Representation

The rule of representation is not generally recognized in Islamic law. The heir's apparent right of succession do not pass to his own heir.[15] It means the children of pre-deceased child will not represent their father or mother at the time of succession. In *Abdul Huq* v *Seetaram Sethi,*[16] it is said that children in Islamic family were not co-owner in the sense that what was purchased by one person was also for the benefit of another. In this case the children of the deceased Muslim were minor at the time of his death. Their paternal uncle on their behalf had purchased some property in the name of one of the minor child. It was held no rule of representation,[17] is recognized in Islamic law, means the children of pre-deceased child will not represent their father or mother at the time of succession.

Illustration: A died leaving behind a son and a son of a predeceased son. The whole property will go to his son and the son's son will get nothing.

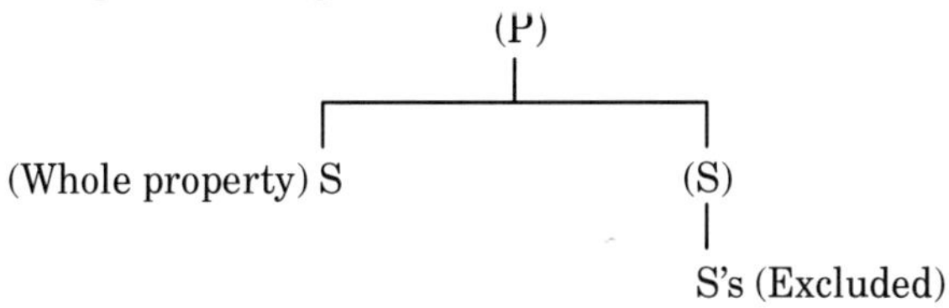

Rule of Spes-Successionis

A chance of an heir, it means there will be a chance to inherit. But under Islamic law, the inheritance open on the death of a person and no birthright or rule of representation is recognized. So there is no question of mere an expectation, to be an heir because it may happen that one will not survive the other. In the life of a Muslim no one can be a heir of his property.[18]

No Concept of Joint Family

In Muslims there is no concept of joint family. Under Islamic law the property acquired by some members will not be deemed to be the joint family property[19] but it is not contrary to Islamic law, if a family trade is carrying on, for the benefit of all members.[20] If the members of an Islamic family live in commonsality they do not form a joint family.

No Rule of Primogeniture

The preference to eldest son in the matter of succession was given by near about all the legal system in ancient time. It is said that it was originated in the English feudal system and also prevalent among Jews.[21] But under Islamic law there is no concept of the rule to give the entire property to the eldest son excluding the other heirs or to leave them on whims and caprice of the eldest son. Every heir shall inherit in his or her own capacity.

No Birth Right

In Muslims the children are not born with the right of property as in Hindu law. Under Islamic law there is no distinction between ancestral or self acquired property.[22] or they do not form a coparcenary in which the child has property right from his birth.

No Concept of Survivorship

Under Islamic law there is no concept of joint family, so no survivorship is recognized, which is the main characteristic of joint family of Hindu Law. The principle is unknown to Islamic law and the heirs of deceased take their share as are tenants in common and not as joint tenants.

Rules Relating to Illegitimate Children

An illegitimate child and its father are not related in law so they are not competent to inherit from each other.[24] An illegitimate child cannot inherit to a legitimate child born to the mother of subsequent marriage.[25] Under Sunni law there is a provision that an illegitimate child can inherit from her mother but under Shia law he or she is not entitle to inherit from any parents.[26] Under Hanafi law an illegitimate child also inherits from a person to whom, it is related through it's mother as distant kindred. The putative parents do not inherit from an illegitimate child under Shia Law.[27]

Insanity and Unchastity

In Islamic law mental derangement is not an impediment on succession.[28] Wife run away from her house and live in adultery, it was held that she was entitled to inherit unless she was divorced.[29]

Non-Muslim Can Not be an Heir

"A Muslim cannot be the heir of a disbeliever, nor can a disbeliever be the heir of a Muslim,"[30] narrated by Usman bin Zaid. *K.P. Chandrashekar Appa v Government of Mysore.*,[31] the facts of the case were, that a converted Muslim woman died, intestate leaving considerable property but have no issue. The brother of the wife who was still Hindu claimed her property as brother. It was held that brother is not entitled to succeed. A daughter, being a sole heir of a converted Muslim, was held to inherit the whole property as a heir and by way of Return.[32] In 1947, a question before the court was whether succession and inheritance of a converted Muslim be governed by Islamic law?[33] It was held that Islamic law applied to a Muslim not only by birth but by religion also. A converted Muslim would be governed in all matters by Islamic law as his personal law.

Homicide

A person, who has caused the death of another, whether intentionally or by mistake or by negligence or by accident, is not entitled to inherit the property of that deceased.[34] Though according to Sirajiyah,[35] the descendants of the murderer were not be excluded. Shia law excludes the murderer, only in the case of intentional murder.

Missing Person

The rule of Islamic law is that missing person must be regarded alive till lapse of 90 years from his birth, which is abrogated by the Indian Evidence Act. If the person is to be presumed alive his property cannot be distributed among his heirs, the part of the estate, which he is entitled to be inherited, kept apart.[36]

Unborn Person as being Heir

If the female relative of the deceased is pregnant at the time of the death, the child in mother womb will be considered competent to inherit but born alive and the share kept for him or her will be the maximum.

Several Deaths at a Time

If there are several deaths among the heirs of the deceased before final distribution of his estate, the shares of different heirs must be determined on the basis of each death working out final distribution.[37] In the leading case of *Jafri Begum* v *Amir Mohd,*[38] the court held that the jus representation is being absolutely unknown to Islamic law of inheritance, the right of inheritance depends upon the exact time of death when the person, through whom the heir claims otherwise, died, the orders of death being the sole guide in such cases. At this time the rule that younger survive the elder will apply.

After discussing the general principles of the law of inheritance. It is suitable to know briefly the heirs and quantum of their shares in the heritage of the deceased.

Kinds of Heirs

"To benefit everyone we have appointed heirs and shares to the property, left by partner and near relatives."[39]

The heirs are divided into three classes according to the order of succession.

- Sharers
- Residuaries
- Distant kindred

Sharers

The sharers are those persons who are entitled to a prescribed share of inheritance by Holy Quran. They are twelve in number, four males and eight females. These are also called the Quranic sharers, who consist of those relations, which were excluded from the inheritance, under the customary law. Though their claims on the score of priority are not inferior to them.[40] The male sharers are father, grandfather (paternal), uterine brother and husband. The female sharers are wife, daughter, son's dauther (how low so ever) full sister, consanguine sister, uterine sister, mother and grandmother (paternal and maternal). The fractional quantum of the share is also fixed by Holy Quran in *Surah Nisan,* which deals elaborately in different verses about the inheritance. The fixed shares are 1/2 1/4,1/8,

2/3, 1/3, 1/6. The ascertainment of heirs, as well as allocation of their share is decided in every case, according to the principle of the school, to which the deceased belonged at his/her death. The difference of the School of heirs will make no effect.[41] The quantum of the share be determined at each death.[42] The estate vests immediately in each heir at the death according to the quantum of share ordained by Holy Quran.[43] This ownership cannot be suspended till the payment of the debt.[44] Next to sharer the residuaries come and after that the distant kindred.

Example: If only father, mother and husband are survived, they all are sharer and the property will immediately vest in them. In this case the father will inherit as residuary because there are no children.

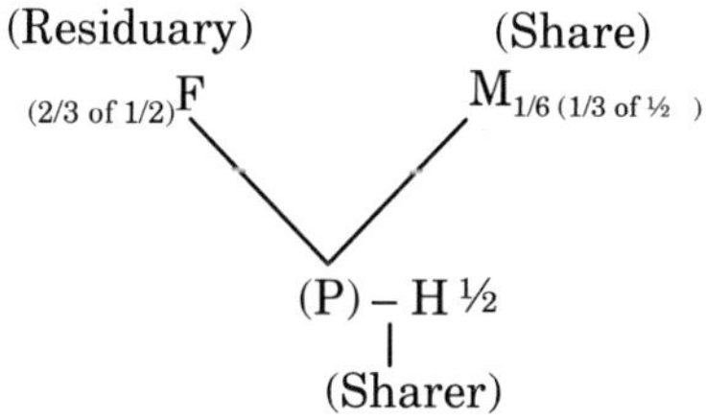

Residuaries

All those persons, whose shares are not prescribed by the Holy Quran and inherit the residue after the prescribed shares been given to the sharers, are called the residuaries. Relating to residuaries there is a Hadith of Prophet (PBUH) narrated by Abu Hurrairah, "The Prophet (PBUH) of Allah (SWT) said *"who are nearer to the believers than themselves and who so ever dies and leave property it is for the residuaries if no sharer."*[45]

It means that after allotting the prescribed shares to the sharers if the property left that residue will go to residuaries. Some times if there is no sharer the residuaries inherit the whole property. If there are widow, son and daughter, after allotting the prescribed share of widow (as she is sharer) the residue will be inherited by son and daughter (as residuaries).

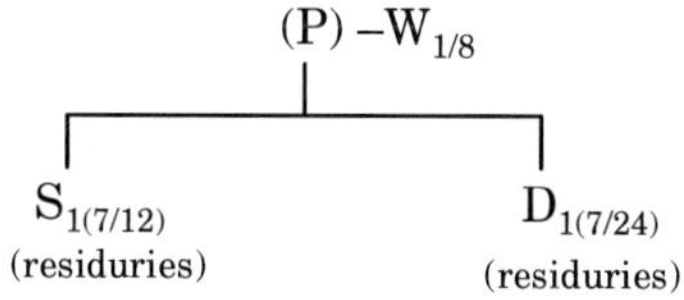

According to Sirajiyah there arc three types of residuaries—

- Residuary in their own right
- Residuary in another right
- Residuary together with another

Residuaries in their own Rights

Those, who are related with the deceased without the intervention of the females, are said to be the residuaries in their own rights. They are four and all are males.

- Deceased's descendants (hls)
- Deceased's ascendants (hhs)
- Deceased's father's descendants (hls)
- Deceased's grand father's descendants (hls)

Residuaries in Another Right

The residuary, in another right is every female who becomes or is made a residuary by the presence of a male, who is parallel to her. These are four females:

Daughter with son,

- Daughter with son.
- Son's daughter with son's son
- Full sister with full brother
- A half sister with father and half brother

Residuaries together with Another

The residuary with another is every female who becomes a residuary with another female; as full sisters or half sisters by father, who become residuaries with daughters or son's daughters.[46]

Among residuaries the nearer will be preferred. There are six sharers who under certain conditions become the residuaries_father, grand father, daughter, son's daughter, full sister and consanguine sister. Father and grand-father sometimes inherits in both the capacities as sharer and as residuary. Daughter, son's daughter, full sister and consanguine sister are four females who inherits either as a sharer or as residuaries under certain circumstances.

Distant Kindred

About the distant kindred there is a Hadith narrated by Ibn Abbas, the Prophet (PBUH) of Allah (SWT) said, "*give the faraid to those who are entitled to receive it. Then whatever remains, should be given to closest male relatives of the deceased.*"[47] Distant kindred are meant those blood relations who are not competent to inherit either as sharers or as residuaries.[48] These distant kindred are consist of cognates and females. Majority of the companions of the Prophet (PBUH) accepted that the distant kindred be entitled to get property as heir. In the absence of any general and special custom to the contrary, the distant kindred would succeed against any person whose relations are undefined.[49] But Imam Malik and Imam Shafai do not subscribe to this view.[50] Distant kindred are also of four kinds-

- Descendants of the deceased
- Ascendants of the deceased
- Descendants of parents of the deceased
- Descendants of the grand parents of the deceased.

There is an acute controversy about to whom the preference should be given over the other. According to Abu Hanifa preference should be given to second class over first class then third then fourth. But Abu Yusuf and Mohd Hasan bin Ziyad reported from Abu Hanifa that the order of preference should be according to the first, second, third and fourth.[51] The remotest relative will inherit under this head.[52]

The fluctuation of Shares among the Sharers and Residuaries

Though the shares of the sharers are prescribed in the Holy Quran and fixed, but according to the situational circumstances, sometimes the share also fluctuate. All the twelve sharers can not get their shares at a one and the same time. There are some conditions which are also prescribed in Holy Quran, which govern the actual succession and the position of sharers, residuaries and distant kindred, at the time of the fluctuation of property of the deceased. Now the position of each sharer in different condition is necessary to be discussed to understand the succession easily.

Male Sharer

Father -"*And to parents each of them shall have 1/6 part of the inheritance if he has son, but if he has no issue (son) and his parents are the heirs then his mother shall be entitled to 1/3 and if he have brethren, then his mother must come 1/6 after any bequest or debts.*"[53]

No one can exclude the father

- He is a sharer of 1/6 along with son or son's son (hls)
- He is sharer and residuary both, when there is a daughter or son's daughter (hls) and no son or son's son.
- He becomes residuary with mother if there is no child or son's child.

Examples :

1. Father - 1/6

   Son (hls) - 5/6

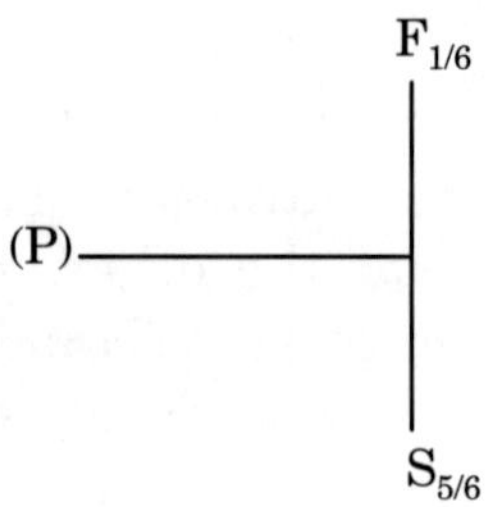

2. Father - 1/2

   Daughter - 1/2

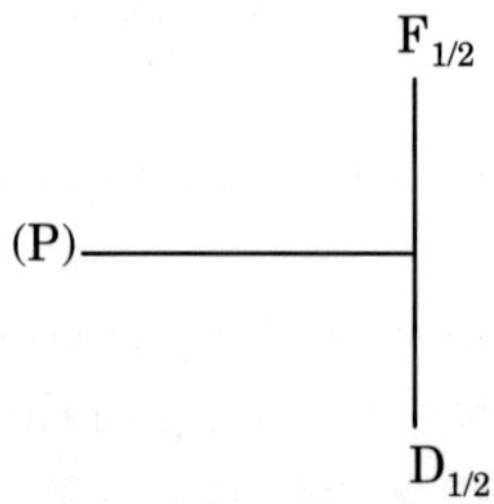

3. Father - 2/3

   Mother - 1/3

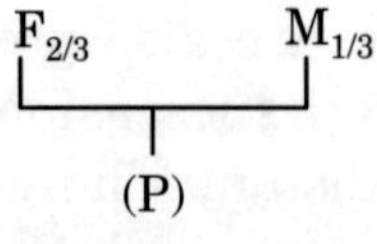

True Grandfather - There are two Hadiths relating to the right of true grand father from Ibn Abbas, "*grand father is either treated or dealt with as the father,*" Bukhari, from Maqbal bin

Yasar. *"The Prophet (PBUH) of Allah (SWT) gave to the grand father among us 1/6"*, Ibn Majah.

- True grandfather can be entirely excluded by father
- In the absence of father the true grand father inherit like the father but—
    - o He can not reduce the mother's share to the 1/3 of the residue.
    - o He can not exclude paternal grand father.
    - o The full or consanguine brother, in existence of the grand father shall not be excluded and the grand father shall get the share equal to that of the brother.
    - o Father's mother in the existence of father, stands excluded but she shall not be excluded by the grand father.

Examples :

2. Father - 1/6

   Grandfather - excluded

   Son (his) - 5/6

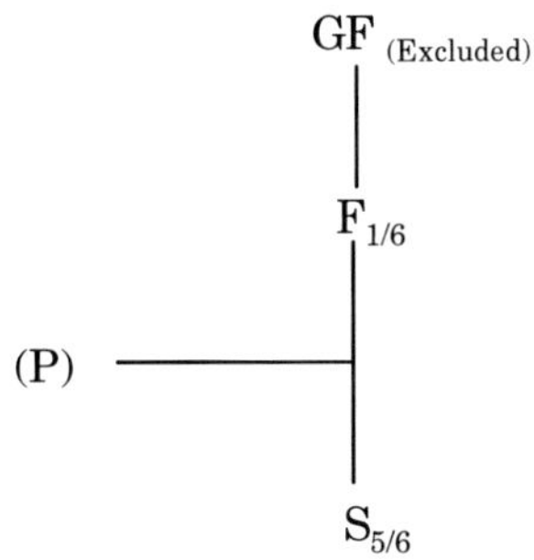

2. Grand Father - 1/2

   Daughter - 1/2

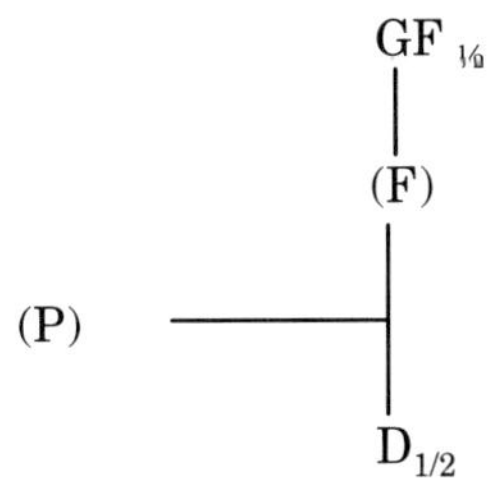

Uterine Brother—*"If a man or a woman be succeeded by a collateral relation (having left neither a parent nor a child) and the deceased have a (uterine) brother or sister then to each of them twain 1/6 and if they be more than two, then they shall be sharers in 1/3 after payment of bequest and debt."*[54]

- Uterine brother be excluded by the child or son's child (hls).

- Uterine brother be excluded by the father and grand father.
- The share will be 1/6.
- If two or more then 1/3 (collectively).

Example :

Father's brother	-	2/3
Uterine brother	-	1/6
Uterine sister	-	1/6

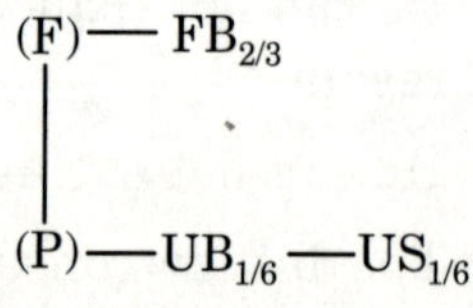

Husband *"And unto you belongeth 1/2 of that which your wives leave if they have no issue but if they have a child then to you 1/4 of what they shall leave after paying bequest and debts."*[55]

- Husband takes $^1/_4$ share along with children or son's children
- He takes $^1/_2$ if there is no children or son's children

Examples :

1.	Husband	-	1/4
	Son	-	2/3 (of residue)
	Daughter	-	1/3

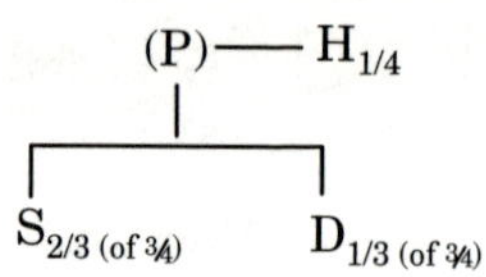

2.	Husband	-	1/2
	Daughter's son	-	1/2

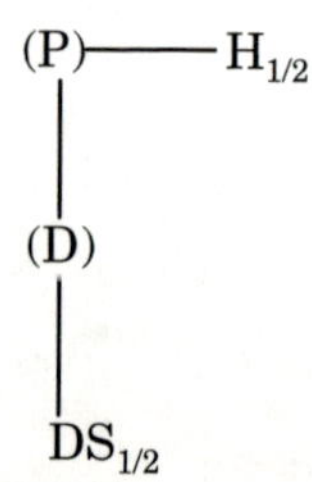

Female Sharers

Wife—*"And unto them (your wives) belongeth 1/4 part of that which ye leave, if ye have no issue, but if ye have issue, then they shall have 1/8 part of what ye leave after paying the bequeth and debts."*[66]

- The wife inherits in every situation.

- The wife or wives take 1/4 if there is no child or child of a son (hls).
- The wife or wives takes 1/8 when there is a child of a son (hls)
- The word wife or widow means the wife of valid marriage. In case of fasid or void marriage there shall pass no inheritance between them.
- The Kitabiah wife (who has not been converted) is not entitle to inherit each other.[57] On the basis of this difference of status several distinctions in law have been maintained between Muslim and Kitabiah wife *e.g.* if a Muslim wife commits adultery she is awarded the fixed 'Hadd' punishment but Kitabiah wife is not punished for adultery with Hadd.[58]
- In the case of divorce, if thc husband has, in his sound health, irrevocably divorce, atonce, breaks off. The divorce having been effect in sound health, the husband dying during the wife's observance of probationary period (Iddat) makes no difference. The wife shall not be his heir.[59]
- In the case of Khula, Mubarat or divorced by court degree they will not inherit each other.

The pronouncement of divorce during the death illness shall not affect the right of inheritance of wife.

Examples :

1. Wife - 1/4 $S_{3/4}$ ——— (P) ——— $W_{1/4}$

   Sister - 3/4 (full of consanguine)

2. Wife - 1/8

   Son's daughter - 7/8

(P)——$W_{1/8}$
|
(S)
|
$S'D_{7/8}$

Daughter—"*Concerning the provision for children, Allah (SWT) chargeth you to the male equivalent of the portion of two* *females and if there be a woman only, if more than two then they shall have 2/3 of the inheritance and if there be only one she have 1/2 ."*[60]

- The daughter cannot be excluded.
- If there is no son.
- The daughter will take $^1/_2$ of the property if she is alone.
- In case there are more than one daughter then 2/3 collectively.
- If there is a son then she will inherit as residuary and her share will be half of a male (brother).

Examples :

1. Wife - 1/8
   Son - 2/3 (of 7/8)
   Daughter - 1/3 (of 7/8)

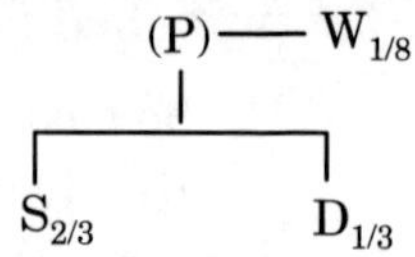

2. Son - 2/3
   Daughter - 1/3

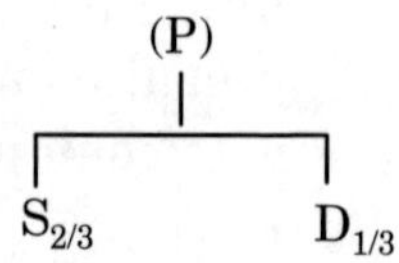

3. Son's son - 1/3
   2 Daughter - 2/3 (Collectively)

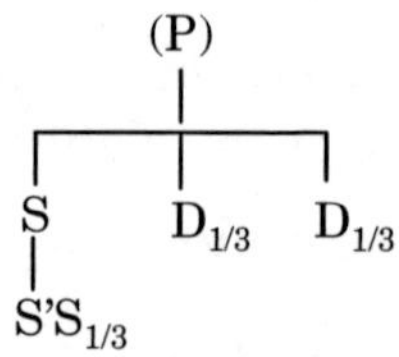

There is also a Hadith relating to the rights of the daughter - from Jabir bin Abdullah—*"A woman came with her two daughters before the Prophet (PBUH) of Allah (SWT) and said "O" Prophet (PBUH) of Allah (SWT) these two daughters are of Sabit bin Qais who was killed in the battle of Uhad, their uncle has taken away the entire property and has left nothing for them. It is not possible to get them married without property. The Prophet (PBUH) answered, 'Allah (SWT) alone could decide". There after recited the Quranic verses as stated in Surah Nisan "Usi Kimullah-I-awladikum" were revealed. The Prophet*

(PBUH) sent for the woman and the uncle and told him to give 2/3 to the two daughters and 1/8 to widow and to take for himself the residue."[61]

Son's Daughter

- If there is no child of the deceased then son's daughter will be sharer if alone 1/2 and if two or more then two 2/3 but with equal son's son she become residuary.
- If there is a son then children of the son will inherit nothing.
- If there is only one daughter and no son, higher son's son or equal son's son then she will inherit 1/6 as sharer.
- If there is more than one daughter and these have taken their 2/3 share then son's daughter shall be excluded and get nothing.
- If there is lower son's son and she does not inherit as sharer she will succeed as a residuary.

Examples :

1. 2 daughters - 2/3
   Son's son - 2/3 (of 1/3)
   Son's daughter - 1/3 (of 1/3)

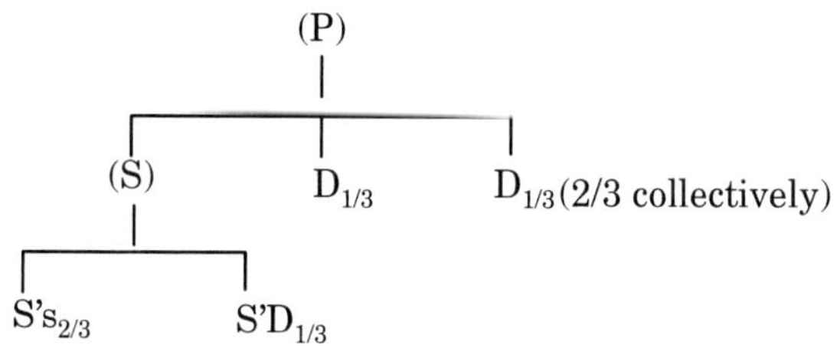

2. Daughter - 1/2
   Son's son - 2/3 (of 1/2)
   Son's daughter - 1/3 (of 1/2)

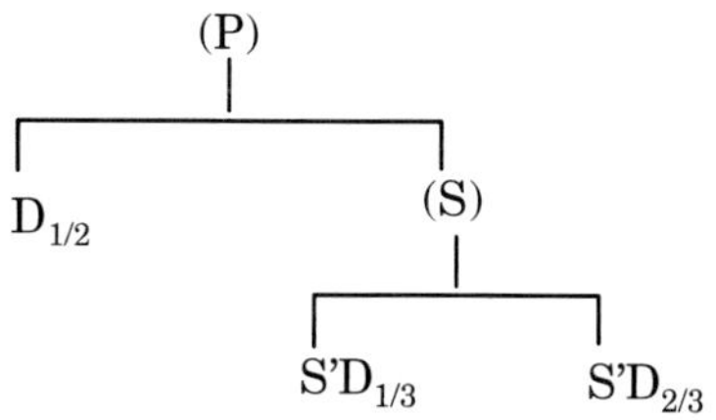

Full Sister—"*If a man die childless and have a sister 1/2 of the heritage shall be hers and he would have inherited from her if she died childless: and if there be two or more then 2/3 of the heritage, and if there be brethren, both males and females, the male shall have portion of two females, Allah (SWT) makes this manifest to you that ye err not, Allah (SWT) knows of all things.*"[62] *Holy Quran declares that the share of male child be equivalent of two females.*[63]

- If there is no son or son's son (his) father, grand father (hhs) or full bother, then full sister will inherit in the capacity of sharer, her share will be 1/2 if alone and 2/3 if more than one.
- With full brother she will become residuary.
- If there is son's daughter the full sister become residuary.

Examples :

1. Mother - 1/6

   Full sisters - 2/3 (collectively)

   Uterine brother - 1/6

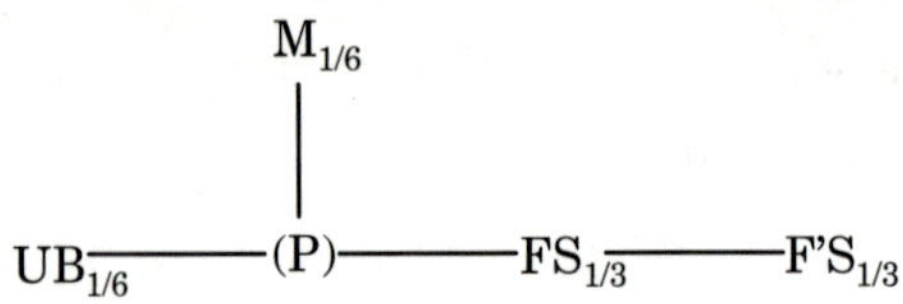

2. Daughter - 1/2

   Son's daughter - 1/6

   Full Sister - 1/3

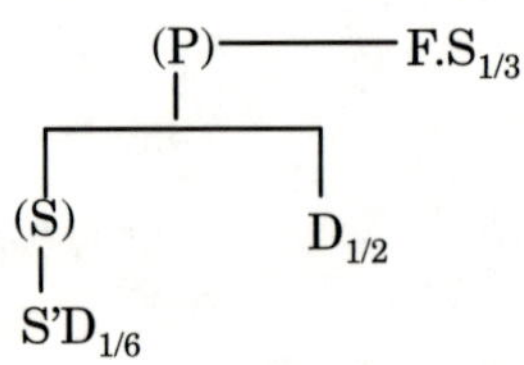

Consanguine Sister

- The consanguine sister will inherit 1/2 if alone and 2/3 if two or more only if there is no child, child of son (hls), father, true grand father (hhs), father's brother full sister and consanguine brother.

- With the consanguine brother she will inherit as residuary.
- If there is only one full sister and one consanguine sister then she will inherit as a sharer 1/6.
- If there is no full sister then she will be a residuary with daughter or with son's daughter.

Example :

1. Full Sister - 1/2

   Consanguine sister - 1/6

   Mother - 1/6

   Brother's son - 1/6

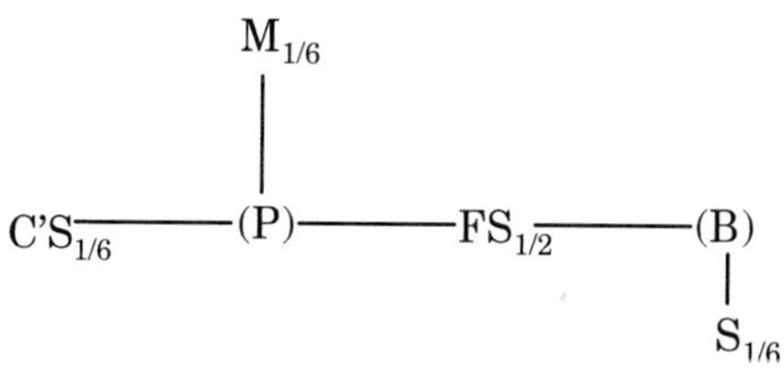

Uterine Sister—There are two situations in which Uterine sister is entitled to inherit.

- If there is no issue of the deceased or his son.
- If there is neither father nor grand father.

There share will be 1/6 if alone, 2/3 if more than one.

Mother

- Mother can never be excluded but her share fluctuate according to the situations.
- The mother will take 1/6 share as sharer with the child or with sister, child (hls) or with two or more brother or sister.
- Her share will be 1/3 if there is no child (hls) and sister or brother.
- If there is husband or a wife and both parents then the mother will inherit 1/3 of what remaining after

satisfying the share of husband or wife and the residue is to father.

- If in a place of father there is grand father mother's share will be 1/3 of the whole property.
- The step mother of the deceased is not entitled to inherit as there is neither relationship by lineage or by affinity.

Example :

1. Father - 1/6
   Mother - 1/6
   Son - 2/3 (of 2/3)
   Daughter - 1/3 (of 2/3)

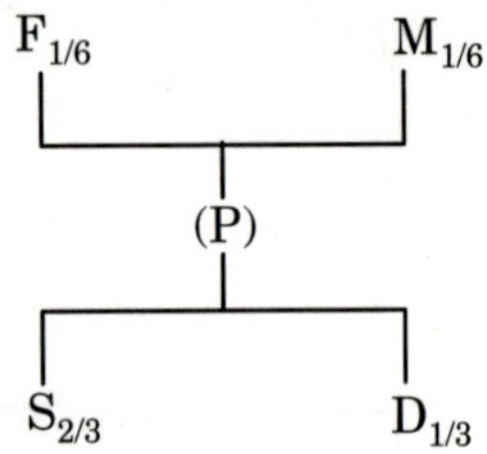

Grandmother

- The share of true grandmother is 1/6 whether one, two or more whether paternal or maternal.
- The paternal grandmother will inherit 1/6 where there is no mother, father or intermediate true grandfather.
- Maternal grandmother will inherit 1/6 if there is no mother.

Example :

Father's mother - (Excluded by father)
Mother's mother - 1/6 (not excluded)
Father - 5/6 (as residuary)

(excluded by father)

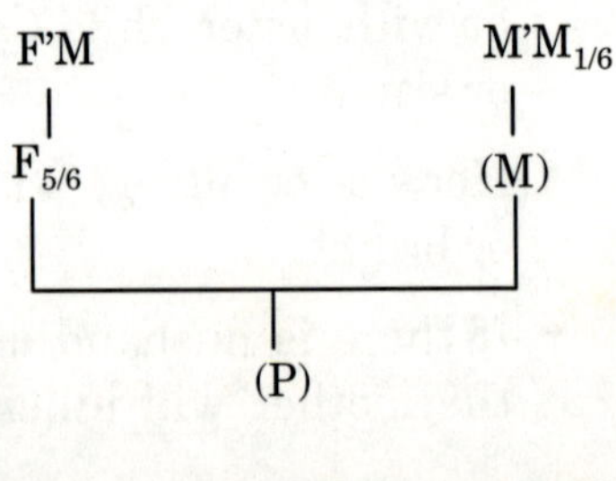

Aportionment or Computation of Heritage

At the time of allocation of shares to the entitled heirs three situation arises—

- The sum of shares is equal to the heritage
- The sum of the shares exceed the heritage
- The sum of shares is less than heritage

There is no practical problem if the sum of shares and heritage is equal but in other two conditions the problem arises which are solved by the special rules provided under Islamic law by the name of Doctrine of Awl and Doctrine of Radd.

Doctrine of Awl

In the situation when the sum of the shares exceed to the heritage, the share of each sharer is diminished or reduced proportionately for example - If a lady dies leaving behind husband and two full sisters. The share of the husband will be 1/2 and sister's share, will be 2/3. The total of these shares will exceed the unity.

Illustration

Husband	—	1/2 = 3/6 reduced to 3/7
2 full sisters	—	2/3 = 4/6 reduced to 4/7
		7/6 reduced to 7/7

Explanation : The proportional shares of $^1/2$ = 3/6 and 2/3 – 4/6 the total will be 7/6, we increases the denominator of 3/6 and 4/6 to make it equal to the numerator.

Doctrine of Radd

In the second situation the problem comes in this way that after allotting the share to the sharer some heritage is left as a residue and there is no residuary. In this situation the residue is returned to the sharers in the proportional way except in the case of husband and wife. In doctrine of Radd to equalize the shares to the heritage the common denominator is decreased. The difference between Awl and Radd is that in the previous case by increasing the common denominator the sum is equalized but in later case by decreasing the common denominator the shares are equalized.

Illustration : A Muslim dies leaving behind mother and daughter the Quranic shares of mother 1/6 and daughter 1/2 will not exhaust the whole heritage and 1/6 will left as residue. This residue, according to rule of Radd, will go by Return to the sharers by decreasing the common denominator of fractional share.

Mother	1/6	=	1/6 increased to 1/4	
Daughter	1/2	=	3/6 increased to 3/4	
			4/6	4/4

In the Case of Husband or Wife

The general exception, of the Doctrine of Radd is that this will not apply in the case of husband or wife. It means they will not get the residue by way of Return.[64] Along with the wife, the sister is not a residuary she will get by Return.[65] With the exception of husband and wife the distant kindred can not succeed so long as there is any sharer or residuary.[66] The doctrine of Return or Radd was discussed at full length in the leading case of *Abdul Hamid* v *Piyare Mirza.* According to Shia law the wife is not entitle to Return but the rigour of law has been modified on equitable consideration. It has been held that the wife even if she had no issue got all property of the deceased husband against the principle of Escheat,[67] and against the classical rule. In Shia law a childless widow is not entitled to take share in landed property.[68] But in *Ali Saheb* v *Hajra Begum*[69] it was held that if there was no residuary the residue reverted to the sharer. It is applicable where the husband or wife is the sharer. In another case of *Abdul Matin* v *Abdul Aziz*[70] the residue was given to distant kindred instead of reverting back to husband.

Shia Law of Inheritance

Hanafis and Ithna Asharis interpret Holy Quran, which is the basic source of Islamic law, differently in relation to the law of inheritance. Hanafi Jurists interpreted the Holy Quran in a literal and strict meaning, while the Ithna Asharis has interpreted it in a liberal and wider sense. The second thing, which makes a contrast between the Sunni and Shia law of inheritance, is that under Hanafi law the pre-Islamic customary laws were kept intact which were not specially abrogated by the Quranic injunctions. On the other hand Ithna-Asharis had abrogated the old customary laws and developed a new set of principles on the basis of Quranic injunctions. Under Shia law the right of inheritance emerged on two bases,[71] either the claimant is related to the deceased by sabab, which means by marriage or by nasab, which means consanguinity.

- By Sabab - Husband and Wife
- By Nasab - All relatives entitle to inherit

All heirs under Shia law are either sharer or residuaries. There is no concept of distant kindred in Shia law.[72]

Comparison of Sunni and Shia Law of Inheritance

- Under Shia law the cognates and agnates were treated equally in the matter of inheritance.[73] Sunni prefer the near in degree to the more remote whilst Shias apply the rule of propinquity to all cases without distinction of class or sex.

Illustration : If a person dies leaving behind him a brother's son and brother's grand son and his own daughter's son. Among the Sunnis the brother's son being a male agnate and nearer to the deceased than the brother's grand son inherit in preference to others but among Shias, the daughter's son being nearer in blood, would exclude the others.[74]

Examples :

Sunni Law **Shia Law**

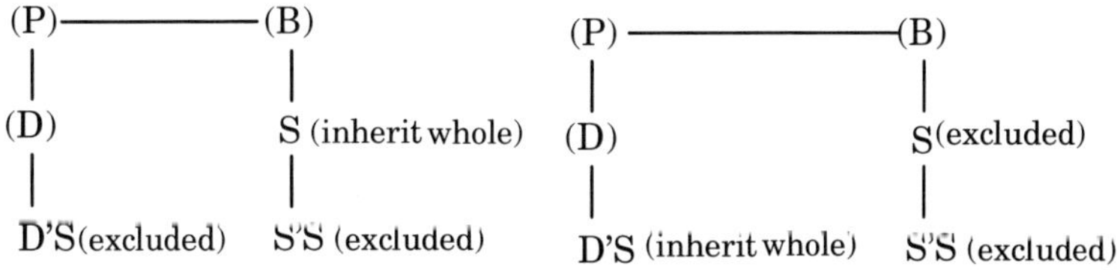

- Under Shia law class I heirs wholly exclude class II and III heirs, class II exclude class three. Among class III nears in degree exclude the remorter.
- Both Shia and Sunni law does not recognize the doctrine of the representation, to entitle the person to inherit,

in the place of his father or mother. But under Shia law it is applied to decide the quantum of the share of any given person, under Sunni law it is not applied at all.[75]

- Under Sunni law a daughter's daughter as an uterine relation has no place in the inheritance until all the heirs and residuaries are exhausted but under Shia law she would inherit the share of her mother.[76]
- When the children of a son coexist with the children of a daughter, the son's children shall take 2/3 and daughter's children 1/3 the respective share of their parents in Shia law. Under Sunni law the children of a daughter are uterine relations and postponed until the sharers and the residuaries are exhausted.[77]
- The Shia law recognized partly the principle of primogeniture, holding that the eldest son is entitle to sabre, the Holy Quran, the signet, the robes of honour and other vestments of his deceased father but not under Sunni law.[78]
- When there is a half brother by the same mother and the son of a full brother, the estate goes to the half brother in Shia law but under Sunni law the half brother get 1/6 and the remainder goes to the son of the full brother.[79]

Examples

Sunni Law

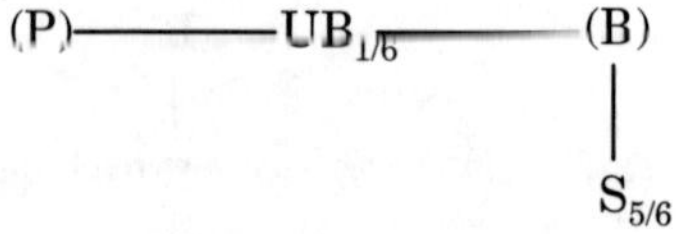

Shia Law

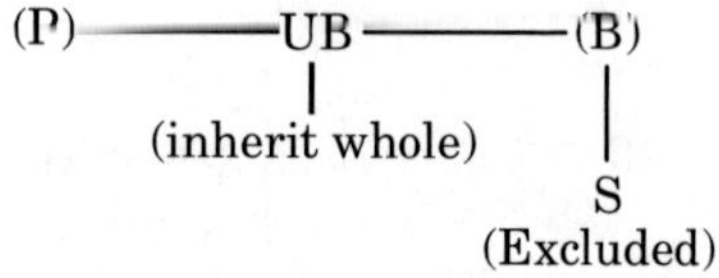

- Where there are paternal uncles and aunts they take the inheritance in the usual portion two to one but under Sunni law the entire estate will go to paternal uncles to the exclusion of aunts.[80]
- Under Shia law the distribution of the property is according to per-stripe but under Sunni law as per capita.[81]

- Under Shia law the females however remote will inherit with the son.[82]
- If a woman be divorced by a husband during an illness of which he does not recover and which eventually causes his death, her inheritance right will continue for the one year under Shia law but under Sunni law until the expiration of the women's period of probation.[83]
- Under Shia law there is a difference between real and personal estate, but not under Sunni law. If there is no child then Shia widow will be entitled to 1/2 of the personal estate only, including house hold trees and buildings but not inherit in real estate. In case there are children then 1/8 of both personal and real property.[84]
- In Shia law if a non-Muslim dies leaving behind a Muslim and a non Muslim heir, the Muslim heir though remote in degree, succeed in preference to the non-Muslim heir but under Sunni law, non-Muslim will not entitle to inherit.[85]
- Under Shia law the doctrine of increase applies only against the daughter and sister but under Sunni law it extends to all sharer alike.[86]
- Under Shia law besides husband or wife, in certain cases the mother and uterine brother or uterine sister also does not share in the Return but under Sunni law the entire sharer except husband or wife share in the Return.
- Under Shia law only intentional murderer is excluded from inheritance but under Sunni law any one who caused the murder is excluded.
- Under Shia law the illegitimate child is entitled to inherit neither from father nor from mother but under Sunni law the illegitimate child will inherit only from the mother but not from the father.[87]
- Both under Shia and Sunni law these heirs are never excluded from succession-father, mother, husband and wife.

On the basis of above discussion, it can be concluded that the Islamic law of inheritance provides minute details about the distribution of heritage and as Sir William correctly said that there is no possible question relating to inheritance which is not rapidly answered by the Islamic system of inheritance. The females have got the right to inherit property with absolute power to appropriate it for the first time in the world by Islam. Number of females was not only made entitled to inherit but the Holy Quran also fixed their shares. These rights were given to females at the time when the females of the rest of the world were not even entitled to hold the property. Though in Hindu legal system there was the concept of stridhana but that was very complicated and not absolute and the daughter were not entitle to inherit the ancestral property. By Act of 1956 the concept of notional partition was introduced by which the daughter and the son equally inherit the property of their father. After the amendment of 2005 she is entitled to inherit the ancestral property as a coparcener in her own right.

B. Under Hindu Law

Knowledge, of isolated details so long as they are not deduced from and connected with their underlying principles, is however as slippery as it is confusing and it is better to have a firm grasp over few fundamental principles than to collect mechanically a mass of disjointed details.[88]

Hindu law developed as a part of religion. There is an acute controversy about it because custom is also acknowledged as one of the main source of law. Myane says,[89] *"Hindu law is the law of the Smrities as expounded in the Sanskrit Commentaries and Digest which as modified and supplemented by custom, is administered by the court."*

The first lawgiver of Hindu law, Manu belonged to the old *basti* of Manali in Himachal Pradesh. From a small temple where there was never an idol, he formulates the basic postulate of the rule of law governing mankind, which was first written on the leaves, now known as Manu Smriti.[90]

The present Hindu law is an outcome of ancient dharamshastras and their commentaries, discordant practices and conflicting decisions. As Derrett pointed out,[91] *"flexibility, diversity, adaptality and genius for adjustment without changing one's entity, are the hallmarks of Hinduism. It is properly not less a way of life than a religion,"*

Definition of Hindu—The meaning of the term Hindu as commonly understood is stated by the court as, *"it is a matter of common knowledge that Hinduism embraces within itself so many diverse forms of beliefs, faiths, practices and worships that it is difficult to define 'Hindu' with in precision.*[92] In Indian Succession Act, 1925, the word 'Hindu' is used in theological sense as distinguished from a national or racial sense as it includes Arya Samajis[93] and Brahmos etc.[94] The Hindu Succession Act 1956, The Hindu Marriage Act, 1955, Hindu Minority and Guardianship Act, 1956, all prescribed three conditions for the purpose of the application of the Act in clause 'a' 'b' and 'c':

- Hindu by religion
- Buddhist, Jain or Sikh by religion
- Who are not Muslim, Christian, Parsi and Jew, is Hindu.

According to Indian Limitation Act, Hindu does not mean a person who is ethnologically a Hindu but also a person who has the legal status of a Hindu and is governed in the matter of inheritance by Hindu law.[95]

Now it is well settled that the term 'Hindu' is so vast that no precise definition can be given. On the basis of above definition given by different statutes and judicial decisions, the applicability of Hindu law will decide whether the person is Hindu or not. Therefore, we can say that barring Muslims, Christians, Jews and Parsis all other habitants, living in India who is subject to Hindu law are considered as Hindus.

Succession

Succession means the acquisition of ownership through kinship to the last holder independent of any voluntary act on his part designed to have this effect.[96]

Before, 1956, there was nothing at much variance in any institution of Hindu Law than the law of succession. No uniform system of succession existed even within the school of Mitakshara. The foundation of the law of succession was based upon the text of Manu—

"Sons take the property to the nearest sapinda the inheritance next belongs."[97]

The difference between the schools and within the schools relating to the laws of succession, was because of the different interpretations, were given by the propounders of different schools. Mitakshara considers that the wealth becomes the property of another solely by reason of his kinship to the owner.[98] According to Dayabhaga ownership to a person's property, by virtue of kinship to that individual arises, only when that person's ownership comes to an end, which happens usually on his death."[99] It means that Dayabhaga recognized the right of heirs in the property of their kinsman arises on the death of that person. On the other hand Mitakshara considers that the accrual of ownership does not depend upon the cession of ownership of previous owner but they acquire the property at the moment of their birth and become the co-owner of the same property. In Dayabhaga it is death, which confirms the ownership, and in Mitakshara it is birth, which confirm the ownership.

Women's Property Right Under Old Hindu Law

The degraded position of women in ancient India precluded entirely the idea of their, having been regarded as heirs of the family property. In early times several writers had quoted a text from Vedas,[100] in which the general unfitness of woman from heritage seemed to be pronounced. At that time even it could not be imagined that females have any property right except Stridhana. Hindu law was very harsh on the point regarding inheritance of females. Baudhyana, reputated founder of one of the school of Yajurveda, excluded females from inheritance on authority of the Sruti text *"woman are considered to be destitute of strength and of a portion"*. Baudhyana says,[101] *"women are devoid of prowess and incompetent to inherit women are use less."* He propounded that the Vedas declared no inheritance to a woman. Some of sayings of Vedas relating to the succession will clarify the position explicitly.

Rig Veda *"speaks about the individual proprietorship of a log of* wood'.[102]

"The text of Vedas *"speaks of the sons dividing father's property after the demise of the father."*[103]

"It speaks of unmarried daughter staying in father's home and asking for a share of father's property"[104]

Rig Veda again says *"A begotten son does not give paternal wealth to his sister. He gets her married."*[105]

In the above mentioned exerts of the Rig Veda, it is evident that only for unmarried daughter there is a provision but for the married girl there is no provision. Instead brother is not bound to give her share in property, his only responsibility is to get her married. It is proved by these exerts that in primitive society, the females had no share in property, except unmarried daughter.

In post Vedic period some changes were brought and the woman who have not got the Stridhana from their husband or father-in-law shall inherit the property of their own father. It is said that after the death of father the son divide the father's wealth and daughters will divide among them the Stridhan, if there is no daughter then the son will take the Stridhana[106]. The position of woman in the joint family was even worse and at the mercy of surviving brothers.

In Smriti period some changes had been brought but heritable capacity was made subject to certain conditions.

The Nirukhta writer Yasha says *"The wise men holds that both the children have the right of inheritance"*[107] About the right of inheritance of widow Kane writes[108] that "Vishwarupa allowed a share of property to the widows of deceased son and grandsons of the intestate when partition take place during his life time. Jimutvahna said that a widow of a deceased person who lived separately or in joint family succeeded her husband's estate.[109] Vijnaneshwara was liberal towards woman and allowed a widow to be the heir of her deceased husband.[110] He also mentioned great grand mothers right to inherit.[111]

By the above discussion it is evident that the old Hindu Law was very insensitive towards women. To remove all the diversities and to improve the condition of woman time to time some legislative steps had been taken *e.g.*- the passing of Indian Succession Act, 1865, which gave very limited rights of property to women. The limitation was removed by the passing of Married Women's Right to Property Act, 1874. After that Indian Succession Act, 1925, came into existence, which was confined to the Parsis, Christians and Jews etc and did not better for Hindu females. Then Hindu Law of Inheritance (Amendment) Act, 1929, was passed. But the fundamental changes had been brought in the condition of Hindu women by the Women's Right to Property Act, 1937. Sec. 3 of the said Act was the most important section, which specially provided provisions for the women's succession. But Hindu female, provided under the Act of 1937, was unfortunate enough to be excluded so long from the domain of Hindu Law of Inheritance simply because they were females. *"Women are devoid of the sense and incompetent to inherit"* is the sharp edge sword that was used to cut their throat.[112]

Though so many efforts have been made to improve the condition of the Hindu females but the radical changes came into being only in 1956, when the Hindu Succession Act of 1956, was passed by the Parliament. It is considered, piecemeal and brought revolutionary changes in the history of women's property right.

Fundamental Changes Brought by the Act of 1956

- All schools are governed by the uniform rules of succession.
- The heirs are divided into four groups and the preference is based upon the blood relationship and other rational conditions.
- The female's share was made equal with her counterpart male member.
- The limited estate of widow is converted into absolute ownership.
- The kinds of the property as Women Estate and Stridhana are abolished whatever kind of property, woman possessed or inherited, is her absolute property.
- All cognates and agnates are made entitle to inherit.
- Sections 14 and 26 have retrospective effect.

- In certain situation the undivided interest of a coparcener may devolve by succession not by survivorship.
- An undivided interest of a coparcenary in a Mitakshara joint family property is made heritable and capable of being disposed of by testamentary documents.

Before going into the discussion of the changes brought and provision made by the said Act, it is better to have a look over the concepts of the coparcenary, joint family and Hindu undivided family.

Coparcenary

A coparcenary is a narrower body *(112-A) (citation)* or an inner circle with in the joint family and consist of only those persons who have taken by birth an interest in the property by birth and also have a right to enforce a partition.[113] It commences with a common ancestor and includes a holder of joint property up to the three degrees. No woman can be a coparcener.[114]

But now by the amendment Act of 2005, daughter is also a coparcener.

Joint Family

Mitakshara joint family is a broader body than coparcenary and includes the wife and unmarried daughter of a copacerner as the member of the joint family. It is purely a creature of law and cannot be created by the acts of the parties.[115] The joint status is a the result of birth and the possession of joint family property, is not necessary to constitute it.[116]

Hindu Undivided Family

It is a normal condition of Hindu society who is joint in estate, food and worship. Hindu undivided family is a concept. Karta does all religious duties and observance.[117] Joint family is a normal characteristics of Hindu family. Presumption of jointness of Hindu family is stronger among nearer relation but weaker in remoter one.

The Position of Women after 1956

After the passing of the Act of 1956, the situation is better though not best. The Act is though considered as the piecemeal in the field of the property rights of woman but it is also criticized by eminent thinker of the Hindu law, like Derrett whose objection, about sections 8 to 13, is that there is a long list of heirs in class I and there is also no limits of agnates and cognates. So the rule of Government escheat is totally disappeared.[118] By analysis of the certain provisions of the Hindu Succession Act of 1956, which relates to the intestate succession and in which certain changes were brought by the Act, it would be clear that whether the said Act really improved the position of women's property right or still it need some changes. So to know the exact position we will have a critical look upon some important sections from sections 6th to 23rd of the Act of 1956, step by step. These sections have elaborate provisions relating to the intestate succession.

Critical Analysis of the Certain Provisions of the Hindu Succession Act of 1956

Section 6 before 2005 *"When a Hindu male dies after the commencement of this Act, having at the time of his death an interest in a Mitakshara coparcenary property, his interest in the property shall devolve by survivorship upon the surviving members of the coparcenary and not in accordance with this Act."*

"Provided that, if the deceased had left him surviving a female relative specified in class I of the Schedule or a male relative specified in that class who claims through such female relative, the interest of the deceased in the Mitakshara coparcenary property, shall devolve by testamentary or intestate succession, as the case may be, under this Act and not by survivorship."

Explanation 1: For the purpose of this section, the interest of a Hindu Mitakshara coparcener shall be deemed, to be the share in the property that would have been allotted to him, if a partition of the property had taken place immediately before his death, irrespective of whether he was entitled to claim partition or not.

Explanation 2: Nothing contained in the proviso of this section shall be construed as enabling a person who has separated himself from the coparcenary before the death of the deceased or any of his heirs to claim on intestacy a share in the interest referred to therein.

Section 6 consists of four paragraphs. The first paragraph says about the devolution of Interest by survivorship in Hindu coparcenary. The second paragraph contains the exceptions to the survivorship by devolution. The third Para, which is an explanation talks about the deemed or notional partition and last one, barred the separated member from claiming the interest in coparcenary.

Section 6 has recognized the female as an heir to inherit the property without abolishing the coparcenary and rule of survivorship. There is also an exception to the rule of survivorship in the Mitakshara coparcenary that if the deceased is survived by a male or female relative who can claim through such female then the interest of the deceased in the property shall be devolve by the intestate succession and not by survivorship. The only male relative specified in class I who first claims through a female relative is the son of a predeceased daughter.[119]

Section 6 has brought revolutionary changes in the history of woman's property right but also bring a number of queries in the mind of legal luminaries and clerics of law which were responded by the judiciary time to time, legal experts also tries to explain the provisions.

Whether the rule of survivorship really exists? The coparcenary or rule of survivorship is not abrogated by sec. 6 but it will be futile to think a family in which there will be no female of class I heir or a person who have an interest through such females. Sec.6 says that the interest of the coparcener would be devolved by survivorship but if there are any female of class I heir or a male who claims through such female then the property shall be devolved according to Act of 1956 or testamentary succession and not by survivorship.[120] So it can be said that apparently the rule of survivorship is not extinguished by the Act of 1956, but in reality it hardly exist. There may be a reason not to abolish the rule altogether because the sudden change in joint family may have adverse effect upon the existing state of things.[121]

The second question, which needs consideration, is, **whether this notional partition is treated as actual**

partition? Sec. 6 talks about the share of females without making them a coparcener, in the property of the deceased, which he has in the coparcenary property. The essence of coparcenary under Mitakshara law is the unity of ownership[122] and there is no question of share during the unity. Retaining the coparcenary how it is possible to ascertain the share. For this purpose the legislature introduced the doctrine of notional partition, which is a legal fiction, apart from actual or real partition without affecting the shares or interest or status of the other coparceners whose interest will be demarcated on the real partition. The Bombay High Court[123] clarified the position by saying that the idea of notional partition should be construed strictly just to ascertain the share of a deceased in the joint family property. It also talked about the position that in the case of only male heir,[124] there was no such partition. Actually to save the rule of survivorship this provision of notional partition was introduced as an exception. As Justice Patel said, that without such fictional partition the share of a deceased could not be ascertained which was necessary for the shares of females who were entitled only in his share in the property and not in whole joint family property as a coparcener.

The next question which comes in mind is that **How the share of a deceased be determined?** As there is a rule of survivorship in the coparcenary so the shares are indefinite till the actual partition took place. The interest of the coparcener fluctuates with each birth and death. That is way the section talked about the deemed partition in which it was imagined that what would be the share of a deceased if the partition took place just before his death, subsequent fluctuation would make no effect in the share of deceased.[125] It is made clear by the explanation, that it is immaterial that the deceased coparcener is entitled to claim partition or not.[126]

Now the next question can be asked **whether the devolution of property by notional partition be binding on the parties?** Supreme Court gives the answer of the above question in the case of *Maharashtra* v *Narayan Rao*,[127] the court observed that this assumption once made is irrevocable. There is a leading case of Bombay High Court *Rangubai* v *Laxmanan*,[128] in which a widow and stepson survived a deceased. In this case there was no possibility of getting any share of the widow in a real partition, as the stepson as a sole surviving coparcener had inherited the whole and there was no one who asked for partition. Though, if the partition took place, she would be entitled to equal share of the son, but the court by the full bench made it clear that the deemed partition would be binding, so treated as actual partition, which got recognition in series of cases by other High Courts. The Supreme Court[129] said that the interpretations of provision of Section 6, directed to enlarge the share of female heirs qualitatively and quantitatively to achieve the intention of the legislature.

It gives the birth to another question, **whether the death of a coparcener would dissolve the coparcenary?** In *P. Govinda Reddy* v *Golla Qbulamma* [130] the full bench of Andhra Pradesh High Court opined that the coparcenary would continue till the actual partition and the death of a coparcenary would not effect the continuance of the coparcener in any way.

An other question which is necessary to be considered is, **whether a woman be a coparcener and a Karta** ? The provision of the Section 6 of Act said that only male member be a coparcener who has a right by birth in the property. Though in some states, equal coparcenary right to daughter has been given as in Andhra Pradesh, Tamil Nadu, Maharashtra and Karnataka etc., but the right conferred by these states has prospective effect. In a case,[131] the deceased left behind his wife, one son and four daughters. He died before the Karnataka Hindu Succession (23 amendment) Act of 1994, came into force by which a new section 6-A was inserted in the Act to give the equal right of coparcenary to the females, but in the given case the court held that succession will be governed by section 6, of the Act of 1956 and son alone was made the coparcener and inherited 1/2 and the daughter and wife inherit equally along with the son from the other half.

Now come to the other part of the question according to the old Hindu law a woman, who is not a coparcener, cannot be the Karta of joint family. It is also supported by the series of judicial decisions.[132] On the other hand in some cases the judiciary[133] encourages the liberal attitude towards it and held,[134] that woman may be a Karta. Some writers also supported on the basis of old Hindu Law.[135]

Another question, which need our attention, is that - **Whether the heirs mentioned in class I be represented by Karta?** The answer was given by the Calcutta High Court,[136] that there was a relation between the joint family property and a Karta when the partition made that relation come to an end though section 6 talked about the notional partition instead of actual partition. Karta could not be imagined in a divided property. So class I heir could not be represented by Karta. In a latest case,[137] the question was raised about the power of Karta to dispose of the property. Supreme Court held that the Karta is competent to dispose of coparcenary property only in two conditions.

- The disposition must be of a reasonable portion of the property.
- That disposition must be for a recognized pious purpose or for legal necessity.

This was also made clear that the permission of the class I heir is also necessary prior to the disposition of the property.

The other important question is - **What would be the effect of section 6 in relation to woman's own right to inherit?** The judiciary, in so many cases has discussed this question from time to time. In a latest case,[138] it is considered that a wife inherited the interest of her deceased husband in the family property. She was also entitled under section 6 as a female heir in the joint family property and continued to be the member of an undivided family. She had the power to dispose of her undivided interest in the coparcenary property by a will or sale for a valuable consideration, though she could not make a gift without the prior consent of the other coparceners.

Whether the quantum of a daughter's share in inheritance is really equal to her brother? Though it seems that sec 6 gives equal right of succession to sons and daughters but the actual position was very different. There was unequal distribution of property between the male and female - as the daughter did not get an interest in the joint family property by birth as son had. She was entitled to inherit only 1/4 of the whole ancestral property. Suppose there is a father sons and a daughter in a Hindu (Coparcenary) family, in the life time of father being coparceners the father and the sons would inherit equal share. After the death of father the other half (which was the share of father) property would be succeeded by the son and daughter equally. Consequently the son's share would have been 3/4 and daughter's share would have been 1/4 of the total property.[139]

Example :

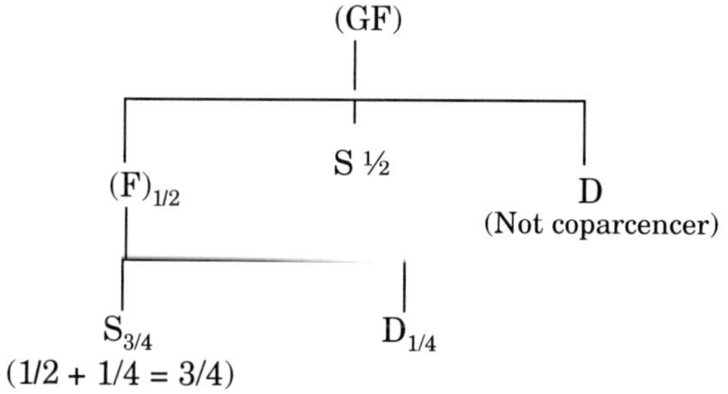

Note: Now the daughter will also inherit as a coparcener along with father and son, the ancestral property, under the provision of thc Amendment Act 2005)

Whether the provision of sec 6-A is discriminatory? A drastic change is introduced by the State of Karnataka[140] in the field of Hindu female right to property by inserting sec 6-A, 'by this section a daughter is made a coparcener by birth and possesses all the rights equal to her brother. But according to clause (d) the married daughter were not entitle to claim such rights as the section 6-A has prospective effect. Although the daughter, who has married, would get benefit of said section after the commencement of the Act and would get the benefit of the said section. This provision is challenged as being discriminatory between the married and unmarried daughter and against to Article 14 of the Constitution. A significant judgement[141] has been given by the court that it is not discriminatory but to avoid the reopening of the partition which would resulted in a chaos in the family and unsettled things which were settled long ago and it is also not in contravention of Article 14 of the Constitution.

Section 6 was considered as a revolutionary piece of social legislation. It was one of the most important section of the Act of 1956 dealt. with coparcenary property of a Hindu male but neither, it had any concern with separate property of the Hindu male which was governed by Sec. 8 of the Act, nor it had any interest in governing the female estate. For which there was a provision in Sec 15 and 16. Though it was very important but it created a lot of anomalies and raised so many questions, which were difficult to be answered. But judiciary tried to answer the questions and gave effect to the intention of the Parliament. The problems arose because, on the basis of old base a new structure was tried to build. As rule of survivorship was not totally abolished but in practice very rarely existed.

Though there were some problems in effecting this section but it did not mean that it had no importance. In the field of woman's right to property its importance could not be denied. As a critique it can be said that Sec. 6 gave a deathblow to the whole concept of joint family property by abolishing up to some extent the rule of survivorship. The continuance of joint family depended on the whims and caprice of a large number of persons who acquired the right to demand partition under the Act. By the notional partition, the status of the heirs of the deceased would be changed and they became the tenants in common instead of joint tenants with the other surviving coparceners. On the other hand the other coparceners continued to be joint tenants.

It is submitted that the rules laid down in Sec. 6 were compromised having some of the merits and demerits which attended such adjustive legislation."[142]

Section 6 After 2005

The most perplex, bewildering, controversial section 6 of Hindu Succession Act, 1956, is now stand amended by the Hindu Succession (amendment) Act of 2005. Section 6, which brought a lot of queries in the mind, which were discussed above, has abolished all the anomalies, ambiguities and confusion. All discriminations between male and female are resolved. By the new (amendment) Act, by providing, equal rights to son and daughter in the Hindu Mitakshara coparcenary. Like son the daughter is now a coparcener by birth. The provision of notional partition, survivorship that had created, so many problems in practice has been amended. The controversial share of son and daughter is equalized as she has got the right to inherit the ancestral property in her own right in the Hindu joint family, which is governed by the Mitakshara School. The new provision substitutes section 6 of the principal Act of 1956, which dealt only with property rights of male heirs. It provides that the daughters shall be equally subject to liabilities and disabilities in respect of said property. These provision which are now amended by the new (amendment) Act of 2005 were already exist in some states which were amended by the state amendment Act of Kerala in 1975, Andhra Pradesh in 1986, Tamil Nadu in 1989 and in Maharashtra in 1994.

Uniform Succession whether really exist after 1956

Prior to the passing of the Act of 1956 there were variety of rules, which governed the Hindu Law of Succession. But now after the passing of the enactment of 1956 there is a uniform system of succession and all the anomalies abrogated.[143] But in reality there are still different rules governing the succession based upon sex and kind of property. As section 6 deals with the coparcenary property, which have no place in, Dayabagha school because there is no coparcenary and therefore not recognized the rule of survivorship, which is the peculiarity of coparcenary. Sec. 8 to 13 deals with the general rules of succession in the case of males. Sec. 15 to 16 deals with the rules relating to succession of females.

Section 8 says that in case of Dayabhaga school all the property of a Hindu male whether separate, self acquired, a share, or an interest in the undivided Hindu family, be governed by this section. But in case of Mitakshara school it would apply only in the case of separate or self-acquired property. The kinds of property arc already discussed.[144]

As the word 'property' is not defined in the Act. Time to time a question came before the court whether agricultural land includes the property? There is no definition of property under the Hindu Women's Right to Property Act 1937, therefore the term property has to be given its ordinary meaning which would include agricultural land also.[145]

Whether Section 8 is prospective or retrospective? Section 8 is silent about its effect as section 6 and 7 clearly says that they are prospective in effect. In the case person died before the Act and succession opened before the Act, there will be no difficulty.[146] If the person died before the Act and succession open after the commencement of the Act which may happen because of widow, or the effect of section 14 which converts the limited estates of widow into full estate. In *Eramma* v *Veeruppana,*[147] learned judges opined that the words "shall devolve" occurring in this section indicate that its operation is prospective.

Kinds of Heirs

Under section 8 a new scheme of heirs is listed on the basis of propinquity and affection. The section 8 prescribes[148] four classes of heirs :

- The heirs specified in class I of the schedule.
- The heirs specified in class II of the schedule.
- The agnates of the deceased.
- The cognates of the deceased.

The order of the succession will be that if there is no class I heir the property will devolve to class II heirs, if no class II heirs then the agnates of the deceased and in failure of that to cognate of the deceased.[149]

Heirs Specified in Class I

In class I there are twelve (and four newly introduced heir by Amendment Act 2005) heirs who have preference over others and who inherits simultaneously and they cannot exclude other heirs of class I. These are as follows :

- Mother
- Widow
- Daughter
- Son
- Widow of pre-deceased son
- Son of pre-deceased son

- Daughter of predeceased son of a predeceased son
- Widow of predeceased son of predeceased son
- Daughter of predeceased son of predeceased son
- Son of predeceased son of a predeceased son
- Daughter of a predeceased daughter
- Son of a predeceased daughter
- Son of a predeceased daughter of a predeceased daughter.[150]
- Daughter of a predeceased daughter of a predeceased daughter.[151]
- Daughter of a predeceased son of a predeceased daughter.[152]
- Daughter of a predeceased daughter of a predeceased son.[153]

Among these heirs there are eight females and four males.

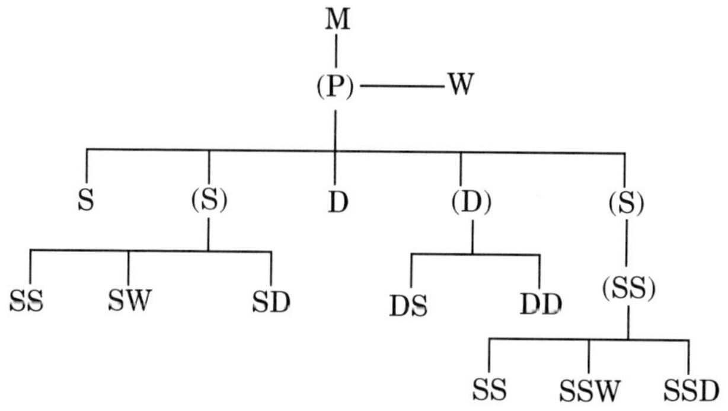

(Note: New heirs are not added in this diagram)

In this given diagram the propositus is indicated by (P) and the predeceased are put in bracket. It shows that a Hindu intestate died leaving behind a widow, a son, a daughter, and son of a predeceased son, a widow of a predeceased son, a daughter of a predeceased son, son of a predeceased daughter, daughter of a predeceased daughter, son of a predeceased son of a predeceased son, daughter of a predeceased son of a predeceased son and a widow of a predeceased son of a predeceased son.

Quantum of the Share of Class I heir

The next question arises what would be the quantum of the share of these heirs whether it will be per-stripes or per-capita? According to the section 10 of the Hindu Succession Act, 1956, three rules would be followed to allot the shares to the heirs.

- The intestate widow or widows shall take one share if more than one then they will distribute among themselves the allotted one share.
- Son's daughter and mother, who survived the intestate will take one share each.
- The heir in the branch of predeceased daughter and son shall take between them one share.

In the diagram given below all the twelve heirs of class I have been indicated: (New heirs are not included in this diagram).

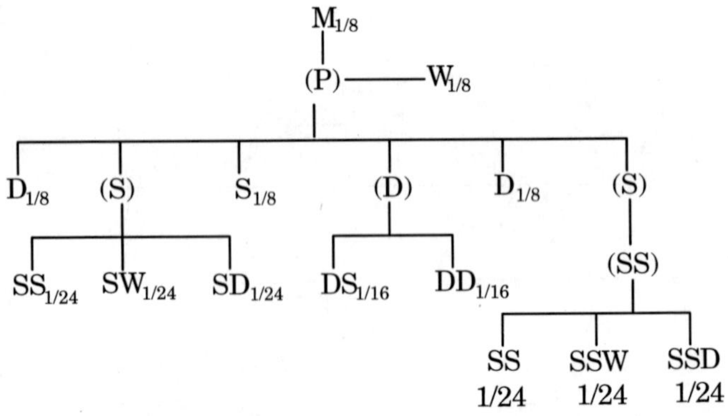

Heirs Specified in Class II

In this class of heirs there are nine categories. The entries in first category would inherit simultaneously according to per capita excluding the heirs of other categories. This rule of preference would continue according to the order of entry. These following heirs are categorized in class II heirs.

- Father (father will inherit all the property if there is no class I heir excluding all heirs mention below).
- Son's daughter's son, son's daughter's daughter, brother, sister.

- Daughter's son's son, daughter's son's daughter, daughter's daughter's son, daughter's daughter's daughter.
- Brother's son, sister's son, brother's daughter, sister's daughter.
- Father's father, father's mother.
- Father's widow, brother's widow.
- Father's brother, father's sister.
- Mother's father, mother's mother.
- Mother's brother, mother's sister.

Example: If a Hindu male died leaving behind father, son's daughter's son and daughter, brother and sister. In this problem father will inherit whole excluding all other heirs.

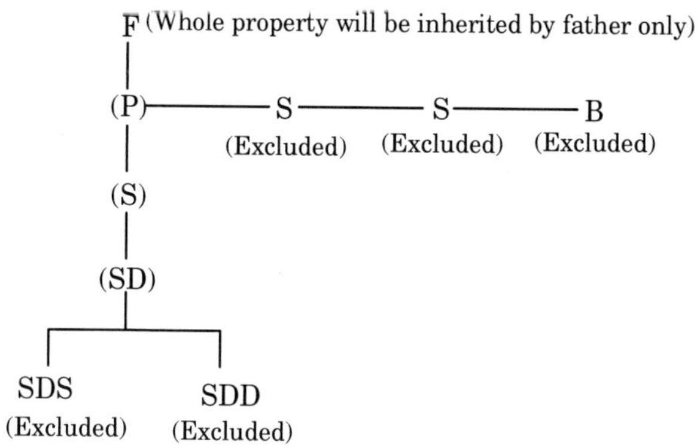

Problem: Take another problem if a Hindu dies leaving behind, son's daughter's son and daughter, brother, sister and brother's son and daughter. The brother's son and daughter will be excluded and all other heirs will inherit simultaneously.

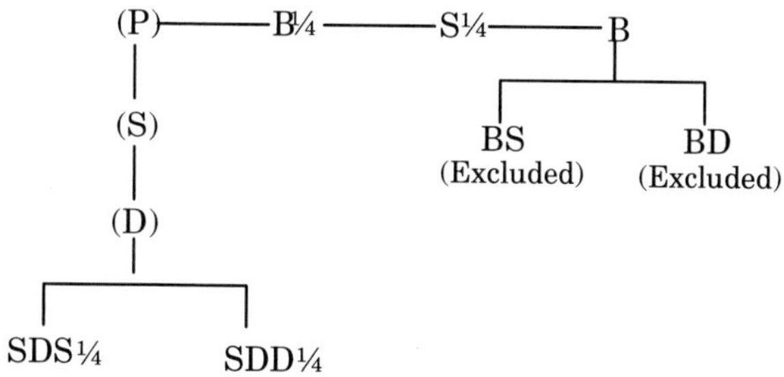

The heirs specified in class III

The heirs in this class are agnates, means the persons related with the propositus through male without the intervention of any females. They may be the descendants, ascendants and collaterals. They will inherit simultaneously.

The heirs specified in class IV

In this class all cognates are made heirs. The cognates are related with the propositus through females. Till all the heirs of class I, II, III were not exhausted the cognates cannot be entitle to inherit. Agnates are preferred over cognates.

SOME CONTROVERSIAL HEIRS

Legitimate and Illegitimate Heirs

Now proceed towards some issues, which were raised before the court with the passage of time, whether an illegitimate son or daughter is included in the category of son and daughter, or not? Under section 3(1)(i) of Hindu Succession Act of 1956, the term 'child' is defined as *'related by legitimate kinship and illegitimate children are not mentioned in the list of heirs of any class of heirs.*[154]

In another latest case[155] the right of the widow of an illegitimate child was questioned. The facts of this case were as such that the husband of the widow was the illegitimate child, so he had no right of inheritance. But the father in law of the widow of an illegitimate son had given some property to the son and daughter-in-law by a deed and possession had also been transferred. The property, which was given to the daughter-in-law, was only for lifetime. By the effect of section 14(1) of the Hindu Succession Act, 1956, that limited interest ripened into absolute one. But in this case court held that daughter-in-law with reference to section 8 means a legitimate daughter-in-law and the widow of an illegitimate son is no heir of her putative father-in-law.

Remarried Widow

Whether the widow would lost her right to inheritance if she remarry before the succession opened? In *Ram Sharan* v *Ujiyaril*[156] the widow of the pre-deceased son had remarried before the succession opened, it was held that she was not entitled to inherit. But the remarriage of the mother did not affect her right to inherit the property of her son, on his death as his heir.[157]

Remarried Widow after 2005

The bar, of remarriage of the widow to inherit the property under section 24 of the Act ,1956, has now been abolished by the new amendment Act of 2005.

Concubine

Concubine is entitled to be maintained by her paramour and on his death by his legal heirs, under the Shastric Hindu Law and this right is not taken away by the Hindu Women's Right to Property Act, 1937. After the commencement of the Hindu Succession Act, 1956, this limited right gets enlarged into absolute ownership. A house is given to concubine by her paramour in lieu of her maintenance. She disposed of it by a sale deed. This right of a concubine was challenged. The court held that she was entitled to dispose of the house in whatever manner she liked.[158]

Whether full blood heirs are preferred to the heirs related to half blood? The answer is given by the Andhra Pradesh High Court in affirmative in a latest case of *P. Jayramiah* v *Ara Gonda Munnarma.*[159]

Enlargement of women's limited estate

Nothing is much controversial than the provision of Sec. 14 of Hindu Succession Act, 1956, which gives absolute rights of ownership over the properties of women in which she had limited interest before the commencement of the Act. Though the controversies were resolved by the judicial pronouncement time to time. Before going into detail it is better to have a glance on the process through which this controversial section 14 have passed.

Rao Committee Report

The right of woman to hold property had always been subject of controversy. There is a majority of opinion that the doctrine of Hindu woman's limited estate has no real foundation in the smritis. It is also very strange that on one hand the Hindu law recognizes the right of woman to hold and dispose of her

Stridhan property, on the other hand the same law finds her incompetent to deal with other kind of property.[160]

In between 1954 and 1956 many legislative measures have been taken, to emancipate the Hindu women on the recommendation of Rao Committee.[161] A Bill was drafted to abolish woman's limited estate, polygamy and exclusion of female heirs by male heir. The Orthodox Hindus condemned the Bill. The matter was again taken up after independence and the Bill dealing with the law of succession was first introduced in Rajya Sabha.

The provision, which changes the limited right of Hindu female into absolute right in the estate, was clause 16 of Hindu Code Bill, which later came into the shape of sec 14 of Hindu Succession Act, 1956.

Section 14(1): *"Any property possessed by a female Hindu whether acquired before or after the commencement of this Act, shall be held by her as full owner thereof and not as a limited owner."*

Section 14, has swept away all the traditional limitations, on her powers of disposition of the property. The women's limited estate, which was a peculiar kind of property almost in any other jurisprudence, was ripened into absolute ownership by this section. She has come out from the state of perpetual tutelage of the old Hindu concept about women and got the status of full and independent ownership, with the full right to enjoy the property in whatever manner she like.

The expression covered by the words used in section 14(1) of Hindu Succession Act, 1956 can be better understood through the pronouncements of the court.

'Any Property'

The words 'any property' have wider meaning to cover all types of properties movable or immovable tangible or intangible. It also includes any right or interest.[162] The mode of acquisition of property is made immaterial.[163] The explanation attached to the section has removed all doubts, which were attached to constitute the Stridhana, and for Stridhana the mode of acquisition of the property was very important.

'Possessed by female Hindu'

In Lok Sabha a debate was held over the bill and the suggestions were given that instead of the word 'possessed' there should be the word acquired' in Section 14(1) because this word can be misused as the female can claim for the property as an absolute owner, given to her in mortgage etc.

The emphasis is given by the Act over the words '*possessed by female Hindu*' because it is a pre-requisite to ripe the women's limited estate into an absolute ownership. The meaning of the words '*possessed by*' is discussed by the Supreme Court,[164] as '*the state of owning or having in one hand or power*'. In another case,[165] the courts made it clear that the expression of the word '*possessed*' will also cover that case in which a female Hindu owns the property, though she is not in actual or physical or constructive possession over the property. The court,[166] also opined that the ambit must not be so extended to cover those cases in which, though the property is in possession of the widow but she has no right over that. The court has not given the benefit of section 14(1) in the case where the property was sold by the widow before the commencement of the Act stating that she would not be considered to be in possession.[167]

In a latest case of *Jamuna Bai* v *Bhola Ram,*[168] a widow was in the continuous possession since the death of her husband, along with the brother of her husband. The husband died before the Act of 1937 and the coparcenary property are inherited by survivorship and the brother was the only survivor. So widow had no right. But court held that she was in the possession of the said property and her limited interest would ripen into absolute ownership.

'Female Hindu'

An interesting question came before the Supreme Court in *Beni Bai* v *Raghubir Prasad,*[169] whether the third wife of a Hindu includes the '*wife*' in Hindu law to give the benefit of this section? The argument were given that under Hindu law one could not have more than one wife so the third marriage was invalid and third wife was not a wife. But the court held that to read '*female Hindu*' as only first wife was totally misconceived and third wife was also a wife and would entitle to get the benefit of this section. Recently in *Jose v Rama*

Krishna[170] the question before the court was that whether the benefit of section 14 be given to daughter also and her limited interest in property would get enlarged to full right? The court held that the female Hindu includes the daughter also and her limited interest would ripen into absolute ownership.

'Whether acquired before or after the Commencement of the Act !'

According to section 14 there are two kinds of Property–

- Property acquired before the commencement of the Act.
- Property acquired after the commencement of the Act.

The property which is acquired before the Act, was women's estate or limited estate'. It is distinguished from Stridhana over which she had absolute right, even before the commencement of the Act. By the effect of the said Act, all the differences between limited estate or women's estate or Stridhana were abolished and all the property in which she has interest and that is also in her possession was made her absolute property. The property acquired after the Act being came into existence, is her absolute property with the limitation of sub-section (2) of section 14,[171] Sub-section (2) has creates a great chaos and controversies and left the task over the judiciary to determine that in particular circumstances, the property will be governed by which sub-section (1) or (2).

'Shall' be held by her as full owner there of and not as a limited owner'?

Under old Hindu law, no female could be a coparcener she was only entitled to maintenance and residence, but no right to demand partition. The widow succeeds only if there is no male issue, except in case of an illegitimate son of Sudra. The widow of predeceased son and the widow of pre-deceased son's son were not entitled to inherit at all, barring the Bombay school. But by the Act of 1937,[172] some revolutionary changes were introduced in the field of women's property rights. Two principal changes brought by the Act, were - that the widow become entitled to the same share as her husband had, in the joint family property and got a right to claim partition, as a male owner, in other words she has put her feet in the shoes of her husband, except in Dayabhaga or the Hindu family governed by the customary law.

The second change was that the widow of a deceased was made entitled to equal share to the son and if no male issue then would inherit the whole property. In all these cases the widow had only a limited interest, means - she has an interest in the property till death without any power to dispose of or alienate the property and on her death the property, would revert back to the heirs of the person from whom she had inherited the property.

After the Act of 1956,[173] absolute ownership in Austinian sense had been confirmed over her inherited property to redress the problem faced by the Hindu female.[174]

According to Austin "*ownership is a right over a determinate thing indefinite in point of user, unrestricted in point of disposition and unlimited in point of duration.*"[175]

In order to get the benefit of the Act, it is necessary that the Hindu female have some interest or title in the property, which is in her possession at the commencement of the Act.[176]

In *Vankamanidi Venkata Subba Rao* v *Chatta Palli Seetharamartana*,[177] the question was that the right of a Hindu female under an instrument is, whether a recognition of a pre-existing right or right created for the first time? In this case, in a gift deed the interest of a widow was acknowledged, as a limited interest and also mentions that after her death it would revert to her husband's heirs. This deed was made prior to the Act of 1956. It was argued that it was a pre-existing right so the benefit of sub-sec (1) be given. But court held that the deed was made in terms of compromise so sub-section (2) would apply.

In *Raghubir Singh* v *Gulab Singh*[178] the court in relation to section 14 of the Act considered three points :

- Whether right to maintain was created by the Acts of 1937 or 1946 or it was a pre-existing right under the Shastric law?

- What was the nature and scope of sub-section (2) of section 14 ?
- How the enlargement of widows interest be effected ?

On the first point, Supreme Court opined that the maintenance right was existed in the Shartic law and this Act only gave them recognition and statutory backing.

About the nature and scope of sub-section (2)' of section 14, Supreme Court upheld the position of Tulsamma case,[179] as it applied only to the instruments, decrees, awards, and gifts, which create a new title.

On the third point, which was discussed elaborately in the instant case of Raghubir Singh,[180] the court views were in affirmative. In this case the husband, (of widow) had executed a will in favour of her grand child with the stipulation that till the life of testator and his wife they would enjoy full control over the property. The issue was, whether this right of wiodw would enlarge or not ? As, it was not in lieu of maintenance. The court held, that it would be enlarged into absolute ownership.

In another case court opined that where the widow had relinquished her right through a sale, her limited interest would not ripen in the absolute ownership,[181] or surrendered her share in the favour of her only son.[182] If the husband had created life interest by a will, only in the half share of the properties that would ripen into absolute one.[183] But it is also not necessary, that all limited interest would be enlarged into absolute one. It depends, upon the facts of each case where the property is inherited by the wife in lieu of her maintenance and the husband himself has got, only a life interest, over the property from his aunt, by a will in a clear and unambiguous language then it would not ripen into absolute one.[184]

Where in partition deed the widow take the property for life and she had herself directed with a clear stipulation that after her death the property would go to her sons, the daughter's claim was not maintainable. Very recently the court held it.[185]

Section 14 of Hindu Succession Act, 1956, has upgraded the position of Hindu female. So, far as the property right is concerned, now the Hindu woman is absolutely entitled, to hold the property. More over if she has any sort of right in the property of her husband then she will become the actual owner of that property because of the effect of section 14 of Hindu Succession Act, 1956. Provided that she is in possession of that property either actually or constructively.

Succession of a Hindu female

The Act of 1956 though considered as that it gave a deathblow to the old Hindu law of succession and forms a total new structure of the rules of succession. In reality it does not totally depart from the old values. As it supports different scheme of devolution of the property of Hindu females. However it demolishes the differences of school and sub-schools. It also makes no difference about the status and forms of marriages and paid no head to the kind of Stridhana which was the basis and the deciding factor in the old Hindu law of succession. However the Act still divided the property of a female Hindu into two categories and provides different sets of rules of succession of these two kinds. The source, from which the Hindu female inherits the property, is still a governing factor of Hindu succession in case of an issueless Hindu female. Though it is immaterial when she died leaving behind her own issue.

Sub-section (1) of section 15, prescribed the general rules of succession, which applied to every kind of property of Hindu female, which is capable of being inheritance but sub-section (2) of Section 15 state about the exception, which has received a heavy criticism.[186] It talks about the sources from which the property is inherited. There are also two other exceptions of the general rule of succession to which sections 15 and 16 will not apply. Which are as follows:-

- To any property which is subject of any other existing law as for the prevention of fragmentation of agricultural land etc.
- Any property, which is described in section 5 of the Act.

Section 15 says that the property of a Hindu female shall devolve according to the rules prescribed in Section 16, Section 15 has divided the heirs of a Hindu female into five categories:-

Class I Heirs

The son, daughter, the children of predeceased son or daughter and husband are class I heirs.

Illustration: Suppose a Hindu female died leaving behind son, daughter, husband and son of a predeceased son and daughter and son of a predeceased daughter. The shares will be as follows:

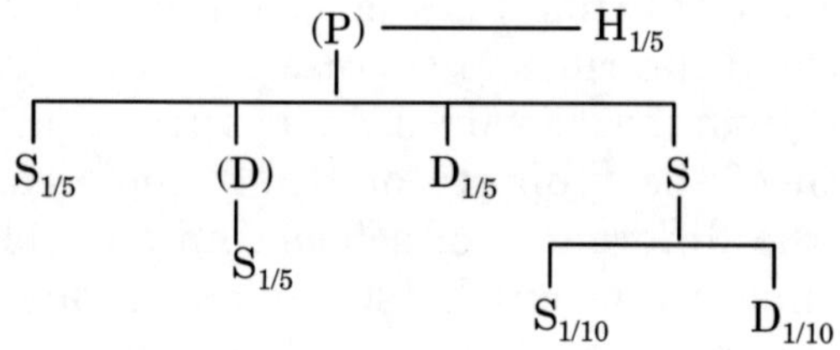

The son and daughter include the children of any predeceased son or daughter[187] and the son and daughter by natural birth legitimate or illegitimate[188] and validly adopted child.[189] The question about the stepson is very controversial and raised time to time. Recently the question before the court,[190] was, whether the stepson of a female was entitled to succeed the estate as her legal heir? The appellate court with reference to the provision of Sec. 15 and 16 of Hindu Succession Act held that stepson is not a preferential heir. However, this controversy was not resolved. To resolve the matter Supreme Court in *Lachman Singh* v *Kripa Singh*,[191] had observed the distinction between 'son' and 'step son'. According to the Collins English Dictionary - a 'son' means - a male offspring and 'step son' means - a son of one's husband or wife by a former union. Relying on that Delhi High Court held that girl had preferential right over the stepson.[192] Instead of it very recently the issue is decided by Jharkhand High Court in favour of the step son,[193] where the original owner died prior to coming in force of Hindu Woman's Right to Property Act, 1937 leaving behind his widow and two sons. The claim was made that the share of widow be inherited by her own son and not by stepson. But the court held that as the original owner died prior to the coming of the Act of 1937, so property should be devolved upon son and stepson equally.

Class II Heirs

If there is no heir in class I, means no daughter, son and husband and the children of predeceased son or daughter then property will go to heirs of husband.[194]

Illustration: Suppose a Hindu female died leaving behind no heir of class I but a brother, a sister and a son of a predeceased brother of her husband, the property will devolve among them if the property is inherited by the deceased female from the husband or in-laws.

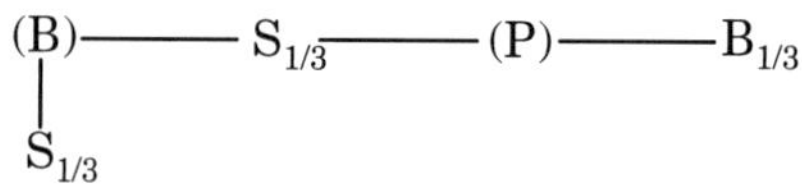

Illustration:- Suppose a Hindu female died leaving behind no heir of class I and II the property will devolve upon the father and mother if inherited from parents. They will take simultaneously.

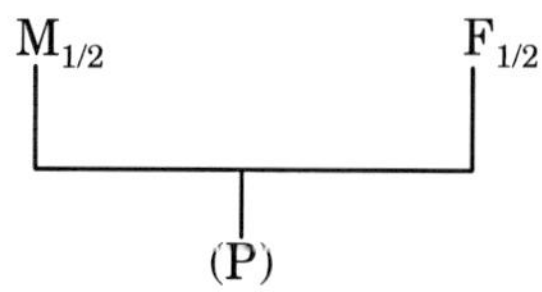

In *Chatro v Sahayak Chakbandi Meerut,*[195] the question came before the Supreme Court that who would inherit the land of a widow landholder dying intestate survived by only daughter? The woman purchased the land in the lifetime of husband. The husband possessed some part of the land, as tenant, after his death the widow repossessed as proprietor holder. On the death of widow, the brother of husband claimed that widow had succeeded the tenancy so her right would not get the benefit of section 14, but Supreme Court held that in the absence of son the only daughter will inherit the property.

From the decision of the above case we have inferred that the Zamindari Abolition and Land Reform Act will apply only when husband died leaving behind the agricultural land and only daughter as an heir. But where a female holder of an agricultural land died leaving behind a daughter as an heir then she will inherit the land as an heir and Uttar Pradesh Zamindari Abolition Land Reform Act and Tenancy Act will not apply.

The heir of the husband mentioned in section 15 means the heirs who would have succeeded under the Act if the husband had died just moment next after the females death.[196]

Class III Heirs

The father and mother will be entitled to inherit the property if there is no child, child of predeceased children, husband and husband's heir. If both parents alive they would inherit simultaneously. The father and mother mean the natural father and mother and not step parents[197] or putative father.

Class IV Heirs

The property will devolve if there is no heir in first three categories, among the heirs of class IV according to the entry.

Sub-sec. (2) says that if there is no child and no child of predeceased children or husband, or mother or father, and then the property will go to one, from whom it is inherited. As if the property is inherited from the husband or father-in-law then it will go to the heirs of the husband. If it is inherited from the parents then it would revert back, first to the heir of father then to the heirs of mothers.

Class V Heirs

If the property comes through the natal family of the female and there is no heir in classes I, II, III and IV, then the property will devolve, among the heirs of mothers. If the number of heirs is more than one, of equal degree relation, then they will take simultaneously.[198] An unmarried Hindu female died issueless leaving behind her, a brother and a widow sister in law. She inherits the property in question from her mother. Brother's claim to be only heir excluding widow (sister-in-law) as being the last heir of his father was not approved by the court. The court held that widow had an equal share in the property.[199] But where the female has inherited the property from her brother then this property will be governed by the rules of sec. 15(a) of the Act.[200]

Section 15

Sub-section (2) of section 15 says that:

"Notwithstanding any thing contained in sub-section (1)

- *Any property inherited by a female Hindu from her father or mother shall devolve, in the absence of any son or daughter of the deceased (including the children of any predeceased son or daughter) not upon the other heirs referred to in sub-section (1) in the order specified therein, but upon the heirs of the father; and-*
- *Any property inherited by a female Hindu from her husband or from father-in-law shall devolve, in the absence of any son or daughter of the deceased (including the children of any pre-deceased son or daughter) not upon the other heirs referred to in sub-section (1) in the order specified therein, but upon the heirs of the husband.*

Section 15(2)(b) is engrafted to prevent the person from inheritance who is not even remotely related to the person, whose property is in question. This section ensure that the property of a Hindu female in the absence of children and children of predeceased children and husband and even parents always revert to the heirs of real owner from whom the property is inherited.[201] If the property is allowed to be drifted away from the source, which is more important for the purpose of devolution of her property, the object of section 15 (2) will be defeated.[202]

The object of section 15(2) is to ensure that the property left by a Hindu female does not lose the real source from which the deceased female had inherited the property. If there is no children of a Hindu female from the husband from whom she inherited the property but from second husband she had children they would not entitle to inherit the property. In fact the Hindu Succession Bill, 1954, when originally introduced in the Rajya Sabha did not contain any clause corresponding to Sub Section (2) of Section 15. It comes to be incorporated on the recommendation of Joint Committee of the two houses of the Parliament.[203]

Section 15 (2)(a) says that if a Hindu female leaves behind no heir of entry 1, 2, and 3 then the property will devolve upon the heirs of her father or mother if inherited from the natal family and does not go to the heirs of husband-Section 15(2)(b) says that if the property inherited from husband father-in-law then in similar circumstances it will devolve among the heir of husband.[204]

In *Vijay Singh* v *Dy. Director Consolidation*[205] the apex court has recognized the absolute ownership of widow, who was in possession of property when the Act came into force, consequently, it was held that on her death intestate her only daughter would become full owner of property as class I heir.

At another place the mother became an absolute owner of the property by virtue of section 14 of the Act, which she has inherited from her husband. It was held that it be devolved upon the son and daughter under the provision of section 15 (1)(a) and not under any other provision of law.[206] To ascertain that who will be the heir of a Hindu female under category (b) of section 15 (1) the time of the wife's death be considered instead of husband because the succession opens only at the time of her death.[207] In a case property inherited by a wife from her second husband which become her absolute property. The widow made a will in favour of her son from the first husband. The heirs of her second husband made the claim. The court in this case held that the property will be devolved according to the will of the widow.[208] In this instant case the court does not apply the provision of sub-section (2) of Section 15 of Hindu Succession Act 1956 and give preference to the will of the deceased. It is submitted that by this decision court has defeated the object of sub-section (2) of section 15.

A very different type of case came to the court. The facts of the case were that one Yamuna Bai had 7 (seven) daughters. One of them was widowed at very early age and lived with her mother over twenty years. She had got nothing from her late husband. In such circumstances, Yamuna Devi had executed a will in favour of her widow daughter excluding all other daughters, which was challenged by the other daughters. It was held by the court that testator and all daughters would get equal share and the widowed daughter would be entitled to the 1/8 share of her mother in addition of her own share[209] It is a case of natural love and affection.

Sub (2) is restricted only to the inheritance and does not deal the property acquired by any other means as through will gift or dowry. Though it is difficult to say why Parliament has restricted its application to the inherited property only, whether dowry and gifts received by a female are not property inherited from the father and husband.[210] It was held where the identity of the property was changed sub (2) would not apply.[211]

The Order and Manner of Distribution

Section 16 is technical and explains the order of succession and manners of distribution among the heirs of a female Hindu. It talks about the simultaneous succession and support the rule of representation. It prescribed three rules:-

Rule 1: Among the heirs specified in sub-section (1) of section 15 those in entry one, shall be preferred to those in any succeeding entry, and those included in the same entry shall take simultaneously.

Rule 2: If any son or daughter of intestate had pre-deceased, the intestate leaving his or her own children alive at the time of intestate's death, the children of such son or daughter shall take between them, the share which such son or daughter would have taken, if living at the intestate's death.

Rule 3: The devolution of the property of the intestate on the heirs referred to, in clauses (b), (d) and (e) of sub-section (1) and in sub-section (2) to section 15, shall be in the same order and according to the same rules as would have applied, if the property had been the father's or mother's or the husband's as the case may be and such person had died intestate in respect there of, immediately after the intestate's death.

The heirs of the father or the husband will be determined according to section 8. The heirs of the mother will be determined according to section 15 of the Hindu Succession Act, 1956. The heirs of mother, father or husband who are entitled to inherit the property of a Hindu female according to section

15, are actually the heirs of Hindu female herself and not of the person through whom the heirship is traced.[212] In *Shankarappa* v *Gauramma*[213] it was held that where a Hindu female inheriting the property of her parents jointly with her sister, died childless and intestate leaving behind a sister and the son of the predeceased sister, the surviving sister will take 3/4 share of the property held jointly and the son of the predeceased sister 1/4.

Some General Principles

Sections 18, 19, 20, 21, and 22 talks about the general principle of the succession which are as follows -

Preference of Full Blood over Half Blood

Section 18 says that the heir who is relative to the deceased by full blood will be preferred in comparison of half blood,[214] if the nature of the relationship is the same in every other respect. In section 18 the legislative intent is to codify the earlier rule of Hindu Law preferring relations of full blood to half blood. It is a substantial reproduction of the previous rules.

Mode of Succession of Two or More Heirs

Section 19 says that if there are two or more heirs they will succeed together as per capita and as a tenant in common. But if a man dies leaving behind three children by a predeceased daughter and four children by a predeceased son, the property will be divided half and half. Here the property will be divided as per stripes. If there are two widows, they both will succeed together as tenants in common and if any one of them die then her share will not pass to her co-sharer but to her own heirs.[215]

Unborn Child

Section 20 talks about the right of the child in the womb. In law he deemed to be present at the death of the intestate Hindu. It does not confine to the children of deceased or predeceased son but to any person who is otherwise entitled. If the partitioned were done before his or her birth he or she will be entitled to reopen the partition. Section 20 extends to cases of illegitimate children entitled to claim.

Simultaneous Death

If several deaths take place simultaneously, how the share will be decided, it is prescribed in section 21 of the Act. Because of the rule of survivorship this question is raised in simultaneous death that, who survived the other for the purpose of succession. Section 21 says that it will always be presumed that younger has survived the elder until the contrary is proved, when the matter is of relationship, age have no consideration but in general the younger in age be considered survived the elder. As where the mother and daughter, shot dead at the same time it will be presumed that daughter survived the mother.[216]

Preferential Right

Section 22 is designed to give the benefit, to the heirs of deceased, to acquire the family property in preference of others. The intention of the legislature is to ensure that the property should remain within the family members rather than to go in the hands of stranger. Though this preferential right resembles to the right of preemption but in strict sense it is different. This right is only available to the class I heirs. Reversioners not belonging to class I heir have no preference over class II heir,[217] This right extinguished if once the partition took place and specific shares have been allotted,[218] because the intention of the legislature is not to put a clog on the power of alienation of independent owners of the properties.[219] It is personal right neither heritable nor transferable.[220]

Section 23 Before 2005

"The march of economic laws can be thwarted but not stopped for ever and the desire for self acquisition and freedom from the trammel of corporate life, ultimately established the institution of partition and separate ownership necessitated, the formulation of rules of inheritance applicable to property held in absolute sever ability by its own last owner."

Section 23 was considered one of the most discriminatory legislative actions, which discriminate only on the basis of sex. It was opposite to the constitutional provision of Art 15(1), which says that there must not be any discrimination on the ground of sex. It was also a violative of fundamental right.

Section 23, *"where a Hindu intesate has left surviving him or her both male and female heirs specified in class I of the schedule and his or her property includes a dwelling house wholly occupied by members of his or her family then not with standing any thing contained in this Act, the right of any such female heir to claim partition of dwelling house shall not arise until the male heirs choose to divide their respective shares, therein, but the female heir shall be entitled to a right of residence therein."* Provided that where such female heir is daughter, she shall be entitle to a right of residence in dwelling house only if she is unmarried or has been deserted by or has separated from her husband or is a widow.

Said section says that where both male and female heirs of an intestate specified in class I of the schedule succeed. The female heir shall have no right to claim the partition of the dwelling house which is wholly occupied by the male but female heirs shall have the right to reside there till they are unmarried or deserted or widowed. This right to claim partition is not extinguished forever but as soon as the male heirs choose to divide their respective share the female heirs also can claim partition. Section 23 was designed to preserve the heritage of a Hindu Jurisprudence,[221] which had considered the dwelling house as an impartible asset, and to prevent fragmentation it puts a rider,[222] on the absolute and equal enforcement of female's right to claim partition. In the words of Raghavachariars "*....to avoid confusion and chaos in the family created by the female whose moorings are elsewhere on account of their marriage, seeking to take away their shares and throw the male members into the streets...*[223]

Whatever may be the object and reason[224] but it was discriminatory to oust the females from her lawful right merely because it was inconvenient for the male sharers.

Before going into the detail discussion of the provisions of section 23, it is necessary to know about the dwelling house. Dwelling house is not defined in the Act. The Supreme Court has discussed it,[225] in *Narasimha case.* in this case the question before the court was that what is dwelling house? Whether it includes the building, which is partly occupied by members of the family, and other part is in possession of some stranger? The Gujrat High Court opined.[226] That if the literal meaning is to be given to the section which says, *"wholly occupied by members of the family"* it ceases to be as dwelling house and section 23 will have no application in this case.

Another question, which need consideration, is that whether a tenanted house be considered as dwelling house? The apex court said that *"In our considered view a tenanted house is not a dwelling house in the sense the word is used in section* 23".[227] The house ceases to be dwelling house if one or the other part is shared by someone as a tenant. By the majority opinion it was concluded by Supreme Court that the word dwelling house is neither a term of art nor it is synonymous of a residential house. To give the effect to the intention of the legislature who chooses the word dwelling house purposely - *"status quo"* should prevail as existing prior to his or her death.[228]

In this case a Hindu intestate died, leaving behind a son and three daughters. The son has sold half part of the house to a stranger. In these cicumstances the house was ceased to be a dwelling house because to constitute the dwelling house the actual, physical and mental (animus possendi) possession should present in the strict sense. The second question, which has been controversial for a long time is considered by the Supreme Court in this case was whether, restrict female to claim partition where there was only one male heir, is genuine?

Different views have been given by the different High Courts through the passage of time. The arguments made by the courts, were generally in the favour that there should be no application of said section in the case of one male heir. As the object of the section 23 is frustrated where there is only one male member and it would be amounted as a complete denial of the female's right because if there is only one male there is no possibility of the male heir to choose to divide and the female is left at the whims and caprice of their male counterpart. The supporter High Courts was Bombay,[229] Karnataka[230] and Orissa.[231]

But contrary view was also given by High Courts of Calcutta[232] and Madras.[233] The Supreme Court put the controversies at rest.[234] The apex court by majority opinion said according to general clauses Act, 1897, the language in plural would have to be read in singular also and where a Hindu died intestate leaving behind a single male heir section 23 would apply. It is submitted that the views of Supreme Court are not rightful and harsh towards females.

An interesting question came before the court,[235] for the consideration whether a coparcener can resist the daughter's claim for partition? The courts response is that section 23 clearly provides that it will apply only to class I heir and all coparceners are not a class I heir.

In circumstances where the dwelling house is not in the possession of the family members the bar of section 23 will not be applicable.[236] In another case it was held that section 23 could not be extended to adjust the interest of the parties in property without destroying the dwelling house as a unit.[237]

Section 23 After 2005

A very sound step has been taken by the legislature by abolishing section 23 of the principal Act, which was most unfair and discriminatory. Now the daughters have the right to claim the partition in the dwelling house. The provisions, which are critically examined in passing paragraphs, are self-evident that how much hardship, they create for the females. The daughters were totally at the whim and caprice of the male members and had no right to claim partition even in great distress. It is a great relief for the women folk of the Hindu society. In Hindu Succession (Amendment) Bill, 2004, the Law Commission of India has recommended in its 174 report that section 23 which disentitle a female heir to ask for partition in respect of dwelling house should be abolished.[238]

Heirs Not Entitled to Inherit?

The Act of 1956 barred certain persons from inheritance in certain condition. These disqualifications are laid down by the Act from section 24 to 28, which are as follows:

Remarried Widow After 2005

Section 24 of Hindu Succession Act disentitled certain widows from inheritance if they re-marry before the succession open. They were the widow of son, widow of predeceased son's son and brother's widow. But once succession opened and she inherited the property, she could not be divested from that property, by her subsequent marriage.[239] Under the Hindu Woman Re-marriage Act, 1956, there was a provision that if widow re-married even after the succession open, she would be divested from the property, she inherited from her husband. Subsequently this Act was repealed in, 1983. But where the marriage of widow took place prior to the coming into force of this Act and because of the old law the widow lost her right to inherit due to the second marriage, the provision of this section will not apply.[240] Recently Supreme Court gave a significant judgement. In this case the widow remarried in 1953, which was a bigamous marriage and held void. The argument was given in favour of widow that void marriage did not attract the provision of section 2 of Hindu Remarriage Act, Supreme Court said *"voidness of marriage will not remove her disqualification to inherit"*.[241]

A very irregular judgement was given recently by the Gauhati High Court, which defeated the object of the Act. The facts of the case[242] were that the deceased after divorcing her first wife married the plaintiff. After his death the plaintiff remarried. The court held that because of remarriage she had lost her chastity, so not entitled to any share. It is submitted that the case is wrongly decided because unchastity is no bar to inherit and section 24 applies only to the widow of son, son's son and brother's son and does not divest deceased's own widow.

Note : This controversial section 24 has now been abolished by the Hindu Succession (Amendment) Act, 2005. Now remarriage is not a bar to inherit the property of her previous husband.

Murderer

Section 25 disqualified the person who causes the murder of the deceased, from inheriting the property of the murdered who by either way commit the murder or abated or help in the furtherance of the murder. For the application of this section, the term murderer, should be liberally construed and not in the strict sense as defined in section 300 of IPC.[243] This section will apply to disqualify the person only and not his heirs.[244]

Conversion

Section 26 disentitles the heirs of a converted person from inheriting the property of any of their Hindu relative. Because of the Caste Disability Removal Act the effect of conversion will not disentitle the person himself who is converted,[245] section further says that if those heirs subsequently become Hindu the disqualification will be removed.

Disqualified Heir be Deemed Died

Section 27 confine to the person himself who by any reason is disqualified to inherit and does not affect the heir's right of inheritance in any way. It says that it be deemed that the disqualified person is dead before the intestate deceased in whose property otherwise he has right to inherit.

Abolition of the Old Disqualification of Hindu Law

Section 28 has abolished other disqualification of old Hindu law, which disentitle the person suffering from some diseases, from inheritance except those which are expressly mentioned in the above going sections of the Act. The unchastity of widow is no bar to inherit even though in the original Bill, the unchastity was suggested to retain.[246] A Hindu was found to be a lunatic when succession opened. It was claimed that under the text lunancy must be congenital to exclude from inheritance. Under Hindu law lunancy is considered distinct from idiocy. It need not be congenital to exclude from inheritance, if it existed when succession opened.[247]

Succinctly it can be said that there are so many anomalies in Hindu Succession Act, 1956 and it is not exempted from defects but at least it has improved, up to some extent the Hindu female's property rights. The entire previous impediment's, which were imposed upon the female's right, are abolished now and she got absolute property right with full rights to appropriate it, in whatever manner she liked. In comparison of old Hindu law now she was in better position though not at best.

Hindu Succession (Amendment) Act 2005

After the sixty two years of Independence the 5th September 2005 be remembered as a red-letter day in the Hindu Women's World, as another progressive attempt has been made by the legislature for the economic and social empowerment of women folk. Hindu Succession Amendment Bill, 2004 was introduced in the on going winter session of Parliament drafted on the recommendation of the 174th Report (May 2000) of the Law Commission. The Commission pointed out that the earlier law granted arbitrary and unfair benefits to the male heirs of a Hindu, died intestate. It suggests the equal distribution of ancestral property between both male and female heirs. It demands equal treatment and equal partnership in economic and social sphere. The Rajya Sabha passed this Bill on 16th August 2005 and by Lok Sabha on 29th August 2005 and got President assent on 5th September 2005 and came into force on 9th September 2005. It really gives a deathblow to the old Hindu law in which the females were even devoid of any property rights.

It is also an encumbrance upon the government to remove the discrimination as some states had already taken steps to remove these gender inequalities long ago such as Kerala in 1975, Andhra Pardesh in 1986, Tamil Nadu in 1989, Karnataka and Maharashtra in 1994.

The Kerala - Joint Hindu Family System (Abolition Act, 1975)

Kerala is the first Indian state who thought about the women and introduced drastic changes in Hindu succession Act 1956, which was followed by the other states. To have a glance upon these changes is necessary is understand the steps taken by the legislature in 2005.

- The concept of Hindu Joint family came to an end which is evident by the very name of the Act.
- The right to claim property by birth has no place because there is no coparcenary (S. 3)
- Under the provision of Sec. 4 of the Act of 1975, the members of Hindu undivided family have become the tenants in common[248] and are no more joint tenant.[249]
- S. 5 has abolished the rule of pious obligation of son to pay the father, grand-father or great-grand-father debt.

- The Act is prospective so any debt contracted before the commencement of the Act be binding on the members of the joint family.

The Andhra Pradesh Hindu Succession (Amendment) Act 1986. This Amendment Act of 1986 come into force on the 5th September 1986 with the following objects:

The Indian constitution has guaranteed the equality before law but the daughter's are excluded from the coparcenary ownership on the basis of sex, so the Act of 1985 is passed to remove this inequality.

- This exclusion of daughter persuade destructive dowry system with its social ills so to ameliorate the condition of women in the society and to eradicate the dowry system its become necessary to take some positive steps.

  By the Andhra Pradesh succession Amendment Act 1986 a new chapter II. A was inserted in the central Act of 1956 and these following changes have been brought:

- Unlike Kerala the Amendment Act has not abolished the concept of Hindu Joint family.
- By the provision of Sec. 29-A (i) the daughter has been put in the same position as the son in every respect. Now the daughter is the coparcener like son by birth and subject to same benefits and liabilities.
- According to Sec. 29-A (ii) at partition the daughter will get the same share as that of son.
- The daughter of pre-deceased son would get the same share as allotted to her counter part son.
- Sec. 29-A (iii) the daughter is made capable the disposing of her share by will or other testamentary disposition.
- Sec. 29-A (iv) the Act is retrospective, so the partition which took place before the commencement of the Act will not be affected. The daughter who married before this Amendment Act 1986 would not get the benefit of this Act. [250]

- Sec. 29-B - If a Hindu family dies, after the Amendment act 1986, her interest in the coparcenary property shall devolve by survivorship upon the surviving members. But if the deceased had left any child or child of the pre-deceased child her interest in Mitakshara coparcenary shall devolve by testamentary or intestate succession and not by survivorship and the concept of notional partition will apply.
- Sec. 29-C (i) A preferential right to acquire the share of the other coparencers who proposed to transfer his share. According to Sec. 29-C (ii) the consideration in case, there is no agreement between the parties, be determined by the court.

  Sec. 29-C (iii) In case there are more than one claimant the preference will be given to the heir who offer highest consideration.

Amendments in other States :

The aims and objects of Amendments in other states are same as that of Andhra Pradesh and the same model and language and same provisions were made by the other states. To adopt these amendments by the Maharashtra and Karnataka State took twelve years.

In a latest case[251] Amudha Rani VK. Veeraraghavan the court held that as per Sec. 29-A (i) the daughter of a coparcener shall become a coparcener in her own right in the same manner as a son and have the same rights in the coparcenary property as she had been a son and shall be the subject of same liabilities and disabilities.

- Sec. 29-A (iv) nothing in chapter II A shall apply to a daughter married before the commencement of this amendment Act[252]. If the States of married girl would not be changed. This provision is challenged in series of cases as discriminatory and violation of Art. 14 of the constitution.

  In the above mention case of Amudha Rani there were three daughters. Two were married before the commencement of the Act. The court held that they are not entitled to any relief. But the third one was unmarried therefore she is entitle to the same share allotted to the son.

In the case of Ravikirthi Shetty V. Jagathapala Shetty[253] it was held that according to the provision of the Hindu succession Karnataka Amendment Act 1994 only unmarried daughter are made coparcener and entitled to equal rights with son. But about the daughter's, who was married before the Amendment Act came in force, is entitled for the share in the property as a class I heir.[254]

Critical Analysis of the Amendment Act of 2005

Drastic changes have been introduced by the Hindu succession Amendment Act of 2005 and place the daughter at par with those of sons. But, unfortunately it has created a lot of confusion which is bound to increase the litigation.

Deletion of Section 4(2) of Principal Act

By the Amendment Act 2005 S. 4(2)[255] has been deleted which exempts the application of the Hindu succession Act, 1956 to the agricultural holdings, fixation of ceilings and devolution of tenancy rights of such holdings. It means in any state any law for time being enforce to prevent the fragmentation of agricultural land or fixation of ceiling or the cultivating rights of such holding the Act of 1956 had no application such as Uttar Pradesh Zamindari Abolition and Land Reform Act etc. This omission of sub-section (2) of S. 4 of the Act of 1956, arises some point of contentions such as -

- Whether the provisions of the Amended Act of 2005 will over ride the state laws?
- Whether such deletion is violation of Art. 14 of the constitution?
- Whether it is ultra-vires?
- Whether it will adversely affect the agricultural and economic planning of the country?

There is no express provision under the amended Act; the confusion is bound to arise, that in case of conflict between the state law and the provisions of the amended act, which will prevail? Such as the provisions of U.P.Z.A & L.R. Act bars the daughter from inheriting the agricultural holdings. If it is presumed that now the agricultural holdings would be the subject matter of Hindu succession Amendment Act, 2005 and the daughter will have equal rights in respect of agricultural holdings with that the son. Then the other question arises. Whether is it not violation of Article 14 of the constitution? As the Hindu succession Act is applied to Hindus. The Hindu daughter will get the benefit of amended Act and be eligible to inherit the agricultural hold insect. But the females of other religion are the subject of state laws which excludes the daughter from agricultural holdings for the prevention of the fragmentation of agricultural land. It will be discrimination only on the basis of religion which is violation of Article 14 of the constitution.

The other point of contention poses a question mark to the competency of the centre to legislate upon the matter of state list. As land is a subject of state list. The term land in entry 18 of state list is of wide amplitude and covers the land of every description, such as agricultural land[256] list III entry V empowers the legislative to modify the personal laws, such as Hindu or Muslim law,[257] Parliament can enact a law under this entry, to deal with the matter of wills, intestacy and succession of agricultural property in spite of its trenching upon entry 18, List II e.g. - Sec. 14 of Hindu succession Act.[258] But a different opinion has been expressed by the Rajasthan High Court[259] which has ruled that section 22 of the Hindu succession Act does not apply to agricultural land[260]. The other point is that the deletion of this sub-section will adversely affect upon the agricultural and economic planning of the country by the fragmentation of the land?

Amendment of S. 6

The major changes brought by the Amendment act are in section 6 of the Principal act of 1956, which are as follows :

- Induction of daughter as coparcener.
- Prospective effect.

- Hindu Undivided family.
- Distinction between the females of Hindu Joint family.
- Rule of survivorship.
- Mitakshara Coparcenary
- Deemed Partition.
- Discrimination between coparceners.
- No discrimination between married and unmarried daughters.
- No provision for the devolution of the interest of the female coparceners.
- Abrogation of the pious duty of son to pay the father's debt.
- Omission of S. 23.
- Deletion of S. 24
- Amendment in S. 30.
- Heirs under the Amendment Act.

Induction of Daughter as Coparcener

Sec. 6 (i) of the Amendment Act has come to end all the discrimination against the daughter which was only on the basis of sex. Now she is a coparcener of Hindu joint family by birth in her own right in the same manner as the son. She has acquired the same rights and subject to the same liabilities as that of son. This induction of daughter in coparcenary has gave a death blow to the traditional concept of Hindu Mitakshra- coparcenary in which the Hindu females were devoid of any property rights. The legal consequences of such introduction of daughter as coparcener are that the longstanding controversies about certain questions come to an end such as -

- Whether a daughter becomes a karta of joint Hindu family?
- Whether a daughter can start a coparcenary?
- Whether a daughter can demand the partition?
- Whether a daughter can dispose of her property by testamentary disposition etc.?

Prospective Effect

There is a provision under this section that these provisions of conceded-laws would not be applicable to any disposition or alienation or any partition which had taken place before the 20th December 2004. Recently Madras High Court[261] held that amended section 6 is prospective in that sense daughter is treated as coparcener on and from the commencement of the Hindu succession Amendment Act 2005.

Hindu Undivided Family

In a latest case[262] the provision of section 6 of the amended Act of 2005 is came for consideration before the Delhi High Court, the court held that the right of daughters in coparcenary is to be determined if Hindu undivided family is in existence as the very opening words of S. 6 (i) envisages the existence of Hindu undivided family when the amendment came into force. Once a partition is demanded and a suit is filed by the member of Hindu Undivided family the severance in status of coparcenary takes place. It is no more a Hindu undivided family. In this instant case the partition took place by the decree of court mere pendency of execution of court decree does not give right to daughter. Explanation of sub section 5 of section 6 of the Amended Act defines the partition made by execution duly registered, to ensure that false claim of partition may not be put forward.

Distinction between the females of Hindu Joint family

Sec. 6 (2) has made a distinction between the females of Hindu Joint family. The females who acquire the right in coparcenary property by birth like daughters and sisters would be capable to dispose of the property by testamentary disposition but the other females of joint females who have acquired the right the way of marriage would be the subject of previous law not amended.

Rule of Survivorship

Sec. 6 (3) State that were a Hindu does after the commencement of Hindu succession Amendment Act 2005. His interest in the property of a joint Hindu family governed by

Mitakshara law shall devolve by testamentary or intestate succession as the case may be under this Act and not by survivorship and the coparcenary property shall be deemed to have been divided as if a partition had taken place. The cardinal rule of Mitakshara coparcenary of survivorship has been abolished, by the express provision but only in the case male coparcener, as the sub section (3) clearly use the words"... his interest". Therefore the rule of survivorship is retained in the case of female interest in the coparcenary property. If it is said that in reality the rule of survivorship was hardly exist after the Hindu succession Act, 1956, it is very true.[263] The first dent to the classical rule of survivorship was made in 1957 by the Hindu women's Right to property Act 1987 and second in 1956. Now it is totally abolished.

Mitakshara Coparcenary

Whether after the amendment Mitakshara coparcenary really exist? As the main features of Mitakshara coparcenary such as fluctuation of shares by each birth and death, unity of possession and the prerogative of the males to be a coparcener, are no part of Mitakshara coparcenary. By the abolition of the rule of survivorship there would be no fluctuation of shares by each death. As the death of a male coparcener will make no effect upon the share of the other coparceners because his interest in property would not devolve by survivorship but by interests succession on the basis of deemed partition. In case of each birth the share of each coparcener will be diminished.

Deemed Partition

By deemed partition the shares of each coparcener be demarcated and now they would not possessed the property as joint tenant but as tenant in common. In a latest case of Hardev Rai v. Shakuntal Devi[264] the apex court held that Mitakshara coparcenary carries a definite concept. It is a body of individual having been created by law unlike a joint family which can be constituted by agreement of the parties. For the purpose of assigning one's interest in the property. It is not necessary that partition by metes and bounds amongst the coparcener must take place, when an intention is expressed for the partition of the coparcenary property the shares of each coparcener are determined, if cases to be a coparcenary property. The parties in such an event would not possess the property as joint tenants but as tenant in common.

Discrimination between the Coparcener

The other question which pricks the mind is whether it is discriminatory between the surviving coparceners? Suppose there is Hindu undivided family consists of father two sons and on daughter and two grand sons. One of the sons died issueless. The share of the deceased son according to the interest succession would go to the father being class I heir and the brother and sister as a coparcener would not get any interest?

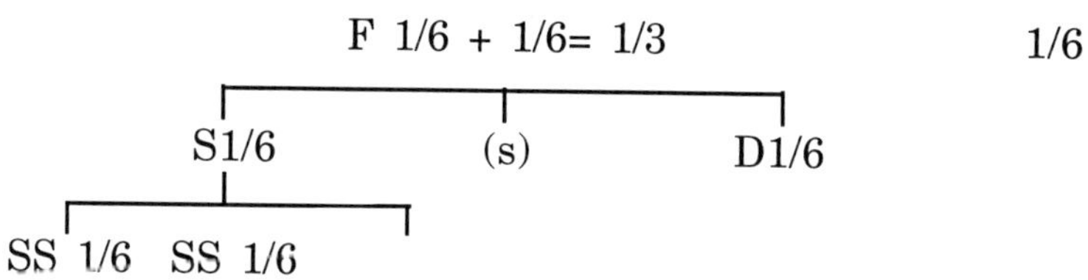

If the rule of survivorship had not been abolished then the share of the deceased son was devolved among the all coparceners then the position was as -

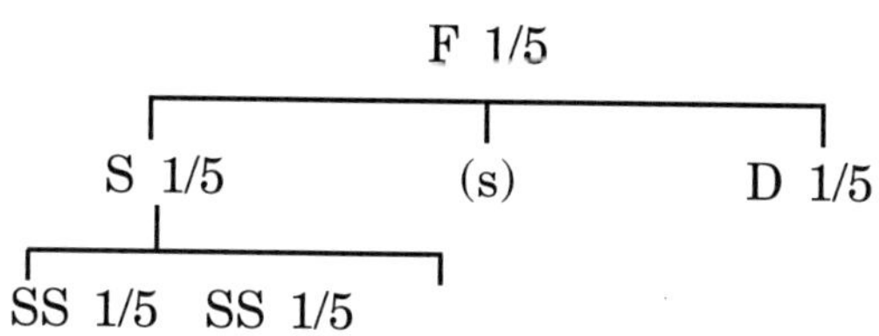

No Discrimination between Marr'ed and Unmarried Daughters

The previous state amendments were discriminatory among the married and unmarried daughters that give the coparcenary rights equal to son only to the daughters who were unmarried at the enforcement of these amended Acts. Though subsequent changes in their status would not effected their right. It was challenged in Majamma v. State of Karnataka[265] which was justified by the court that it would create a chaos and will result in settled things unsettled. But in this amendment Act, the married daughter is given same benefit as unmarried daughter subject to the provision that any disposition, alienation, partition or testamentary disposition effected prior to the 20th December 2004, could not be invalidated. Now she is a coparcener though not the member of the joint Hindu family because the act is silent upon this point. Before the amendment once a daughter is given into marriage ceased to be the member of the Hindu Joint family.

No Provision for the devolution of the interest of female coparcener

There is no express provision that how the interest of female coparcener will devolve because before 2005 she was not a coparcener and her property was subject to the provision of S. 15 of H.S.A. 1956, which is not touched by this Act of 2005. Sec. 6 of the Amendment Act the legislature has used the words 'his interest' which can not be said to be included 'her' also. According to S. 13 (1) of the general clauses Act 1897," words importing the masculine gender shall be taken to includes female. See 3(2) of the Hindu Succession Act, 1956 clearly says that, 'in this act unless the context otherwise requires words importing the masculine gender shall not be taken to include females. Bythis amendment the legislature expressly included the words disposed of by him or her in section 30 of the Act of 1956.

Abrogation of the pious duty of son to pay fathers debt

Sec. 6 (4) clearly states that after the commencement of this Act the son is not bound to pay the debt of father, grand father or great grand father which before the Act was the pious duty of the son, grand son and great grand son. But this Act would not apply away debt contracted before the commencement of the Act.

Ommission of Section 23-

Before the omission of section 23 was considered the most discriminatory provision of Hindu succession Act 1956 which discriminates only on the basis of sex. It was challenged in the series of cases. It is discussed at great length at appropriate place in this book.

Deletion of Section 24-

Section 24 barred the widow of son widow of pre-deceased son and widow of brother from inheritance if they remarried at the time of partition. But the Act was silent about the other widows of the joint family such the widow of pre-deceased son's son and the widow of the son of the pre-deceased daughter and widow of the father's brother. Now the question arises whether the remarriage of these widows did not effect their right to where the property of their pre-deceased husband. The second thing which comes in the mind whether S. 24 was useless? Because as soon as the widow remarried her states is changed and she ceased to be the widow of the deceased. But she would be the wife of the person to whom she married. It is an appreciated step of legislature that deletes the useless and confusing provisions.

Amendment of S. 30

In the principal Act the legislature has substituted the words 'disposed of by him' by the words 'disposed of by him or her'. The amendment has not only made the daughter a coparcener of the coparcenary property but has given the right to dispose of the property by a will just like a son. Now the Hindu female like Hindu male has the same right of testamentary disposition of the coparcenary the daughters and sister in their own right and the widows as the absolute owners.[266] The court held that under the provision of S. 30 of a person bequeaths his or her property the property would devolve according to the will and not by the provision of succession.

Heirs under the Amendment Act

By the Amendment Act 2005 some heirs of class II have got place in the schedule of class I heirs. But they have not been removed from the schedule of class II heirs.

In old Hindu Law there were only these class I heirs who form the Mitakshara coparenary and the property was devolve according to the rule of survivorship not by intestate succession through the self acquired property was devolved as to intestate succession. The Hindu females had no right is acquire property by any way. These heirs were son, son's son and son's sow son. The first induction of heirs was made in 1937, by making certain widows the heir who were:

Widow of the deceased

Widow of the son

Widow of son's son

(But the widow of son's son's son was not included) The revolutionary changes were made in 1956 by the introduction of long list of heirs which were:

Mother

Daughter

Sons' daughter

Daughter's son

Daughter's daughter

Son's son's daughter

Though most of the newly introduced heirs were females yet it was discriminatory among the heirs of same status. Such as though the son's son's daughter has got the right to inherit yet the son's daughter's son and daughter had been placed in second class heirs entry second the daughter's son son, daughers son's daughter daughter's daughter's son and daughter's daughter's daughter were among class II heir entry third . The class I Heirs inherit the property simultaneously but the inheritance among the class II heirs take place according to preference of their entry which means the entry one would got preference over the entry second and entry second over entry third and so on the other flow of the Act of 1956 was that the widow of son's son had been introduced as heir since 1937 but the widow of the daughter's son was not given the same right ever in 1956.

The Amendment Act of 2005 has removed all the flows of 1956 and has abolished all discriminatory provision and has substituted certain heirs of class II to the heirs class I which are:

Daughter's son's son

Daughter's son's daughter

Daughter's daughter's son

Daughters's daughter's daughter

Though apparently it seen is that the Amendment Act has removed all ambiguities and inequalities yet it has its own short comings such as first of all it has not corrected the flow of the Act of 1956 by not introducing the widow of daughter's son. The other discrimination is done with the son's daughter's son and son's daughter's daughter who are still a second class heirs while their counter part daughter's daughter's son and daughter's daughter's daughters are placed in class I. The other notable point is that these heirs who are placed in class I heir are not removed from entry III of class II heirs. How can a heir be in two places. It is submitted that the legislature should remove these anomalies as soon as possible otherwise it will increased lot of litigations.

The Effects of Amendment Act, 2005

The new amended Act of 2005 has itself created a lot of anomalies. For instance it has deleted section 4(2) of the Act of 1956, which has the provision that any law deals with the fragmentation of agricultural holding, or fixation of ceiling, or the devolution of tenancy rights of such holdings, shall be governed by the provision of section 4(2) of the Act of 1956. It means after the amendment the boundations have been extinguished and it would apply to such agricultural holdings also, and by this deletion the female heirs will have a right to inherit the land. Now we will wait and watch how the state would adopt new law as the matter of land is the subject of state list.

Though by giving birth right in the coparcenary property to a female child is a significant step'in the field of women empowerment yet the other female members of the joint family (by a marriage) are in the same position as they were before the amendment of the Act. Thus the present Act has not provided any benefit to the other female members of the joint family. Moreover by making discrimination between married and unmarried daughter, it clearly violates the provisions of part 3rd of the constitutions which guaranteed the equality under article 14.

The words 'with incidents of coparcenary ownerships' in section 6 (2) of the amending Act, are not explained by the legislature as what are those incidents of coparcenary ownership. Consequently the answer would be seeks in the classical law.

The abolition of the rule of survivorship certainly benefited the daughter but instead created a chaos. Suppose a Hindu family comprises of a father, two sons and a daughter who form an undivided coparcenary. By the provision of the Act, 2005 each of them would have one fourth share in the joint family property. But suppose one of the sons dies. The share of the deceased son would go by the testamentary or intestate succession. If there is no Will, the father would be preferred and the brother and sister would be excluded. Under old law on the basis of survivorship the girls being not a coparcener would not inherit the property but now as the deceased brother's share go to the father, the girl would get the share after the death of father.

The use of the words 'his' in section 6 (3) also pricks the mind whether the survivorship is abolished only to the male members and not for females as it is the fundamental rule of inheritance that 'his' does not include her. By this an inference can be drawn that the abolition of survivorship would not apply in the case of female coparcener's death.

The other confusion which is created by the amending Act is whether the devolution of the coparcenary property of female be governed by the old laws of succession, which would go to her husband or her natal family member who died childless.*

By this amendment Act of 2005 many sections of Hindu Succession Act of 1956 are repealed or altered which were unfair towards females. The Hindu daughter of Mitakshara joint family will also be born with a silver spoon in her mouth and the daughter has all the rights and labilities, which her brother has it can be said that the new Act is a total commitment for the women empowerment and protection of her property rights. Now it is turn of judiciary to implement it and give flesh and breath to these laws.

Christian Law

With the establishment of British political authority in India, so many reforms have been made governing the family problems of the Indians though it is said that the Britishers had no interference in the family matters and their respective personal laws had governed these matters. But it is not absolutely true because so many family laws were passed by the English Rulers as Parsi Marriage And Divorce Act, 1865, The Indian Succession Act, 1865, Indian Divorce Act, 1869, Hindu Wills Act, 1870, and Christian Marriage Act, 1872 etc.

The British rule in India began on the legislative front with the Indian Succession Act, 1865 and Parsi Succession Act, 1865. These were based on English Law and was declared, to constitute subject, to certain exceptions, be applicable to all classes of intestate and testamentary succession. These exceptions were so wide that exclude all natives of India,[267] such as Hindus, Muslims, Sikhs, Jains etc., as they were very sentimental about their religions. This law is applicable only to European, Indians-Christians, Jews, and Parsis etc.

Indian Christian

- Indian Christian means a native of India.[268]
- Who is of unmixed Asiatic descent.
- Who in good faith claims to be of unmixed Asiatic descent.
- Who profess any form of the Christian religion.[269]

This definition is taken from the Native Christian Act, 1901. But there, in the place of "Native Christian" the words "Indian Christian" are used. Native Christians are those who were converted Christian whom the Britishers regarded as their faithful slaves.[270] An Anglo Indian does not come with in the definition under clause (d).[271]

Application of the Act

The Act empowers the State Government to exclude any community from the operations of certain sections, which are expressly mentioned in section 3 of the Indian Succession Act, 1925. That are generally related to the domicile, marriage, intestate and testamentary succession etc. As section 4 exempt the Hindus, Muslims, Buddhists, Sikhs and Jains from the operation of section 4 to 19. But under section 21 of the Special

Marriage Act, 1954, the Act will apply to those whose marriage is solemnized under 'Special Marriage Act, irrespective of their religion.[272]

General Principles of the Succession of the Christian

Under section 5 of The Indian Succession Act 1925 two different sets of rules were made to regulate the succession of movable and immovable property of a Christian deceased.

Movable property includes-standing timber, growing crops, grass, fruits upon and juice in, the tree and property of every description except immovable property.[273]

Immovable property means things attached to the earth,[274] as lands, trees, buildings etc. but it does not include standing timber, growing crops or grass etc. Sub (1) of section 5 says that the succession of the immovable property of the person, be governed by the law of the land, where the deceased had his domicile at the time of his death.

Illustration: Suppose, Mr. X having his domiciled in India but he dies in France, leaving some movable property in France and England, and both movable and immovable in India.

The succession of the whole property is to be regulated by the law of India but the status, of the parties, is to be decided by the law of the domicile.[275] In the case where the deceased left both movable and immovable property, sub-section (2) of section 5 says that it will be regulated by the laws of the country in which the person whose property is in question to be governed, domiciled all the time till his death.[276]

Illustration: Suppose Mr. X an Englishman, having his domicile in France, dies in India leaving behind both movable and immovable property in India. In this case the succession to movable is regulated by rules of France and the succession of immovable by the law of India.

Rules Regarding Domicile

The word domicile is not defined in the Indian Succession Act, 1925. In Halsbury's Laws of England[277] the word domicile is defined as *"A person is domiciled in that country in which he either has or is deemed by law to have his permanent home."*

Dicey and Morris has defined domicile as, "*a person is in general domiciled in the country in which he is considered by English law to have his permanent home.*[278]

The Indian Succession Act 1925 laid down from sections 6 to 19 some rules about the domicile of the deceased, which are as follows:

- If a person has more than one domicile the place where he lives with his family is considered his permanent home to regulate the succession. (Sec. 6).[279]
- Unless the new domicile is acquired, the domicile of the Birth prevails.[280]

Traders or Merchant

A, a person whose domicile of origin is in England, proceeds to India where he settles as a merchant, intending to reside here to the rest of the life. His domicile is now in India.[281]

Foreign Representatives

But there is an exception in the case of the representatives of the foreign government and their family, though they permanently resides in foreign country with family but because they have no intention to change their domicile, is considered the domicile of that government, from where they came to represent.[282]

Children Legitimate and Illegitimate

In the case of children, the domicile of the legitimate child be ascertained, by the domicile of his father, at the time of his birth and in case of illegitimate child according to his or her mother's domicile.[283] In the case of posthumous child, his or her domiciled is considered in that country where his or her father domiciled till death.

Illustration: Suppose at the time of the birth of A, his father was domiciled in England. The domicile of A is considered in England though he himself was born in France if. A is a legitimate child.

Illustration: Suppose at the birth of B, an illegitimate child, his putative father was domiciled in England but his mother domiciled in France B's domicile will be considered in France.

- A lunatic person cannot acquire a new domicile.[284]
- If the domicile of the dead is not known and not proved the domicile of another place and he dies leaving movable property in India the succession will be governed by the Indian Law.[285]

The Effect of Marriage to Regulate the Succession

Section 15 says that by marriage a woman acquires the domicile of her husband,[286] if she had not the same domicile before. Section 16 says that during the continuance of marriage the wives domicile follows that of her husband, therefore if a woman in India possessing movable property, marries to a person whose domicile is in England, on her death husband is entitled to inherit her whole movable property to exclude the children according to English law.

Exception: The wife's domicile no longer follows that of her husband if they are separated by the sentence of a competent court, or if the husband is undergoing a sentence of transportation.

Abolition of the English Concept of Marital Property

By the Indian Succession Act of 1925, the English concept of marital property was totally abolished. In English law there was a rule that on marriage the property of female was merged in that of husband's property and she was no longer, authorized to enjoy it in whatever manner she like, though with the approval of husband she was entitle to appropriate it.

Section 20 of the said Act of 1925 provides that, "*no person shall by marriage, acquire any interest in the property of other spouse and the other spouse will not lost, his or her right to appropriate his or her own property which he or she could have done if unmarried.*"

Exception: But the provision of this section would not applied if any one of the spouses professed Hindu, Islam, and Buddhist or Jain religion at the time of marriage.[287]

Different Domiciled of Spouses

According to section, 21 if there is a different domiciled of the spouses neither party shall acquire by marriage any rights in respect of any property of the other spouse which is not comprised in a settlement made previously to the marriage.

Intestate Succession

If there is no will or testamentary document left by the Indian Christian deceased to dispose of his property, the succession of the property is regulated according to the rules of the Indian Succession Act, 1925.

Heirs

The Indian Succession Act, 1925, chooses the heirs on the basis of consanguinity and placed them into three categories:-

- Husband and wife
- Lineal ascendants and descendants
- Collaterals

The relationship is decided according to the consanguinity, which is of two types lineal consanguinity and collateral consanguinity.[288] In lineal consanguinity two persons are connected in one straight line whether descendants or ascendants.[289] A straight line does not connect collateral consanguinity,[290] but they are descendants from the same stock of ancestor. Though there is no consanguinity between husband and wife,[291] but they are heir of each other. It is an exception of the general rule of succession based on consanguinity.

Section 27 abolishes the distinction between cognate and agnate between half and full blood, between the posthumous and normal child. All are equally entitled to succeed.

Illustration: A Christian widow has a daughter B by her first husband. A remarries and have two sons C and D by second husband B has intestate and unmarried leaving property. The property will be divided equally between A, C and D.[292]

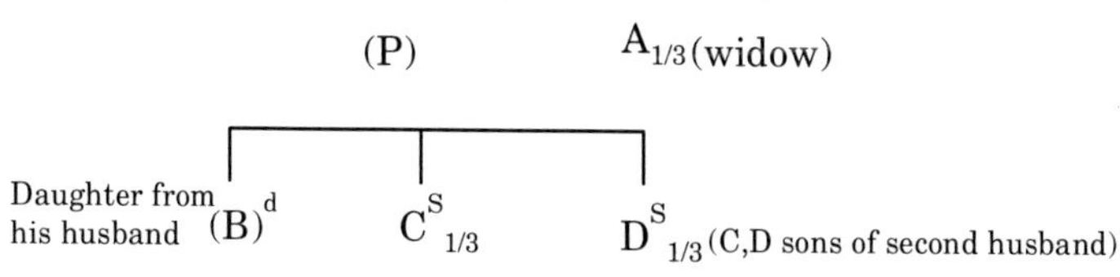

Widow or Widower

There is no difference to the rules regulating the succession of widow or widower both has same rights.

- If there is widow and lineal descendants[293]
- 1/3 will go to the widow or widower as the case may be
- 2/3 will go to the lineal descendants

Illustration: Suppose a Christian intestate died leaving behind a widow, a son and daughter, the share of widow will be 1/3 and son and daughter will inherit 1/3 each from the 2/3 shares of descendants. If they are more, they will inherit from the 2/3 and the widow's share will not be reduced from 1/3.

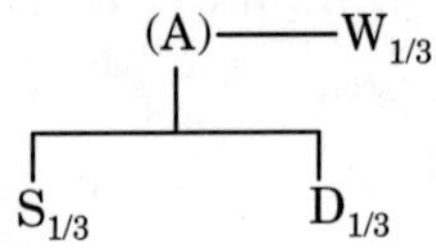

- **If there is widow and collateral and no lineal descendant.**[294]
  - 1/2 will go to widow or widower.
  - 1/2 to collaterals, if one or more they will share from the 1/2 share allotted to collaterals.

Illustration: Suppose, A, died leaving behind widow, a sister and a brother and there is no lineal descendant.

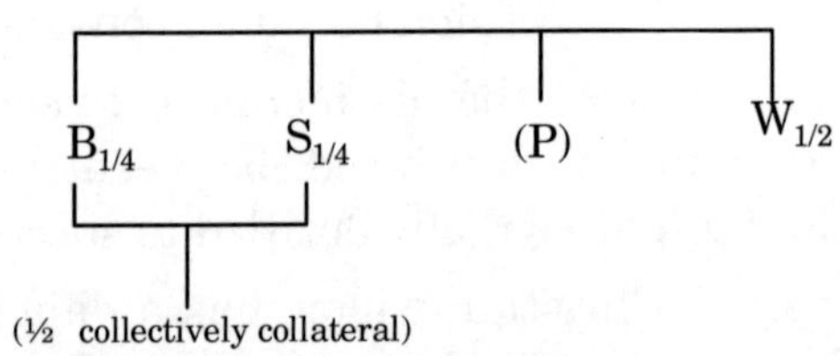

- **If there is only widow or widower and no lineal descendants and no collaterals.**[295]
  - The whole property will go to widow or widower.
- **If there is no widow or widower, no lineal descendants and no collaterals then**
  - the whole property will go to the Government.[296]

Judicial Separation

In case of judicial separation no one is entitled to inherit each other and they presumed to be dead for the purpose of succession.[297] Under the Travancore Succession Act if the mother or the widow become entitled to any immovable property then they have only a life interest, which is on death or remarriage.[298]

Lineal Descendants

The lineal descendants consist of children, grand children, great grand children and remoter lineal descendants. The lineal descendants are divided into three classes—

- lineal descendant of first degree,
- lineal descendant of second degree,
- lineal descendant of third degree remoter.

Lineal Descendants of First Degree

Lineal descendants of first degree are the children of the deceased himself or herself. They take equally and there would be no difference between son and daughter. The child does not include the illegitimate child[299] and the adopted child.[300]

If there is no surviving spouse and deceased has left only a child or children but no more remote lineal descendants through a deceased child, the property shall go to his surviving child or children. If they are more than one they will inherit equally irrespective of sex.[301]

Illustration: Suppose A died leaving behind a son and two daughters they will inherit equally

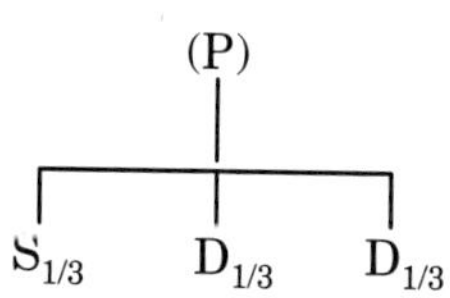

Lineal Descendants of Second Degree

The grand children of the deceased are considered as the second degree of lineal descendants. If the deceased has not left the surviving spouse and no children but has left grand children and no descendant of grand children, then whole property is shared equally. Under English law then property is divided as per stripe, not per capita.[302]

Illustration: A has two sons B and C both died in the life time of A, leaving behind one daughter from C and two sons from B. After the death of A the property will go to all three grandchildren equally as per capita.

English Law

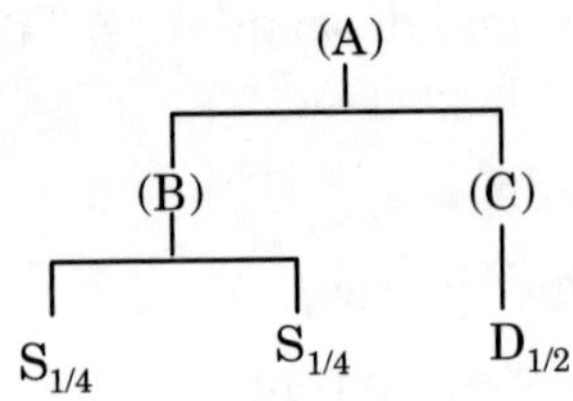

Indian Law

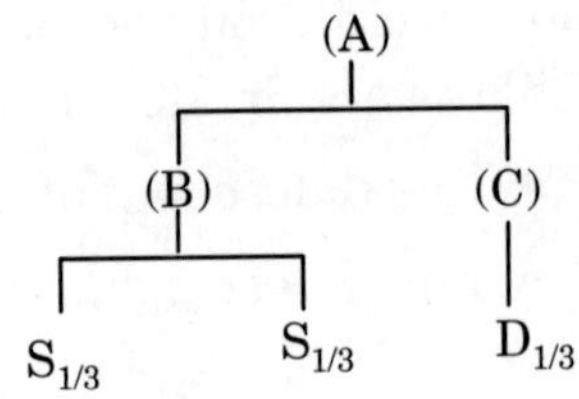

Remoter Lineal Descendants of Third Degree

If there are only great grand children and other remote descendants of same degree, they will inherit equally.[303]

Where Lineal Descendants are not of Same Degree

If the deceased left many lineal descendants who are not of same degree then the property is distributed per stripes.[304] According to the rule of representation they all will inherit the share of their parents for which they would have been entitled if they had survived the intestate.

Illustration: A Christian died leaving behind four children of a predeceased son and one son of a predeceased daughter and one son of his own. Thc property will be divided into three equal shares then 1/3 share of the predeceased be divided among the four children of the predeceased son equally - the other 1/3 will go to the son of predeceased daughter and the other 1/3 be inhertied by the deceased own son.[305]

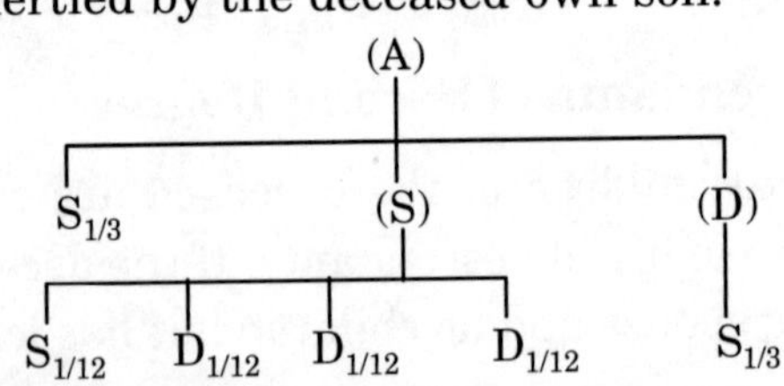

Illustration: If a Christian has left no child of his own but four children of a predeceased daughter and four children of a predeceased son and three children of predeceased son's son. In this case the property will be distributed into nine equal share from which 1/9 will go to each grand child and the remaining 1/9 will be divided among the three great grand childrensequally.

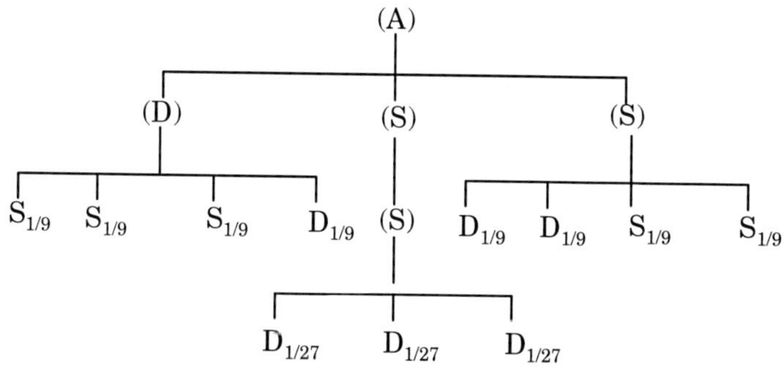

Illustration: A died leaving behind, three children of a predeceased son, two children of a predeceased son's son, one child of his predeceased daughter and one son of his own. In this case 1/3 share will go to his own son, the other 1/3 be divided among the three children of a predeceased son and two children of a predeceased son's son and the other 1/3 will go to the son of his predeceased daughter.

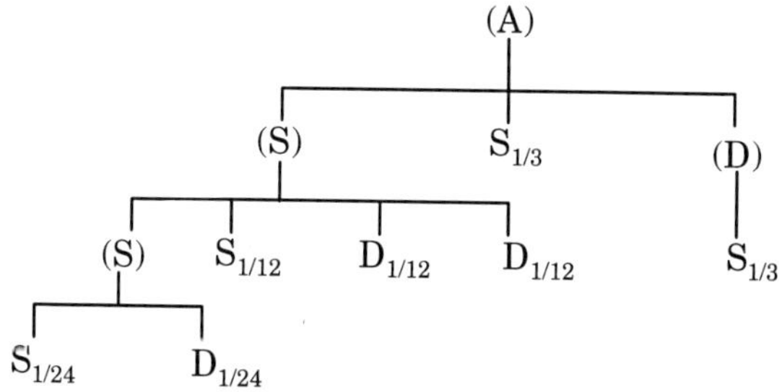

Illustration: A died leaving a daughter and a pregnant wife of a predeceased son. Subsequently a son is born to the pregnant wife of a predeceased son. In this case property will be divided equally among these two surviving heirs.

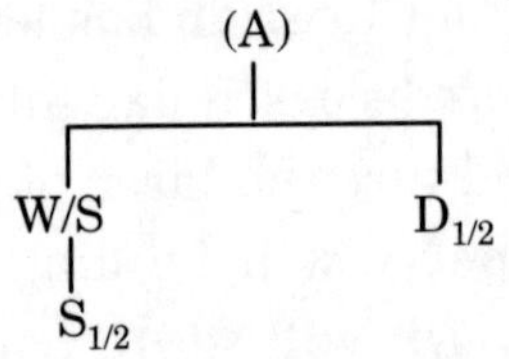

Where there is no Lineal Descendants

If there is no lineal descendants but surviving spouse the property be distributed to the rules laid down in sections 42 to 48 of the Act.[306]

Father

According to the provision of section 42 of the Act of 1925. If the intestate leaves father and widow or widower, then father will take 1/2 and other half will go to widow or widower as the case may be. If there is no surviving spouse then father will inherit the whole property.[307] Father excludes any other kindred.[308] But in case there is son and father though both are of equal degree kindred the father will be excluded by the son.

According to the provision of section 42 of the Act of 1925—

- If the intestate leaves father and widow or widower then father will take 1/2 and other 1/2 will go to the widow or widower as the case may be.

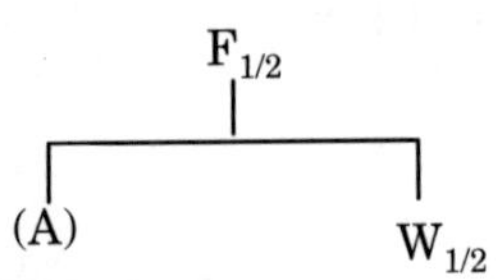

- If there is no surviving spouse but distant kindred the father will inherit the whole excluding the distant kindered.

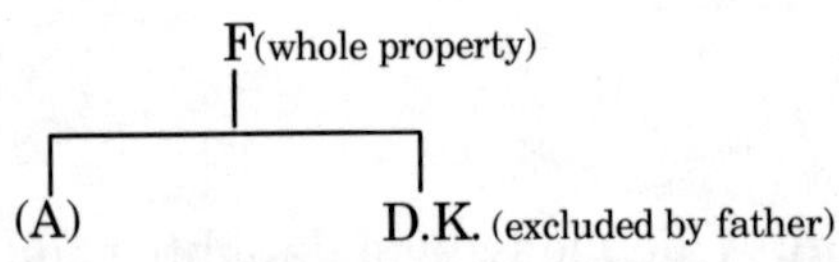

- If there is no son and father though both of them are equal degree kindred but the father will be excluded by the son and whole property will go to son.

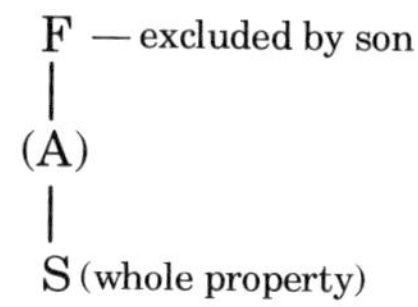

No Father but Mother, Brother and Sister

Section 43 says about the situation, if the deceased is survived only by mother, brother and sister and there is no child of any deceased brother or sister. Father is also dead then the property be distributed among mother, brother and sister equally. Stepmother is not included as mother[309] but uterine sister is treated as a full sister.

Illustration: A died leaving behind his mother and two brothers and a stepsister the property be divided into four equal part and each one will inherit $^1/_4$ share.[310]

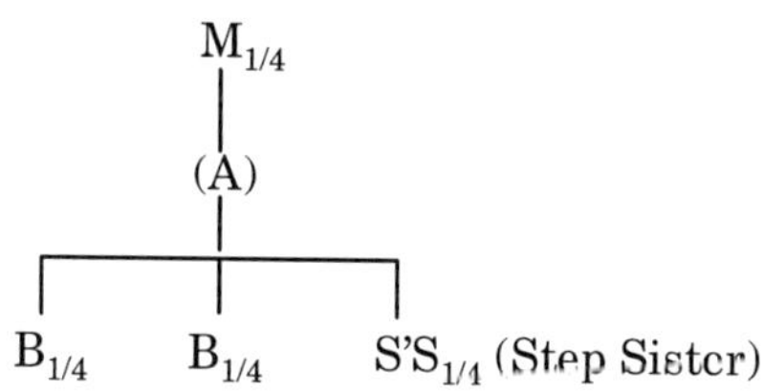

No Father but Mother, Brother and Sister and the Children of Deceased Brother or Sister

In such a situation where the intestate is survived by mother, two brothers and a child of her deceased sister and two children of deceased step brother but no father then the property be divided into five equal shares. 1/5 will go to mother, 1/5 to one brother, 1/5 to another brother, 1/5 to the child of deceased sister and the remaining 1/5 be divided equally among the two children of deceased bother 1/10 each. Here the rule of representation will apply.[311]

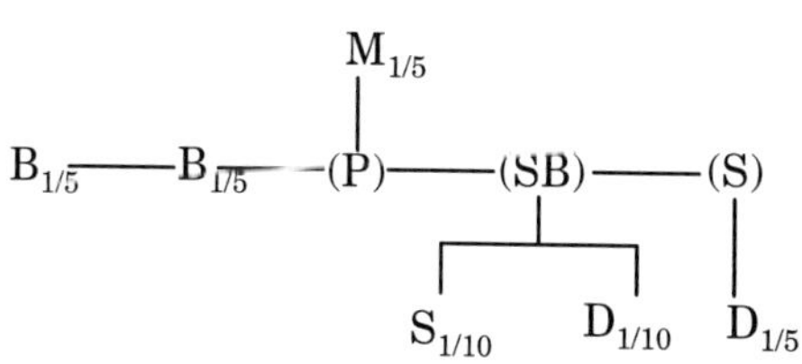

No Father but Mother and Children of Deceased Brother or Sister

If there is no father, brother and sister survived. Only mother and children of deceased brother and sister living then the children of deceased brother or sister will be entitled, to the share of his father or mother according to the rule of representation.

Illustration: A dies leaving behind mother and child of his deceased sister and two children of his deceased brother. The property will be divided into three equal share 1/3 will go to mother, 1/3 to the child of deceased sister and remaining 1/3 is to be inherited by the sons of the deceased brother collectively[312] means 1/6 by each son.

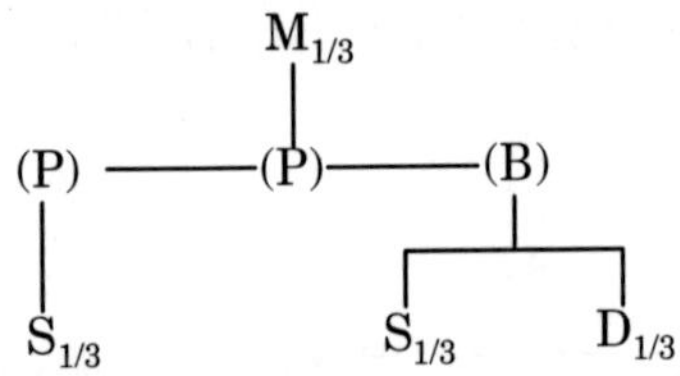

No Father, Brother, Sister, Nephew or Niece but Mother

If mother survives the deceased only and by no one else of first and second degree of lineal descendant then the whole property will go to mother.[313]

No Parents and Lineal Descendants but Grand Parents, Brother and Sister and Children of Brother and Sister

In case the deceased is survived by grandfather, brother, sister and children of predeceased brother and sister. The children of predeceased brother or sister are entitled to the share of their respective parents.[314]

Illustration: A died leaving behind grandfather and two sister, one brother and three children of his deceased sister. The property will be divided into four equal shares. $^1/_4$ will go to brother, 1/4 will go to each sister and 1/4 will go to the children of deceased which they will share equally and grand father will get nothing because he is excluded by brothers and sisters.

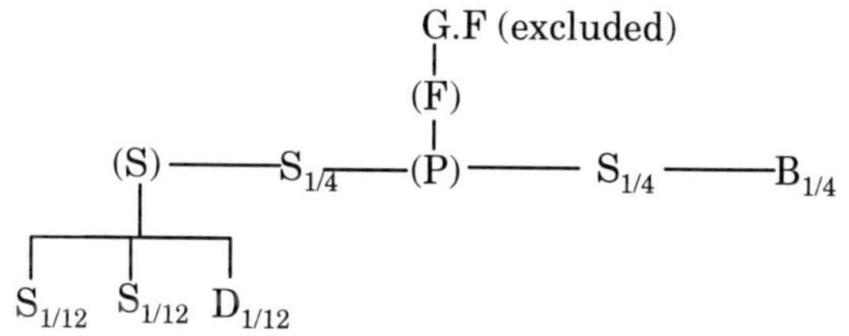

No Parents, no Lineal Descendants and no Brother and Sisters

In a situation where parent's brother and sisters do not survive the deceased and also there are no lineal descendants the property will go to the relatives of same degree and they will share equally.[315]

Illustration: A died leaving behind grand father, and grand mother and relative of the same degree then both the grand parents will inherit equally if there is uncle and aunt also they will be excluded by the grand parents because uncle and aunts are the relative of third degree.[316]

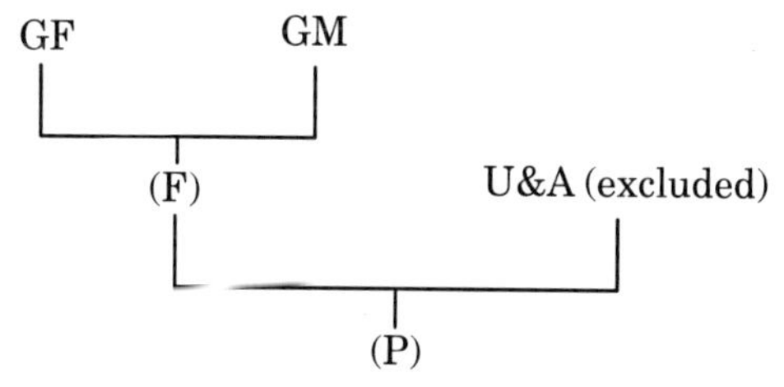

In second situation if great grand parents and uncles and aunts survive the deceased then because they all are of third degree relatives will inherit equally.[317]

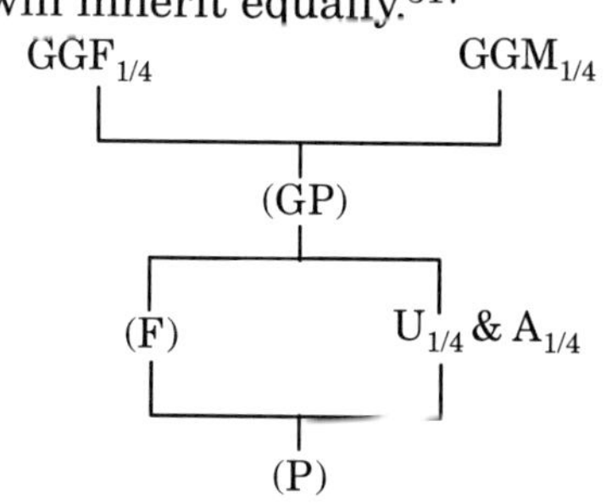

Doctrine of Escheat

If there is no one to inherit as no widow, lineal descendants or ascendants and distant kindred then whole property will go to the government.[318]

In case of nun

There is no provision, which restrict a nun from the inheritance either in religion or in Statutes. If his wife survives a Christian male, son and daughters one of who is nun the court held it that nun is eligible to inherit the property of her father.[319]

Travancore Christian Succession Act and The Cochin Succession Act

The Indian Succession Acts which governs the succession of the property of Indian Christian was extended to the State of Travancore and Cochin by the State (Laws) Act 1951. The above mentioned Acts were highly discriminatory,[320] which govern the Christians of Kerala Supreme Court held that, all Indian Christians be governed by the Indian Succession Act of 1925.

Recently in *Land Board* v *Cyriac Thomas*,[321] Supreme Court has reaffirmed his earlier decision. The facts of the case were that Kerala Land Reforms Act made a provision that the person who had more land than a specified limit, will have to surrender the excess land to the government. A man had more land but he claimed that this belonged to his sister. The government claimed that under Travancore Christian Succession Act, daughter's share is limited to Rs. 5000/- only and she can not inherit the land of her father but Supreme Court held that after the death of Christian father the sons and daughters have succeed the property equally according to the provision of Indian Succession Act, 1925.

Christian law of succession is a codified law. Though it is no more a religious law even in Christian dominated States. It is not much discriminatory towards women. The old concept of marital property is no more in existence in this codified law and females have got absolute property right with independent right to appropriate it, in what ever manner they like.

Parsi Law

It is one of the most important and best-known religions of pre-Islamic era. It took its name from that of its founder Zorathushtra (Zoroaster). The roots of the Zorastrianism can be located in an Eastern Iranian tribal area and basically pastoral society. The religion originated around 1000 BCE and developed further, under the Persian Empire. The problems of evil and suffering was basic to Zoroastrian thought and the urgent human necessity of providing an answer to the problem was reconciled with an abiding faith in the dignity and freedom of humanity by means of belief, in the so called myth of choice. The famous codes are "*The Syrian Law Books*" and "The Zorastrian *Madigni - Hazar Dadastan*"[322]

The word '*Parsi*' is originated from the word '*pars*' or '*fars*' a province in Persia from which the original Persian emigrants came to Indian sub-continent.[323] The expression Parsi has no religious connotation. It carries a more territorial connotation. The religion of every Parsi is Zoroastrian but it's not necessary that every Zoroastrian be a Parsi. For example, an Iranian who is registered as a foreigner and who is not domiciled in India but follows the Zoroastrian, is not a Parsi with in the meaning of the Act and the Parsi Matrimonial Court has no jurisdiction over him.[324]

The Parsi Marriage and Divorce Act 1936 as "Parsi Zorostrian" has defined the word "Parsi", that cannot be confined to Indian Parsi Zoroastrian but extended to include the Zoroastrian of Iran also and that the court constituted under the Act has jurisdiction over them.[325]

The Succession of Parsis

After the passing of the Indian Succession Act 1925 the succession of the property of a Parsi was governed by the Act of 1925. There are social rules regulating the succession of a Parsi intestate in sections 50 to 56 of the Act of 1925.

Before the passing of the Act of 1925, the Indian Parsis were governed by the English common law in matter of succession because of the claiming of the English law of primogeniture by a Parsi. The Parsi Chattels Real Act of 1837, was passed by which the Parsis to a great extent were excluded from the operation of the English law. But the English Statute of Distribution governed the intestate succession. The Parsis were not satisfied with that, so they demanded their separate laws of inheritance because they do not want to be exploited by the laws of England, where wife had no power over her own property. With the result of their struggle Parsis Intestate Succession Act, 1865, was passed which introduced the widow and daughter as heir and entitled them to inherit the property. Before that they were only entitled for the maintenance. But mother and sister were not made the heirs and they were incapable to inherit.

Beside all these Acts that worked for the Parsis till 1925, the rules governing the Parsis in the Act of 1925, are totally based on previous Act of 1865. The present provision of the Act of 1925, relating to the succession of the Parsis was passed through various amendments[326] and Judicial decisions.[327] In 1939, drastic changes were made that the widow of predeceased lineal descendants were also introduced as heirs and the widowers were excluded from the list of the heirs.

General Principles of Intestate Succession of a Parsi

The Indian Succession Act of 1925 laid down some general principles. From sections 50 to 56 deals with the principles regulating the intestate succession of a Parsi. Drastic changes were introduced by the amendment Act of 1991, in the governing rules of Parsi intestate succession.

Posthumous Child

Clause (a) of Section 50 abolished the difference between the posthumous child and the child born in the lifetime of father. In the matter of succession both are equally treated.[328] Though before 1939, there were different rules.

Predeceased Child

If a lineal descendant of a Parsi intestate has predeceased him then his or her share would be lapsed into two conditions.[329]

- If he has left no widow or widower, or
- If he has left no lineal descendant of such predeceased child.

Prior 1991 there was another condition, which was abolished now that if he has left no widow or widower of any lineal descendants.

Remarriage

In the case a widow or widower remarry in the lifetime of the intestate then he or she will not be entitled to inherit and be deemed non-existent.[330] The word widower is inserted by the Act of 1991. Previously this provision was only for the widows. The widower of a predeceased daughter was held entitle to share even he had remarried.[331]

Distribution of Property among Widow, Widower Children and Parents

If a widow or widower and children survive a Parsi, they will take equal share.[332] This section was very discriminatory when introduced in 1925, towards woman. Prior to the amendment of 1939, the widow's share was half the share of the son but by the Act of 1939 it was made equal to the share of the son, and the daughters share was 1/4 share of the son. It was made $^1/_2$ by the amendment Act of 1939, but by the amendment Act of 1991, all sex-based discrimination had been resolved, now they all entitle to equal share.

Illustration: Suppose a Parsi died leaving behind widow, son and daughter they all inherit equal share.

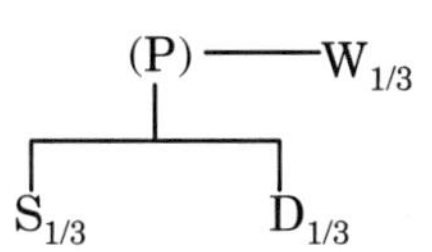

In second situation if there is no widow or widower and only children irrespective of sex they will inherit equally.[333] Prior to 1939 the share of the daughter was 1/4 of the son, which was made of 1/2 and now by the Act of 1991 equal to the son.

Illustration: Suppose a Parsi died leaving behind only a son and two daughters and no widow, each will take 1/3.

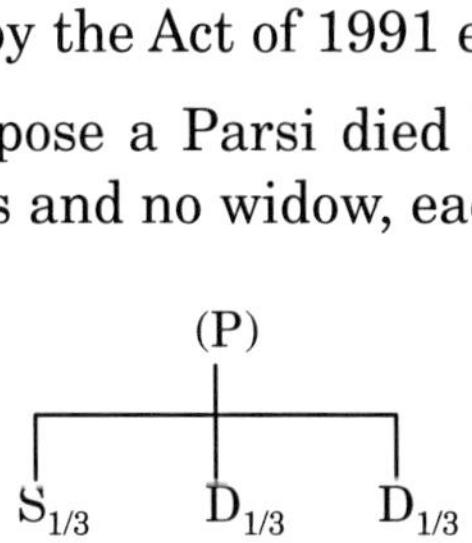

In third situation if one or both parents survive a Parsi and there is also a widow or widower and children, the share of each parent be $^{1}/_{2}$ of the share of each child.[334] The share of the parents was introduced by the Act of 1939 but at that time the father's share was $^{1}/_{2}$ of the son and mother's share was $^{1}/_{2}$ of the daughter. The stepparents were not included in the word 'parent' in the Act.[335]

Illustration: Suppose an intestate Parsi dies leaving behind parents, widow, son and daughter. The share of the parent will be half of the child rest heirs will inherit equally.

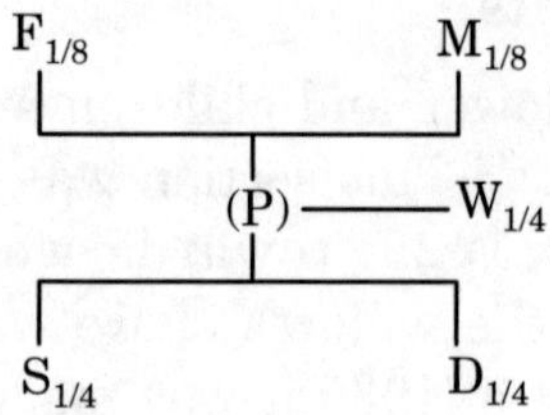

Section 52 was repealed by the Act of 1991, which prior to the amendment dealt with the succession of the property of the female Parsi because like Hindu Law there was two different sets of rules governing the estate of male and female.

Distribution of Share of predeceased Child of Intestate Leaving lineal Descendants

- If any Parsi died leaving behind the lineal descendants of a pre-deceased child, the share, of that predeceased child, will be that share, for which, he was entitled if surviving at the death of the intestate Parsi and that share will go to his or her lineal descendants according to the rules.[336] The rule of representation will apply here.
- Clause (a) says if that deceased child is son and leaves behind his widow and children then the share of that child will be distributed among them equally.[337]

Illustration : Suppose a Parsi died leaving behind his son, daughter and predeceased son's widow, son and daughter. At first the property will be divided into three equal share one share will go to son, one to daughter and the remaining 1/3 will be distributed among the heirs of predeceased son.

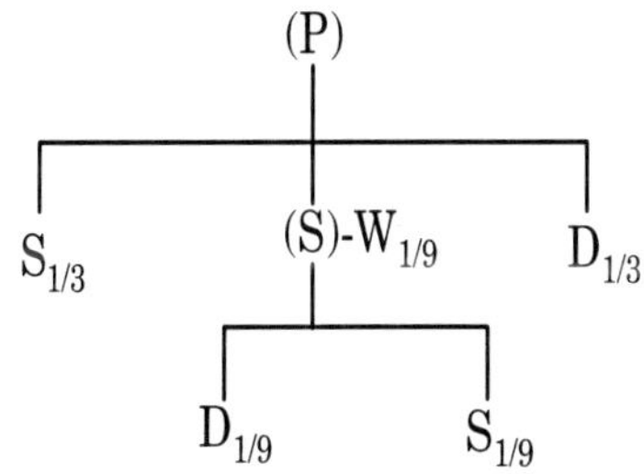

There is a proviso attached with clause (a) of section 53, which says about another situation in which if predeceased child has left no lineal descendant but a widow or widower of his lineal descendants. Then she or he will be entitled of 1/3 of the property.[338]

- Clause (b) says about another situation, in which if the deceased child was a daughter her share be divided, among her children equally. In this clause, the widower is excluded from the inheritance. It is difficult to say, why there is contrast between two sections as 50 and the provision of this section in that section the widower is included as heir[339] even he remarried.[340]

In condition where the child of such predeceased also died in the lifetime of intestate his or her share will be ascertained and dispose of according to the provision of clause (a) and (b).[341]

If any remoter lineal descendants of the intestate died in the life time of intestate his or her share be ascertained as if he or she is living at the time of the intestate death and his or her share be distributed among his or her heirs.[342]

Before going in to detail study of the provisions of sections 54 and 55 it is necessary to know the heirs mentioned in schedule II part I of section 54 and part II of section 55.

The Heirs of the Deceased

Schedule II

Part I (Section 54)

- Father and mother.
- Brother and sister and lineal descendants of them as shall have predeceased the intestate. Other than half brother and sister.

- Paternal and maternal grand parents.
- Children of paternal and maternal grand parents and the lineal descendants of such of them as have predeceased the intestate.
- Paternal and maternal grandparent's parents.
- Paternal and maternal grandparent's parents children and the lineal descendants of such of them as have predeceased the intestate.

Part II Section 55

- Father and Mother.
- Brother and Sister and lineal descendants of them as shall have predeceased the intestate. Other than half brother and sister.
- Paternal and maternal grand parents.
- Children of paternal and maternal grand parents and the lineal descendants of such of them as have predeceased the intestate.
- Paternal and maternal grandparent's parents.
- Paternal and maternal grandparent's parents children and the lineal descendants of such of them as have predeceased the intestate.
- Half brothers and sisters and the lineal descendants of such of them as have predeceased the intestate.
- Widows of brothers or half brothers and widower of sisters or half sisters.
- Paternal or maternal grandparents children's widows or widowers.
- Widows or widowers of deceased lineal descendants of the intestate who have not remarried before the death of the intestate.

If there is no Lineal Descendant but a Widow or Widower or a Widow of any Lineal Descendant

If there is no lineal descendant but only widow or widower his or her share[343] would be 1/2, the other half would go to the relatives mentioned above according to the order specified. The next kin would be preferred to those preferred in second and so on.[344]

Illustration : Suppose a Parsi died leaving behind a widow, a brother and a sister but no lineal descendant the half will go to widow and other half will be equally distributed among brother and sister.

$S_{1/4}$ —— $B_{1/4}$ —— (P) —— $W_{1/4}$

If there is a widow or widower of an intestate and also widow or widower of lineal descendants then the share of his or her widow or widower be 1/3 and 1/3 will go to the lineal widow or widower and the other 1/3 will go to the relatives,[345] but if there is more lineal widow or widower they will inherit 1/3 collectively.

Illustration: Suppose a Parsi dies leaving behind widow, sister, brother and a widow of pre-deceased son the property will be divided into three equal parts, 1/3 will go to each widow and 1/3 will be distributed among sister and brother.

$S_{1/6}$ —— $B_{1/6}$ —— (P) —— $W_{1/6}$

$SW_{1/3}$

If there is only one widow or widower of lineal descendant she or he will take 1/3 but if no widow or widower of intestate and there is more than one lineal descendant's widow or widowers then 2/3 will go to them which be distributed equally among them the other 1/3 will go to the relatives.[346]

Illustration: Suppose A dies leaving behind brother, sister, widow of his pre-deceased son and widower of her pre-deceased daughter. The brother and sister will take 1/3 collectively it means 1/6 each; the other 2/3 will be inherited by the widow and widower collectively.

$B_{1/6}$ —— $S_{1/6}$ —— (P)

(1/3 Collectively)

$DW_{1/3}$ $SW_{1/3}$

(2/3 Collectively)

After deducting the share of widow or widower of all description the residue property will be distributed among the relatives according to rule of nearer exclude the remote one. The share will be equal irrespective of sex among the same degree of propinquity.

If there is no relatives then the whole of the residue shall be distributed in proportion to the share specified among them, like Islamic law the rule of Return prevails, in Parsi law also.

If there is no Lineal Descendants nor a Widow nor Widower nor a Widow of any Lineal Descendant

If a Parsi dies leaving behind no lineal descendant nor a widow or widower nor a widow or widower of lineal descendant then his or her next kin is entitled to inherit the property according to the order mentioned. The rule apply here will be the nearness of blood to relation to the intestate. The agnate will be first exhausted then cognate if there is neither agnate nor cognate then the widow or widower of brother and sister will be entitled.

The Relatives who are not Otherwise Entitled to Inherit

If there is no above mentioned heir then the property will be divided, among the relatives who are not otherwise entitled to inherit according to the above mentioned provisions. The rule nearer will exclude the remote one is applied.

This is the whole law of inheritance of a Parsi who died intestate. But there are different rules, which govern the testamentary succession of a Parsi. The whole law of Parsi, intestate succession passed through revolutionary changes. The Parsis were much exploited in the British period by governing their succession according to the rules of common law. After a long struggle, the Act of 1865 was passed. That too was much discriminatory towards females. Though some important amendments were made in 1939 but it can be said that after the amendment of 1991 it is evident that the female of Parsi got their due share.

The Parsi law recognized the rule of representation and the nearer exclude the remote one. Like Muslim Law it also recognized the Doctrine of Return. Now if any discrimination seems in succession that is the share of parents is half of the child but it cannot be said that it is discriminatory in any form because the parents have no responsibility.

Lastly, it is inferred from the above discussion that by the amendment of 1991 in the rules governing the Parsi intestate succession provided under Indian Succession Act of 1925 is not discriminatory towards females.

References

1. Encyclopaedia Britanica Vol. 6, p. 317.
2. *Ibid.*
3. Fatwa e-Aalmagiri, Vol. 10, Urdu Translation by Amir Ali (1982) p.421, see Sir Ronald K. Wilson: Anglo Mohammadan Law (a digest) 2nd ed. p. 283.
4. Macnaugthen W.H.: Principles and Precedents of Muslim Law (preliminary remark) p.1.
5. Fitzgerald S.V.: Muslim Law and Abridgement, London (1931) p. 182.
6. See Smith: *op cit.,* p. 801.
7. Op cit Id pp. 56-66; See, Tayyabji: Muslim Law, p. 801.
8. *Ibid* p. 802.
9. Quran: XXXIII, Surah Nisan.
10. Hasan Ali v Nazo (1889) 11 All 456.
11. Razia Begum v Anwar Begum (1958) S.C.R. (India) 1111, 1137.
12. Dhan Pal v Faluman, AIR (1935) Lah. 203.
13. Murtaza Hussain Khan v Md. Ali Khan, ILR 33 All 532 (P.C).
14. Karamat Ali v Sadat Ali (1932) 8 Luck. 228, See also Smt. Kulsumunnisa v Smt. Ahmadi Begum AIR (1972) All 219, Agha Walyat v Mahbub, AIR (1972) Pesh. 83.
15. Dakshan Chandra v Takim Dhait AIR (1924), Cal. 558.
16. (1927) 106-1-C, 76.
17. Walliullah: Mohammadan Law p. 268 See: also Maimoona Bibi v Khawaja Mohiuddin (1970) 1 MLJ 266, Jafri Begum v Amir Mohd Khan (1886) 7 All 842, Bhagirathi Bai v Roshan Bibi, ILR 43 Bom. 412.
18. Jayyabji F.B. Mohammadan Law, IIIrd ed. Sec. 382.
19. Abdul Samad v Biwi Jan AIR (1933) All 206, See: Also Sukrullah v Zehra Bibi AIR (1932), All 512.
20. Mohd. Abdul Rahim v Abdul Hakim, AIR (1921) Cal. 653.
21. Encyclopaedia Britanica, Vol. 12, p. 254.
22. Ram Abidi v Mirza Ahmad, AIR (1925), Oudh 190.

23. M. Khazir Bhat v Ahmad Dar AIR (1960) Jammu and Kashmir 57, See : also Ma Bi v Ma Khatun AIR (1930) Rang 72.
24. Boodhun v Jan Khan (1870) W.R. 265.
25. Rahmatullah v Maqsood Ahmad AIR (1952) All 640 at p. 641.
26. Jayyabji *op. cit.,* p. 819.
27. Bafatan v Bilaiti Khanam (1903) Cal. 683.
28. Khyratun v Amanee, ii, W.R. 212.
29. Mohd. Bakhsh v Hayat Khan (1888) 23, Punj, Rec. No. 37 (98, 100).
30. Sahih-Al-Bukhari, Vol. 8.
31. AIR (1953) Mys. 621.
32. Rukmanibai v Bishmillabai, AIR (1993) M.P. 45.
33. Bai Khatya v Karim Bahi, AIR (1947) Guj. 4 at p. 7.
34. Kenchava v Girimallapa AIR (1924) p.c. 209.
35. Sir William Jones *op cit.*, 22-28.
36. Jayyabji *op. cit.,* p. 824.
37. Mst Jawai v Hussain Baksh (1922) 3 Lah. 80, 67, 1C, 154.
38. (1886) 7 All 822, 834 Moola Qasim v Moola Ali AIR (1905) 32-1-A. 177-179, para 2.
39. Holy Quran IV : 33.
40. Jayyabji *op. cit.,* p. 827.
41. Hayat-un-Nisan v Mohd (1890) 1 All 290.
42. Supra note 36.
43. Supra note 12.
44. Faiz v Abdul Jabbar. AIR (1943) Pesh, 65.
45. Sahih Bukhari Vol. 8, translated by M.M. Khan, chapter 5, Tr. No. 2309.
46. Sir Edward Ryan: Digest of Mohammadan Law.
47. Sahih Bukhari Vol. 8, translated by M.M. Khan, Chapter 5, Jr. No 2309.
48. Jayyabji *op.cit.,* p. 818.
49. Inayat v Mst. Bhasin AIR (1928) Lah. 291 at p. 294.
50. Al-Haj-Mohd Ullah: The Muslim Law of Inheritance.
51. Al-Sirajiah, cited by Mohd Ullah.

52. Abdul Serang v Putlee Bibi (1902) 29, Cal. 738.
53. Holy Quran IV : II
54. Holy Quran IV: 11-12.
55. Holy Quran IV : 12.
56. Holy Quran IV : XII.
57. Abu Zehra : Ahkam-Al-Tarka wal Mawarith, Dar-Al-Fikr-al-Arabi, Cairo, pp. 141-142.
58. Tanzilur Rehman, Dr : *op. cit.,* p. 479.
59. *Ibid.,* p. 132.
60. Holy Quran IV : 11.
61. Abu Daud Tirmizi.
62. Holy Quran : IV-177.
63. Smt. Halima Bibi v S.A. Fatima Bibi (1987) MLJ 353.
64. Ali Saheb v Hajra Begum (1963) 2 Mys., L.J. 14 at p. 14.
65. Mubarak Begum v Suhail Kumar AIR (1957) Raj. 154 at p. 157.
66. Mst Zainab v Jamal Khan AIR (1957) Nag. 428 at p. 430. See Koonasi v Datun (1884) I Cal. 14 (ILR).
67. Isab v Isab (1920) 44 Bomb. 947.
68. Muzaffar Ali v Prabhavati (1907) 29 All 640.
69. Supra note 64.
70. AIR (1991) Gau. 70.
71. Ameer Ali-Mohammadan Law, Vol. 2. pp.
72. Tayyabji *op cit.,* p. 867, See Waliullah: Mohammadan Law (B.R. Vermas) 5th ed. 1978, p. 400.
73. *Ibid.,* p. 894.
74. Syed Ameer Ali: The Personal Law of the Mohammadans (1880) (Comparative Sketch of the Law of inheritance among Shia and Sunnis) p. 44.
75. Md. Khan M.A.: Islamic Law of Inheritance, p. 179.
76. *Ibid.,* p. 78.
77. *Ibid.,* p. 79.
78. *Ibid.,* p. 74.
79. *Ibid.,* p. 84.
80. *Ibid.,* p. 86.

81. Tayyabji *op. cit.,* p. 895.
82. *Ibid.,* p. 896.
83. Khan M.A. *op cit.,* p. 90.
84. *Ibid.,* 92.
85. *Ibid.,* p. 97.
86. Ahmad Aqil: Muslim Law (revised by Prof. I.A. Khan), p. 375.
87. *Ibid.*
88. Priya Nath Sen: The General Principles of Hindu Jurisprudence Tagores Law Lecture 1909.
89. Mayne J.D. and Ayengar: Treaties On Hindu Law and Usage-10th ed. 1938.
90. Chaudhary VKS former Advocate General of U.P. : Times of India 27th Dec. 2004.
91. Derret : *Op cit.,* 1970 p. 13.
92. Commissioner of Wealth Tax Madras and others v R. Sridharam (1976) Supp. SCR 478.
93. Mst. Suraj v Attar 1 Pat. 706.
94. In Goods of Gyanedra Nath 49 Cal. 1069.
95. Rajah Chattar Singh v Diwan Roshan Singh ILR (1946) Nag. 159.
96. Supra note 1 p. 125.
97. Manu IX-187, See Adit Narayan v Mahabir Parasad 48 : IA 86.
98. Supra note 1 p. 126.
99. *Ibid.*
100. Jain Prakash Chand. "Women's Property Right under Traditional Hindu Law." Journal of LI, Vol. 45-384 (2003) p. 510.
101. Baudhyana's Dharamshastra 11 22, 47.
102. X: 155: 3
103. III : 51 : 12.
104. 17.7
105. 312
106. Yajnavalakya 11. 116-119.
107. *vide* L. Swarup's Translation : p. 40.
108. Kane, *op cit.,* p. 266.
109. Dayabhaga p. 256.
110. Kane : *op. cit.,* p. 260.

111. Mayne and lyengar, *op cit.*
112. Singh Raghunath "The Hindu Women's Right to Property Act, 1 937", AIR (1937), p. 107.
112A. Bhupatrai Hira Chand v Comms. of I.T. (1977) 1091 TR 97 Cal.
113. Bishnil Kumar Rai v Miner Mahendra Bai Lama and others, AIR (2005) Sikkim 33. See also Gowli Budhana v C.I.T. (1966) I.S.C.R. 224.
114. Pushpa Devi v Commissioner of Income Tax (1977), S.C. 2230.
115. Manjunath Gowda v CED (1977) 10 SCC 684.
116. Haridas v Devkuvarban, 50 Bomb. 443 at 447.
117. Hankari Devi v Raj Bhawani Devi AIR (2007) NOC 2008 (Raj).
118. Derrett : *op. cit.,* pp. 255-56, See also Kacharu Baban Kotthawala v State of Maharashtra (1969) 71. Bomb. L.R. 663.
119. Prof. Raman S. Venkata : N.R. Rag havachariar's Hindu Law VIII ed. (1987), P.N. 926, See also Ranganathan Chettiar v Annamali Mudaliar 80, L.E. 258 (1967) 1 MLJ 389.
120. Laxmi N. Tudu v Basti Mahajan AIR (2004) Jhar 121.
121. Pataskar LSD 2 v 56 Col. 6996.
122. Katama Natchair v Raja of Sivaganga (1861-) G.M. IA 543, Supreme Court Encyclopaedia, Vol. 3, p. 246.
123. Shivgonda v Director of Settlement, (1992) Bom. 72
124. Rangubai v Laxaman AIR (1966) Bom. 169.
125. Karupa v Palaniammal, AIR (1963), Mad. 254.
126. Sushila v Narayan Rao, AIR (1975), Bom. 257.
127. AIR (1985) SC 716.
128. AIR (966), Bom. 169.
129. Gurupad v Hira Bai AIR (1978) SC 1239.
130. AIR (1971) AP. 363.
131. (2000) AIHC 4013 (karn).
132. Commissioner of I.T. v G.S. Mill, AIR (1966) SC 24, Ram Avadh v Kedar Nath, AIR (1976) All 283, Parida v Gobinda, AIR (1970) Orri 32, Sahadeo Singh v Ram Chabila Singh AIR (1978) Pat. 258.
133. Commissioner of I.T. v Seth Govind Ram, AIR (1966) SC 2.
134. Pandurang Dhake v Pandurang Gorle, AIR (1947) Nag. 178.

135. Derrett : Essay in Classical and Modern Hindu Law, New Delhi Universal Book Traders, (1995) p. 136.
136. Naryan Prasad Ruia v Mutuni Kohain, AIR (1969) Cal. 69.
137. Thimmaiah v Ningamma (2000) 7 SCC 409.
138. Kanna Gounder v Arjuna Gounder, AIR (2003) Mad 157.
139. Gansalves Lina; *op. cit.,* p. 36.
140. Vide, Karnataka Act. 23 of 1999, Sec. 2.
141. Manjamma v State of Karnataka (1999) AIHC 3003 (Karn.)
142. Mulla : Principles of Hindu Law, revised by Sundar Lal Desai Bombay, N.M. Tripathi Pvt. Ltd. (1982), p. 926.
143. Kesharbai v St. of Maharashtra AIR (1981) Bom. 115.
144. Supra note Chapter II.
145. A.L. Vaijnath v Guramma (1979) 1 SCC See also Tukaram Genba v Laxman Genba Jadhav, AIR (1994) Bom. 247.
146. Appa Saheb v Gurubaswwa, AIR (1960) Mysore 79.
147. AIR (1966), SC 1879.
148. Hindu Succession Act, 1956.
149. See : Her Jesa Kachara v Lakshman, AIR (1979), Guj. 45.
150. The heir has been included by the Hindu Succession (Amendment) Act, 2005.
151. The heir has been included by the Hindu Succession (Amendment) Act, 2005.
152. The heir has been included by the Hindu Succession (Amendment) Act, 2005.
153. The heir has been included by the Hindu Succession (Amendment) Act, 2005.
154. Ramkali v Mahila Shayamwati, AIR (2000) M.P. 288 see also Daddo Atmaram Patil v Raghunath Atmaram Patil, AIR (1979) Bomb. 176.
155. AIR (2002) Kant 134. See also : Appa v Mulhani (1975) Ker. L.T. 699.
156. (2000) AIHC 938 (M.P.).
157. Ratni Bai v Mankuwar (1978) MPLJ 515.
158. Prakash v Pushpa Rani (2004) A.P. 463 NOC.
159. AIR (2005) (A.P.) 27.
160. Sri Partashar H.V. : Parliamentary Debate Rajya Sabha (1955) Vol. 9, 2711, 2722.

161. Rao Committee Report 116, 119, 120, 1947.
162. V. Tulsamma v V. Shesha Reddy, AIR (1977) SC 1947.
163. See the explanation attach the section 14.
164. Gumalapura Taggina Mutoda Kothuru Sami v Setra Verravva (1959) Supp. (1) SCR 968, AIR (1959) SC 577.
165. Mangal Singh v Smt. Ratno, AIR (1967) SC 1786.
166. Eramma v Verruppanna, AIR (1966) SC 1879.
167. Keshav v Padmavati Shantibai and Others C.A. No. 79 of 1963 (referred in Supreme Court Encyclopaedia, Vol. 3, p. 246.
168. AIR (2003) M.P. 40, see also : Naresh Kumari v Shashi Lal, AIR (1999) SC 928, AIR (1999) SC 1147.
169. AIR (1999) SC 1147, see also : Naresh Kumari v Shashi Lal, AIR (1999) SC 928, (from H.P.)
170. AIR (2004) Ker. 16.
171. Sub. (2) Sec. 24 "Nothing contained in Sub. Sec. (1) shall apply to any property acquired by way of gift under a will or any other instrument or under a decree or order of civil court or under an award where the terms of the gift will or other instrument of the decree order or award prescribe a restricted estate in such instrument or the decree order or award prescribe a restricted estate in such property."
172. The Hindu Women's Right to Property Act, 1937.
173. Hindu Succession Act, 1956.
174. Pratap Singh v Union of India, AIR (1985) SC 1695.
175. Tripathi B.N. : An Introduction to Jurisprudence, p. 394.
176. Krishna v Akhil (1958) Cal. 671.
177. (1997) SCC 460, AIR (1997) SC 3082.
178. AIR (1998) SC 2401, See also Ram Kali v Chowdhri Ajit Shankar (1997) SCC 619, Bhommireddy v Bhoospalli (1997) 10 SC 673, AIR (1997) SC 2311.
179. Supra.
180. Supra.
181. Naresh Kumar v Shashi Lal, AIR (1999) SC 928.
182. D.V. Jagannathan v P.R. Sriniwasan (1999) AICH 444.
183. Yadala Venkata Subbama v Yadala Chinna, AIR (2001) SC 1664, (2001) SCC 393, See also Bhusa v Kashiram, AIR (1994) SC 1202.

184. Muninanjappa v R. Mannal (2001) 5 SCC 363, AIR (2001) Sc 1754. See also Gorachand Mukherjee v Malabika Dutta, AIR (2002) Cal. 26.
185. Sheri v Savitri, AIR (2005) Kant 33, See also : Laxmi Kantha v Vijay Laxmi, AIR (2004) Ker. 295.
186. Shri Jain D.C. at 1968 I.S.J.J. 1-4. He shows that Mulla's explanation is impossible and hopes that Parliament will act to cure the anomalies (referred by Derrett - A Critique of Modern Hindu) p. 258.
187. Mannikyamma v Venkata Subba Rao (1978) 2 AN W.R. 18.
188. Gurbachan Singh v Khichan Singh, AIR (1971) Punj. 240.
189. Bhagwania v Kushali (1977) M.P.L.J. 99.
190. Bhagwan Dass v Prabhawati Ram, AIR (2004) Delhi 37.
191. AIR (1987) SC 1616 at 1619.
192. Prakash v Bela Sihare, AIR (1996) Del. 336.
193. Naresh Jha v Prakash Kumar Jha AIR (2004) Jhar. 2.
194. Keshri v Har Prasad (1971) M.P. 129.
195. AIR (1997) SC 1702.
196. Gopikabai v Bajya (1971) M.P.L.J. 335.
197. Anhio v Baijnath (1974) Pat. 177.
198. Mallapa v Shivappa (1962) Mys. 140.
199. Yogindra Prakash Duggal v Om Prakash Duggal (2000) AIHC 2905 (Del.)
200. Bala Sahab v Jamila, AIR (1978) Bom. 44.
201. Bagat Ram v Teja Singh, AIR (2002) SC 1.
202. Dhanistha Kalita v Ramakanta Kalita, AIR (2003) Gau. 92.
203. (2001) 252 ITR 324.
204. Mahesh Kumar Pate v Mahesh Kumar Vyas (2000) AIHC 485.
205. AIR (1996) SC 855.
206. Debahari Kumbhar v Sribasta Patra, AIR (1994) Ori. 86.
207. Seetha Lakshmi Ammal v Mutthuvenkataremma Iyenger (1998) 5 SCC 368, AIR (1998) SC 1692.
208. Chintaram Rushibai (2000) AIHC 1308 M.P.
209. Ramabi Padmaker Patil v Rukminibai Vishnu (2003) 7 ACE 395.

210. Ajit Singh v State of Punjab (1983) Cri. L.J. (NOC 271).
211. Veera Ragva Amma v Subba Rao (1976) AP. 337.
212. (1971) 3 SCC 847.
213. (1973) Mys. 142.
214. P. Jayarmaiah v Aragonda Munemma AIR (2005) A.P. 27.
215. Nagamma Naicker v Ponnuchunnayyyan 81, LW 23 (1970.
216. Padmaraja v Gyan Chandra Appa (1970) Mys. 87.
217. (1997) 11 SCC 310.
218. Krishna Pada Roy v Parimal Chandra Saha, AIR (2000) Gau. 117, See also Dhobel Rout v Paheli Raut, AIR (1998) Ori. 74.
219. Bhagirathi Chetoi v Adhikanada Chetoi, AIR (1988), Ori. 285 at 288.
220. Kamal Goel v Puroshatama Das, AIR (1999) P & H 254.
221. Mookammal v Chitra Vadi Ammal (1980) AIR Mad. 293.
222. Anant v Janki Bai, AIR (1984) Bom. 319.
223. The Leading case Narashimha Mury v Susheela Bai, AIR (1996) SC at 1831.
224. The Object and the analysis of Sec. 23 was discussed by Patna High Court in Raghunathan v Rambalak. AIR (1964) Pat. 206 and Later on by Allahabad High Court in Katara v Smt. Hoshiari (1967) All L.J 1031.
225. Supra.
226. Supra.
227. Supra.
228. Supra.
229. Anant v Janki Bai, AIR (1984) Bom. 319.
230. Kasiyavva v Hanuman Tappa (1984) 1 Kant. L.J. 273.
231. Mohanti Motyalue v Oluru Appanama, AIR (1993) Ori. 36, Hemlata Devi v Umashankari, AIR (1975) Ori. 908.
232. Surya Kumar Das v Maya Datta 86 Cal. W.N. 359, Arun Kumar v Jitendra, AIR (1975) Cal. 232.
233. Janabai Ammal v Palahi, AIR (1981) Mad. 62.
234. Supra. 223.
235. Fulsing Ramsingh Rajput v Durgabai, AIR (1997) Bom. 201.
236. Purusotham Bachara v Rangabati Barik (1999) AIHC 4760 Ori.
237. D.M. Jayamma v Munniyamma (2000) AIHC 4013 (Karn).

238. 174th Law Commission Report para 1.18.
239. Bhuribai v Chamabai (1968) Raj. 139.
240. Shankar Prasad v Usha Bala, AIR (1978) Cal. 525.
241. Velamuri Venkata Siva Prasad v Kothuri Venkateshware, AIR (2000) SC 434 See also Ram Sahran v Ujiyari (2000) AIHC 938, M.P.
242. Lalramchanni v Lalthachungi, AIR (2002) Gau. 96.
243. Indian Penal Code.
244. Seetharamiah v Ram Krishaniah, AIR (1970) A.P. 407.
245. Ashok Naidu v Raymond S. Mulu (1976), Cal. 272.
246. Clause (39) of the Hindu Code Bill 1954.
247. Parameshwari Thayaininah v Shri Subramanium, (1960) 2 SCR 729.
248. Dharamambal Vs Laxmi Ammal AIR (2003) NOC 117 (Ker)
249. WTO V.K. Madhavan Nambiar (1 988) 1 69 ITR 8 1 0
250. B. Chandra Shekhar Reddy V. State of Andhra Pradesh AIR (2003) S.C. 2322
251. AIR (2008) Mad 64
252. The Hindu succession Tamil Nadu Amendment Act 1989
253. AIR (2005) Kar. 194
254. Subbayyajoga Naik v Narayni AIR (2004) Kar. 430
255. S.4 (2)" for the removal of doubts it is hereby declared that nothing contained in this Act shall be deemed to effect the provision of any law for the time being in force providing for the prevention of fragmentation of agricultural holdings or for the fixation of cealing or for the devolution of tenancy rights in respect of such holdings" omitted by Amendment Act 2005.
256. State of Punjab v. Amar Singh AIR (1974)SC 994
257. Ameerunnission V. Mehboob AIR (1953) SC 91
258. Kashiram V Umapada AIR (1968) Cal 83, Hari Das v. Hukumi AIR (1965) Punj 254
259. Jeewansam v.Lich Madevi AIR (1981) Raj 16
260. Jain M.P; Indian Constitutional law Vthed (2007) P.N. 508.
261. Bhagirath VS. Manivaman AIR (2008) Mad 251
262. Brij Narain Agarwal v. Anup Kumar Goyal AIR (2007) Del 254
263. For detail see page no 96-100 of this book

264. AIR (2008) SC 2489
265. (1999) AIHC (2003) Kar
266. Section 14(1) Hindu succession Act 1956
267. Ilbert: Government of India, 3rd ed. p. 36.
268. Section 2 clause (d) Indian Succession Act. 1925.
269. Ma Khun v Ma Ahma, 12 Rang. 184.
270. Mehmood Tahir : *op. cit.*, p. 99.
271. In re. T.R. Farle (1976) IMLJ 257 : 89 Mad. 147.
272. Kashiba v Stripat 19 Bom. 697.
273. General Clauses Act X of 1897.
274. *Ibid.*
275. Ratan Shaw v Bamoji, 40 Bom. L.R. 141.
276. See the illustration No. 2 of Sec. 5 of Indian Succession Act, 1925.
277. 4th *ed*. Vol. 8, para 421.
278. Morris : op. cit. p. 100.
279. Somerville v Somerville S. Ves 758.
280. Sec. 9 of Indian Succession Act, 1925.
281. See the Illustration of Sec. 10.
282. Sec. 12 of Indian Succession Act, 1925.
283. Sec. 7, 8 of Indian Succession Act, 1925.
284. Sec. 18 of Indian Succession Act, 1925.
285. Sec. 19 of Indian Succession Act, 1925.
286. Miller v Administrative General 1 Cal. 412.
287. Sub. Section (2)(b) of section 20 of Indian Succession Act, 1925.
288. Sec. 24 of Indian Succession Act, 1925.
289. Sec. 25 of Indian Succession Act, 1925.
290. Sec. 26 of Indian Succession Act, 1925.
291. Administrator General v Simpson 26 Mad. 532.
292. Jessopp v Watson 1 M and K 665.
293. Sec. 33 (a) with Sec. 35.
294. Sec. 33 (b) with Sec. 35.
295. Sec. 33 (c) with Sec. 35.
296. Sec. 34 of Indian Succession Act, 1925.

297. Sec. 24 of Indian Divorce Act, 1925.
298. E.D. Devadasson : Christian Law in India 319.
299. In the Goods of Sarah Ezra, AIR (1931) C. 560.
300. Ma Khun v Ma Ahma, 12 Rang. 184.
301. Sec. 37 of Indian Succession Act. 1925.
302. Sec. 38 of Indian Succession Act, 1925.
303. Sec. 39 of Indian Succession Act, 1925.
304. Sec. 40 of Indian Succession Act, 1925.
305. See the Illustration of Sec. 40.
306. Sec. 41 of Indian Succession Act 1925.
307. Sec. 42 of Indian Succession Act, 1925.
308. Administrator General v Anandachari, 9. Mad. 466.
309. Rutland v Rutland, 2 P. Wms. 216.
310. See the Illustration of Sec. 43.
311. See 44 of Indian Succession Act, 1925.
312. Sec. 45, see the Illustration also.
313. Sec. 46 of Indian Succession Act, 925.
314. Sec. 47 of Indian Succession Act, 1925.
315. Sec. 48 of Indian Succession Act, 1925.
316. See the Illustration of Sec. 48.
317. *Ibid.*
318. Secretary of State v Girdharilal, 54 All 226.
319. G.K. Kempegowda v Lucinda, AIR (1985) Kant. 231.
320. This aspect is remedied by the case of Mary Roy v State of Kerala (1986) 2 SCC, 209.
321. AIR (2002) S C 3161.
322. Encyclopaedia of Religion, Vol. 15.
323. Sir Dinshaw Mulla Petil v Jamestji Jijabai, 11 Bom. L.R. 85 at 113 (quoted by Mohd. Shabbir : Parsi Law in India).
324. Vazifdar v Vazifdar ILR (1951), Bom. 279, 52 Bom. LR 875.
325. Singh Jaspal - Law of Marriage and Divorce in India p. 481 (1983) Delhi, See also : Jamshed Irani v Banu Irani (1967) Mah. L.J. 33.
326. Indian Succession Amendment Act, 1939, Act 51 of 1991.
327. Ratan Shaw v Bamaji 40, Bom. L.R. 141.

328. Manchaerji v Mithabai 1 Bom. 506.
329. Clause (b) of Sec. 50.
330. Clause (c) of Sec. 50.
331. Jehangir v Pirojbai 11 Bom. 1.
332. Sec. 51, 11 (a).
333. Clause (b) of Sub. Sec. (1) of Sec. 51.
334. Sub. (2) of Sec. 51.
335. Rutland v Rutland 2 p. Wms. 216.
336. Sec. 53 of Indian Succession Act, 1925.
337. According to the provision of this chapter.
338. Supra.
339. Clause (b) of Sec. 50.
340. Supra.
341. Clause (c) of Sec. 53.
342. Clause (d) of Sec. 53.
343. Clause (a) of Sec. 54.
344. Clause (d) of Sec. 54.
345. Clause (b) with (d) of Sec. 54.
346. Clause (c) with (d) of Sec. 54.

4

Comparative Study of Women's Property Rights under Different Legal System

An Overview

"The richest source of all discoveries in every empirical science is comparison and combination. Only by many fold contrast the contrary becomes completely clear; only by the observation of similarities and differences and the reason for both, may the peculiarity and inner nature of each thing be thoroughly established...."[1]

When we observe different cultures which embodies different ethical theories and which uses such beliefs to produce different legal results, we are able to distinguish the respective places which ethical rules, legal norms or other techniques of social control hold in different societies. The rush of social problems and the ensuring maladjustments compelled new changes in the law. Sometimes the elite attempted to impose their legal concepts on a custom bound peasant society, which is equally true in a colonial situation. For instance, Britishers attempted to come, to term with the Hindu and Muslim's legal traditions in India and in the far-flung Halsburg Empire before the First World War.

According to Lepaulle,[2] the unity of one legal system was more apparent than real. Moral economic, religious and many other forces in different proportions had come into play, in the composition of a legal system and all these forces must be taken into account and weighted in the process of comparison.

It centered on the application of the comparative methods to the date provided by the different legal system of the world's past and present. This involved the assignment to each of a place with in a scheme of progress, development or evolution and the assessment of their values.

The aim of comparative method is obviously to promote better understanding of the laws and legal systems of different religions. To make understand of acknowledged objectives of comparative law, the comparative analysis is necessary. By that, one always gets better understanding of one's own legal norms, system or structure.

Definition of Comparative Law

According to H. C. Gulteridge, *"Comparative law is a process or a method by which two or more legal systems or part thereof are compared with a definite aim"*.[3]

According to O'Kahn Freund, *"Comparative law is neither a professional tool nor an academic toy, it has a higher purpose of providing an insight into the social purpose of law."*[4]

About the meaning of comparative law M. Rheinstein says, *"The term comparative law has been used for denominating the descriptive analytical observation of a special field of positive law."*[5]

On the basis of the sayings of these jurists, it is said that comparative law is a theory of evolution as stated in social term by Comte and Spencer or in biological term by Darwin, all against a background of geological and palaeontological discovery. Comparative law never possessed one single method accepted by all. As comparative law also claimed to be a science and made use of scientific theories of the time, to build up comprehensive picture of the natural history of the legal system, on evolutionary basis.

Different families of Law

Before comparing the position of women's property right under different religious laws, it is necessary to know something about the different families of law, in a very short glance, to which the religious laws are also a branch. The legal system had tried, to classify the laws into four major categories, to which they termed four families of laws. Though one cannot aspire to mathematical exactitude in the social sciences, yet to ascertain the family of law, there are so many factors, which are taken into consideration such as the sources of laws, the working method of jurists, the philosophical, political and economic principles of the society etc. The religious law with which, we are mainly concerned is also among these four family of law which are as follows :-

- Romano - Germanic family
- The family of Common law
- The family of Socialist law
- The family of Religious law

Romano-Germanic family

The Romano - Germanic family of law originated in Europe in 12th Century, on the basis of the compilations of the Emperor Justinian and developed a judicial science common to all and adapted to the condition of modern world. Through the colonization by European Nations, the Romano-Germanic family of law had conquered vast territories, where the laws were either belonged or related to this family. Outside Europe these Romano-Germanic laws were though adapted but they retained their own indigenous institutions also, as in Muslim world and in the countries of Far East. French law is an apt example of Romano-Germanic family of law.[6]

The family of Common Law

The family of common law belonged to the laws of England and also to the laws of those countries, which were modeled on the basis of English law. The origin of the common law is linked to royal power. It was developed as a system to re-establish peace rather than articulate a moral basis for the social order. The common law is very different in its concepts, vocabulary and method from the Romano-Germanic family. The common law had expanded through out the world because of colonization and reception. Like Romano-Germanic law, the common law was also partially adopted in religious world like Muslim and Hindu laws etc. It is also true with respect to the United States and Canada, where the civilization was very different in many respects from that of England.[7]

The family of Socialist Law

The family of Socialist laws originated in the Union of Soviet Socialist Republic (USSR the old name of Russia) since the 1917, Revolution. The members of this socialist camp were of those countries, which formerly had laws belonging to the Romano-Germanic law. The distinct feature of Socialist law is, its revolutionary nature in opposition of the static character of Romano-Germanic laws. The sole source of socialist rules of law lies in the work of the legislators, who express the popular will. The new concept subtracted from the realm of law, a whole series of rules which jurists of the bourgeois country would consider legal rules.

The family of Religious laws

The above-mentioned three principal families of law attracted the whole world to have certain elements from one or other of these families. But beside these, there are other philosophical and religious systems of laws, which in strict sense do not constitute families as such. They are entirely independent of each other such as Muslim law, Hindu law, Christian law, Parsi law and Jewish law etc. This is the oldest family of law. These are not the laws, of any particular state, but it is the law of a community of believers and applied universally to the believers of that community wherever they live. These laws are mainly concerned with the matters of the way of life such as marriage, succession, divorce, adoption etc. These religious laws are actually the sum of the rules derived from the religion concerning human relationship. Because of its connection with revealed religion, it has entirely original concepts, and theory of the sources of law. These religious laws are different from each other and do not constitute a family of law. These religious laws can be grouped as a family only because they are based on their religious faith.

For the purpose of comparative study of religion the term in German *Religious is senschaft* and in French *la science de religion,* are used.[8] The function of comparative religion, said by an early twentieth century scholar, *"consists in placing the numerous religions of the world side by side, in order, that deliberately comparing and contrasting them, it may frame a reliable estimate of their respective claims and values."*

Development of Different Religious Laws

The Romano-Germanic, Socialist and Common laws are primarily linked to the development of European civilization. They reflect a way of thinking and living, which is European. But in Asia and Africa a vast population have already established a form of civilization, which could not be considered inferior to that of the west. They also had religious beliefs which have to a certain extent, blocked the reception of western laws and legal concepts. Now we consider the development of each religious laws separately and very precisely.

Development of Muslim Law

Islamic Law, which is a body of rules, gives practical expression to the religious faith and aspiration of the Muslims. In the beginning of Islam in early seventeenth century, Arabia, the task assumed by Muslim Jurisprudence was, the discovery of the terms of Allah's (SWT) law for Muslim society. Legal scholar had gradually built up a corpus of doctrine, which was elaborated and systematized in a large number of commentaries and the voluminous literature. The practical problem faced by Prophet Mohammad (PBUH) and his successors in their judicial capacity was, the relationship between Quranic laws and the prevailing customary laws.[10]

The conflict and tension apparent mainly in the system of inheritance, as the patrilineal pre-islamic Arabian society had confined the succession to the male agnate relatives. Contrary to it Islam emphasized upon the closer family tie, in which the female was given a higher and more responsible status. Holy Quran had given the rights of property to certain females for the first time in the era of woman world. The females have their prescribed Quranic fractional shares in different capacities as wife, daughter, mother, sister and grandmother etc. The new Quranic heirs and the old customary heirs were merged into a composite system of succession. As in Sad's case the brother of the deceased was allowed to inherit along with the new heirs wife and daughters. Under customary law the brother was alone entitle to inherit the whole property, the wife and daughter have no share in this case.

Derrett says, *"Holy Quran expressly declares that a brother does not inherit when the deceased is survived by* a *child."*[11] The word *'child'* was apparently taken to mean *'male child',* so that a brother would be excluded from succession by a son of the deceased but not by a daughter. Such consideration makes it clear that the early authorities interpret the Quranic precepts in the light of the accepted standards of customary law. The Quranic heirs were simply superimposed upon the customary system and confined strictly to the portions prescribed for them by the holy Quran. This restrictive interpretation of the Quranic provisions and the perpetuation of the traditional standards of customary law was by no means confined to inheritance, but was a central feature of general legal development in the Medinan period.

The Development of Hindu Law

The Hindu law exists, since the origin of Indian Civilization. It is one of the oldest laws of India. Laws which regulate the life of the believers mentioned in the Vedic literature of about 1500 BC. Though the exact date of its origin is missing in the traditional materials. Some fundamental rules of law are available, which have spiritual backing between 200 AD and 500 BC.[12] The earliest lawgivers were Manu and Smritikars. Manu chose, the visionary of ultimate truth to formulate the basic postulate of the rule of law governing the mankind.

The laws were developed with the development of civilization, because of the patriarchal system; only male agnate had the right to hold, to inherit and to dispose of the property. But at the time when the Western world was totally unknown to the concept of women's property right the Hindu and Muslim laws gave some property right to females. In Hindu law it existed in the form of Stridhana, though very limited rights had been attributed to them and that also can be exercised only to a certain type of property called Stridhana. On the other hand Muslim females had more and absolute rights in relation to property.

When the Portuguese, the French and the Britisher acquired some Indian territories, the Dharamshastras were injected with the principles of their respective laws. The Dharmashastras were reanimated so far as the natural conservatism of lawyers and special caution of Privy Councilors was allowed.[13] After the Independence of India, new codified laws were passed and it would not be wrong to say that old Hindu law rarely existed in matters of succession, marriage and adoption etc.

The Development of Christian Law

The Common law system came into being in England largely as the result of the activity of Royal courts of justice from the time of Norman Conquest. It is called the Anglo Saxon law and is very little known. The mission of St. Augustine of Centerbury converted England to Christianity in 597. Just as in continental Europe, laws were drafted shortly after the conversion. Ecclesiastical courts were set up to apply common law, common to all Christianity. But again like other countries these laws were very similar to other barbarian laws and regulated very limited aspects of that social relationship to which our present idea of law now extends.[14]

Christian law does not occupy a place in the world comparable to that of Muslim and Hindu laws because of two reasons. Unlike Muslim law, the Christian law has none of the feature of a revealed law nor does it again like Muslim Law purport to regulate totality of human relationships. Compared to Muslim law, it is very fragmentary and essentially the public law of that particular society made up by the Roman Catholic Church. Cannon law has generally left the regulation of private laws and other matters relevant to public law to the laws of individual states. In these areas Cannonists are content to formulate certain principles, which in order to satisfy Christian morality, of secular laws put into effect, and which in any case the faithful must observe.[15]

In Christian world there was no concept of women's property right till the 19th century. Even the assets, which the female possessed before marriage, were merged in the property of her husband after marriage, to which they termed as marital or matrimonial property. Over this property the females have no independent right. They could not appropriate it without the consent of her husband. In 19th century, laws were made and the females were given their own independent property rights.

The concept of women equality has been constantly tinkered, tempered and fiddled with quite frequently, the fact is that it has been evolving throughout human history. The women's rights have been intricately tied to the laws, customs and religions throughout the ages. The Holy Quran, the Bible, the Vedas, the Babylonian Code of Hummurabi and the analects of Confucius are the source through which the religious laws are governed. These religious laws define and demarcate the people's rights, duties and responsibilities. In India generally these laws fail to give women their due. Though the law exists but women are afraid to seek remedy through law enforcing agencies. There is a large gap between the law, social attitudes and beliefs, which acts as barriers in the enforcement of laws for women's emancipation. Because of the complexity of the social institutions like marriage, adoption, divorce and succession the women empowerment is not possible. The succession law is also discriminatory. Consequently, divorce remains theoretical possibility due to women's economic dependence on men and the social ostracism suffered by divorced women. India is an agricultural state. Gender equality in agricultural land can enhance women's right and can accord a better social status in the family. Property may be helpful in eradicating the domestic violence, dowry deaths and reduce family's poverty. It will be helpful in acquiring education and means of livelihood. Studies have already shown that women's risk of physical violence from husband is dramatically less if they own land or house.

Social justice is an inseparable component of women's right and equality without which it is empty and meaningless. Equalities in basic liberties, equality of opportunity for advancement and positive discrimination in favour of women ensure social justice and human rights. In her milieu, human rights expect a change in the perception and the value characteristics of Indian culture. Social justice, women's empowerment and equal status of women are easily said than put in practice. Especially in the society ridden with orthodox and conservative ideals and ideologies for which religious sanction and support are not lacking. In such societies any improvement in the status of women is almost impossible without the co-operation and change of hearts from the part of men.

With this background and on the basis of the discussion in the previous chapters an effort is made to compare firstly, the general rules of the law of succession secondly the shares of females in different capacities in different laws, to understand the actual position.

Comparison of the General Rules of Succession

Islamic Law	*Hindu Law*	*Christian Law*	*Parsi Law*
Islamic Law of Inheritance is based on Quran and pre-Islamic Customs which were not abrogated by the Holy Quran	At present the Hindu law of inheritance is governed by the Hindu Succession Act of 1956,[16] in India. If the Act is silent then by Mitakshara and Dayabhaga school of Hindu Law.	The provisions of the Indian Succession Act of 1925 in India govern succession of a Christian Intestate.	In India the provisions of India Succession Act, 1925 now govern the Parsis intestate Succession.
The nearer in degree excluded the remoter.	Same rule applied to Hindu except in the case of coparcenary.[17]	The nearer in degree exclude the remoter one	The nearer in degree excludes the remoter one
Rules of representation is not applied in general under Muslim law.	Rule of representation is recognized in Hindu law.	Rule of representation is recognized.	Rule of representation is recognized.
There is no concept of joint family in Muslim law.	The concept of joint family is the salient feature of Hindu law.	There is no concept of joint family in Christian law.	There is no concept of joint family in Parsi law.
The right to inherit the property arises only on the death of the propositus.	There is a difference between the two main schools of Hindu law. In Dayabhaga the right to inherit arises on the death but in Mitakshara it arises on the birth of the coparcener. Here the word 'coparcener' includes both son and daughter.	The right to inherit arises on the death of propositus.	The right to inherit arises on the death of propositus.

Islamic Law	*Hindu Law*	*Christian Law*	*Parsi Law*
Rule of primogeniture is not recognized in Muslim law at any time.	It prevailed at ancient time in Hindu law but not at present.	Rule of primogeniture is not recognized at present.	Rule of primogeniture is not recognized at present.
There is no concept of the rule of survivorship in Muslim law.	It is salient feature of Hindu coparcenary.	There is no concept of the rule of the survivorship.	There is no concept of the rule of the survivorship.
An illegitimate child is not entitled to inherit his or her father's property but he or she is entitle to inherit mother's property (Shia law is an exception) the father of an illegitimate child is not entitled to inherit his son or daughter only mother is entitled.	Like Muslim law an illegitimate child is only related to her/his mother and is entitled to inherit each other U/sec 3(1)(j) of Hindu Succession Act, 1956. By virtue of Section 16 of Hindu Marriage Act, 1956, an illegitimate son has been conferred the status of a legitimate son and he also has a right of survivorship.	The succession to the immovable property is regulated by the law of the place where the person domiciles at the time of his death and the domicile of the person of legitimate birth, is in the country in which his father domiciled at the time of his or her birth but the domicile of an illegitimate child be determined by the domicile of his or her mother.	The Act is silent at this point.
Under Muslim law a non Muslim can not be the heir of a Muslim intestate.	Under Hindu law conversion is not a bar to succession but the children of the converted person would not be entitled to represent his father if predeceased or if born after conversion, unless such children or descendants are Hindu at the time when the succession opens.	The Act is silent at this point.	The Act is silent at this point.
The murderer is not entitled to inherit.	Under Section 25 of Hindu Succession Act 1956, a murderer or the abettor is not entitled to inherit the property.	The Act is silent at this point.	The Act is silent at this point.

Islamic Law	*Hindu Law*	*Christian Law*	*Parsi Law*
The posthumous Child is entitled to inherit but born alive.	The posthumous child is entitled to inherit but born alive.	Section 27 of the Indian Succession Act, 1925 abolish the distinction between posthumous and the child born in life times of his or her father, all are equally entitled to inherit.	Clause (2) of section 50 of Indian Succession Act, 1925 abolished the distinction between posthumous and the child born in the life time of father, all are equally entitled to inherit.
If several death took place simultaneously and is difficult to ascertain who survive the other the rule younger survived the elder will apply.	Under Hindu Succession Act of 1956, same provision like Islamic Law is provided.	The Indian Succession Act, 1925 is silent on this point.	The Indian Succession Act, 1925 is silent on this point.
In Muslim Law the property is immediately devolve among the surviving heirs and the subsequent marriage of the widow will not affect the inheritance.	Under Section[18] 24 of Hindu Succession Act, 1956 the son's widow, son's son's widow and brother's widow would be disentitled from inheritance if they have remarried before the succession open but widowed mother and step mother are not disqualified from inheritance even if they have remarried. Now by the new Amendment Act of 2005 section 24 is omitted.	The Act is silent at the point.	In the case the widow or widower remarried in the lifetime of the intestate he or she will not be entitled to inherit, Under Section 50 clause (c) of Indian Succession Act, 1925.
There is no difference between self-acquired or ancestral property movable or immovable property.	Both self acquired and ancestral property is treated differently but no difference between movable and immovable.	Under Section 5 of Indian Succession Act 1925 two different sets of rules were made to regulate the Succession of movable and immovable property.	No difference between movable and immovable, and personal, self-acquired and ancestral property.
There is no difference between The governing rules of succession of male and female	The inheritance of Hindu male's property would be governed by the provision of section 8	No different rules governing the succession of male and female intestate.	No different rules governing the succession of male and female intestate.

Islamic Law	*Hindu Law*	*Christian Law*	*Parsi Law*
Intestate	of Hindu Succession Act, 1956 and the female's property would be governed by the provision of section 15 and 16 of Hindu Succession Act, 1956.		

Comparison of the Shares Allotted to Females in Different Capacities under Different Laws

Mother, grand mother, great grand mother, step mother and mother of illegitimate child

Islamic Law	*Hindu Law*	*Christian Law*	*Parsi Law*
The true mother is always entitled to inherit if survived the son or daughter.	The true mother as class I heir is always entitled to inherit if survived, the son or daughter.	The true mother is not always entitled to inherit the property of her deceased son or daughter.	The true mother is always entitled to inherit if survived the son or daughter.
The mother's share shall be 1/6 if there is daughter or son or son's issues or two brothers or two sisters of any sort, of the deceased or one brother and one sister.	There is no difference in the share of class I heir they shall get equal share.	The true mother is entitled to share if there is no lineal descendants, widow and father but brother or sister her share shall be equal.	If there is widow or widower, children and parents the mother's share shall be the half share of each child.
If there is no daughter or sons or son's issues or two brother or two sister or one brother and one sister then she is entitled to 1/3 of entire property.	If there is no class I heir only mother, she will inherit the whole property.	If there is mother, brother or sister and children of predeceased brother or sister then mother and living brother and sister will inherit equally and the children of predeceased children will take the share of there parents.	The Act is silent at this situation.

Islamic Law	*Hindu Law*	*Christian Law*	*Parsi Law*
In case there is only husband or wife then after deducting the share of husband or wife, the mother shall be entitle 1/3 share of the remaining estate.	The wife being class I heir will inherit with mother if no other class I heir survived. In the case of husband if there are no children the whole property would go to husband.	The mother is excluded by the presence of wife or husband.	The Act issilent at this situation.
Stepmother is not entitled to inherit the property of his stepchild.	Same provision is under Hindu law.	The Act is silent.	The Act is silent
Mother of an illegitimate child is entitled to inherit the property of her child.	Same provision in Hindu Law.	Same provision is in Christian law.	Same provision is in Parsi law.
If there is no mother then grand mother paternal and maternal shall be entitled to 1/6 share, paternal grandmother is excluded by grandfather.	If there is no class I heir and no father, brother sister and their descendants and no lineal descendants of children then grand father and grand mother will be entitled to equal share.	If there is neither lineal descendant, nor parent, nor brother nor sister but grandfather or grand mother and uncle and aunts their grand parents will inherit equally excluding the uncle and aunts.	If there is no lineal descendants, father mother, brother, sister but leaves widow or widower or widow or widower of lineal descendant after allotting their share the residue will go to grand parents equally.
Great grandmother is entitled as distant kindered.	The great grand mother (hhs) is entitled as distant kindered.	If there is neither lineal descendant, nor parent, nor brother, nor sister and deceased left only great grandmother uncle or aunts they will inherit equal share.	If neither lineal descendant nor widow or widower of lineal descendant father, mother brother, sister paternal and maternal grand parent, children of grand parents then great grand parents are entitled to share equally.

Table-2

Widow, widow of predeceased son, widow of pre deceased son's son (hls), widow of brother

Islamic Law	*Hindu Law*	*Christian Law*	*Parsi Law*
In the case there are children or child then she shall get 1/8 of the estate. If more then they will inherit 1/8 collectively.	Widow of valid marriage shall inherit equal share along with the children and children of predeceased son and predeceased son's son.	Widow of valid marriage is entitled to 1/3 if there are any lineal descendants.	The widow of valid marriage is entitled equal share along with children.
Widow of valid marriage is entitled, if there is no issue, to get ¼ of the estate. If more than one they will inherit ¼ collectively.	In case there is no heir of class I she will inherit the whole property.	If he has left no lineal descendant but kindred then 1/2 share will go to widow. If no issue and no kindred then whole property will go to widow.	If there is no lineal descendant and no widow or widower of a lineal descendant the widow shall take half of the estate. If there is widows or widowers or only one then she will take 1/3 of the estate.
Widow of void marriage is not entitled to inherit.	The widow of void and voidable marriage are not entitled to inherit.	The widow of void marriage is not entitle to inherit.	The widow of void marriage is not entitle to inherit.
A kitabiah or non Muslim widow is not entitled to inherit.		Act is silent at this point.	Act is silent at this point.
Widow of a predeceased son is not entitled to inherit.	Widow of a pre-deceases son is entitled the share of her husband along with the children equally.	The widow of a predeceases son will inherit her husband share equally along with children.	The widow of a predeceases son is entitled to the share of her husband along with the children in equal proportion.
Widow of predeceased son is not entitled to inherit.	If there is no child then the widow of predeceased son is entitled to the whole share of her husband.	If there is no child the widow of a pre-deceased son is entitled to inherit the share of her husband.	If intestate leaves no lineal descendants widow or widower of lineal descendant such widow or widower shall receive 1/3 of the estate.

Islamic Law	*Hindu Law*	*Christian Law*	*Parsi Law*
The widow of pre-deceased son's son is not entitled to inherit.	She be entitled to the share of her husband if alone and will enjoy equal share along with children.	She be entitled the share of her husband if alone and enjoys equal share along with the children.	With children she will enjoy equal share of her husband but if alone then 1/3 of the estate.
The widow of pre-decesased son's son is not entitled to inherit.	She be entitled to the share of her husband if alone and will enjoy equal share along with children.	She be entitled the share of her husband if alone and enjoys equal share along with the children.	With children she will enjoy equal share of her husband but if alone then 1/3 of the estate.
The widow of bother is not entitled to inherit.	The widow of brother is entitled to inherit in some situation.	The widow of brother is entitled as a distant kindred.	If the entries of schedule II part I are exhausted and up to the sixth entry of part II then brother's widow is entitled to inherit.

Table-3

Sister, Consanguine Sister and Uterine Sister

Islamic Law	*Hindu Law*	*Christian Law*	*Parsi Law*
Full sister is not entitled to inherit in the presence of son (hls) or the father (hhs).	Full sister is not entitled to inherit if class I heir and father present.	In the presence of children and widow the full sister is not entitled to inherit.	In the presence of children and widow or widower the full sister is not entitled to inherit.
If she is alone and no son (hls) and father (hhs) then she will inherit ½ of the estate.	If she is alone and no heir of class I heirs and also father she inherits the whole property.	If there is no lineal descendant and father but another, brother and sister they will succeed.	If there is no lineal descendant father and mother a widow or widower and full sister and brother, then after allotting the share of widow or widower the residue will be inherited by the brother and sister equally.

Islamic Law	*Hindu Law*	*Christian Law*	*Parsi Law*
If they are two or more and no son (hls) and father (hhs) then she will get 2/3 of the estate.	If two or more than two they will share equally.	If no father but mother, a brother or sister and children of any deceases brother and sister living then mother, brother and sister succeed equally with the children of predeceased brother.	If there are two or more sisters and no above mentioned heir, or brother they will succeed equally.
If no son and father only brother then she will become residuary.	If there is brother also they will share equally.	If there is only brother and sister and no father, mother, they will inherit equally.	If there is no above-mentioned heir but only brother and sister they will inherit equally.
If no son and father only brother then she will become residuary.	If there is brother also they will share equally.	If there is only brother and sister and no father, mother, they will inherit equally.	If there is no above-mentioned heir but only brother and sister they will inherit equally.
If no son, father and brother but a daughter or son's daughter she will get the residue after their shares are allotted.	If there is son's son's son, or son's daughter's daughter they will entitled to equal share.	In presence of child the sister is not entitled to inherit.	In the presence of any lineal descendant the sister is not entitled to inherit.
Consanguine sister is not entitled to inherit in the presence of two full sister.	Consanguine or half blood sister is not entitled to inherit in the presence of full sister.	Consanguine sister is not entitled to inherit in the presence of any lineal descendant and ascendant widow or widower.	Consanguine sister is not entitled to inherit in the presence of any heir specified in schedule II part I and part II up to entry sixth.
If there is one full sister and one consanguine sister the full sister shall take ½and consanguine 1/6.	If there is any brother or sister of full blood present the brother and sister of half blood be excluded.	In the presence of full sister half sister is not entitled to inherit.	In the presence of full sister half sister is not entitled to inherit.

Islamic Law	*Hindu Law*	*Christian Law*	*Parsi Law*
If there is only Consanguine brother and consanguine sister then she will inherit as residuary.	Where there is a brother of half blood and sister of full blood the former will not be excluded.	If there is no father but mother and full brother and consanguine sister each would inherit equally.	If there is no heir specified in schedule II Part I and no heir up to the entry of sixth In second part then only half sister is entitled to inherit.
Consanguine sister with true daughters and grand daughters become residuary.	In the presence of child or grandchild the consanguine sister be excluded.	In the presence of true daughter and granddaughter the consanguine sister is not be entitled to inherit.	In the presence of true daughter and granddaughter the consanguine sister not be entitled to inherit.
If there is no issue of the deceases or of his son, no father or no grand father and there is one uterine brother and sister they shall take 1/6 each.	If there is no heir of class I and no father and full brother and sister then half sister is entitled to inherit	Uterine sister is entitled to inherit when there is no lineal descendant or ascendants.	Uterine sister is entitled to inherit only when no lineal descendant or ascendant.
If they are two or more uterine sister then they will get 1/3 which be divided equally between brother and sister.	Same as above.	Same as above.	Same as above

Table-4
Daughter, Son's daughter and Daughter's daughter

Islamic Law	*Hindu Law*	*Christian Law*	*Parsi Law*
If there is no son and daughter is alone, then her share is half of the estate and the other half will go to distant kindred.	If there is no other class I heir and daughter is alone then she would inherit the whole property.	If there is no son and no remote lineal descendant (hls) then the surviving daughter will alone be entitled to inherit the whole property.	If no son and no remote lineal descendant and widow or widower or father and mother then the surviving daughter will

Islamic Law	*Hindu Law*	*Christian Law*	*Parsi Law*
			alone be entitled to inherit the whole property.
If there is no son and daughters are more than one their share would be 2/3 of the estate, which they will divide equally among them.	If there is more than one daughter they would inherit equally.[19]	If there is no son and no remote lineal descendants and widow but more than one daughter they will inherit equally.	If there is no son and no remote lineal descendants and widow but more than one daughter they will inherit equally.
If there is son and daughter then they would inherit as residuary.	If there is both son and daughter they would inherit equally.	If only son and daughter survived they would share the property equally.	If only son and daughter survived they would share the property equally.
If there is one daughter and no son and a son's daughter, the son's daughter is entitled to inherit the share of 1/6.	If there is one daughter and no son but son's daughter she be entitled the ½ share (which is of her father if he would have been alived).	If there is one daughter and no son but the son's daughter, both will inherit equally.	If there is one daughter and no son and a son's daughter, the son's daughter will take half estate.
If there is no daughter or son, the son's daughter would inherit like daughter.	If there is no other heirs the son's daughter would inherit the whole.	If there is no daughter or son but the son's daughter and no other heir of lineal descendant she will inherit the whole property.	If there is no daughter or son but the sons daughter and no other heir of lineal descendant then she will inherit the whole property.
If there is more than one daughter and one son's son and sono's daughter. She will inherit the 1/3 of 1/3, means 1/9 of the estate.	If there are two daughters and one son's son and one son's daughter the two daughter will take 1/3 each and the other 1/3 be inherited by the son's son and son's daughter collectively.	If there is more than one daughter and son's son and son's daughter 2/3 will go to two daughters and the remaining 1/3 be equally inherited by son's son and son's daughter.	If there is more than one daughter and son's son and son's daughter 2/3 will go to two daughters and the remaining 1/3 be equally inherited by son's son and son's daughter.

Islamic Law	*Hindu Law*	*Christian Law*	*Parsi Law*
If there is a daughter, son's daughter son's son's son and son's son's daughter, the son's son's daughter be entitled 1/9 share and son's daughter 1/6.	If there is a daughter, son's daughter, son's son's son and son's son and son's son's daughter the daughter shall take 1/3, the son's daughter shall take 1/3 and other 1/3 be equally inherited by the son's son's son and daughter.	If there is a daughter a son's daughter, son's son's son and son's son's daughter then 1/3 will go to daughter, 1/3 to son's daughter and the remaining 1/3 be inherited by son's son's son and son's son's daughter equally.	If there is a daughter, a son's daughter, son's son's son and son's son's daughter then 1/3 will go to daughter 1/3 to son's daughter and the remaining 1/3 be inherited equally by son's son's son and son's son's daughter 1/6 each.
If there are two son's daughters, a son's son's daughter and a son's son's son, the two son's daughters will take 2/3 and son's son's daughter and son's son's son shall take 1/6 share.	If there is two son's daughter, a son's son's daughter and a son's son's son, the two son's daughter will take 1/3 each and the other 1/3 be inherited by son's son's son and son's son's daughter equally, it means 1/6 each.	If there is two son's daughters, a son's son's daughter and a son's son's son the two son's daughter will take 2/3 and son's son's daughter shall take 1/6 share each.	If there is two son's daughters, a son's son's daughter and a son's son's son the two son's daughter will take 2/3 and son's son's daughter will take 1/6 share each.

SOME COMPARATIVE ILLUSTRATIONS

Illustration No. 1

A female died leaving behind her husband, two daughters, and two sons of a pre-deceased son, brother, mother, stepmother and a widow of her brother. The deceased had inherited the property from her father. Divide the property among her heirs according to rules of Muslim, Hindu, Christian and Parsi law.

Under Muslim Law

In this given illustration according to Muslim law of inheritance, the property of Muslim female intestate shall be devolved upon the mother, husband and two daughters. The stepmother is not considered as mother and has no inheritance rights. Brother and the widow of brother are also not entitled to inherit being distant kindred in the presence of sharers. As under Islamic law there is no rule of representation recognized, so the sons of pre-deceased son are also not entitled to inherit.

Under Muslim Law, in the presence of any child the husband's share will be 1/4. Because of the presence of the daughters the mother's share will be 1/6 and the two daughters will inherit the maximum share of 2/3.

In the above illustration the sum total of 1/4 + 1/6 + 2/3 exceeds the unity. Therefore by applying the doctrine of Awl (increase) the share of each sharer will be reduced proportionately.

Husband —	1/4 = 3/12	reduced to 3/13
Mother —	1/6 = 2/12	reduced to 2/13
2 Daughters —	2/3 = 8/12	reduced to 8/13
	13/12	13/13

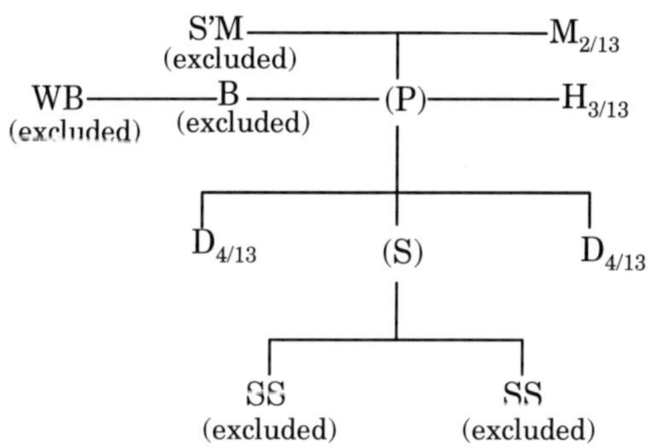

Under Hindu Law

In this illustration the property of female Hindu shall be devolved upon husband, two daughters and two sons of the predeceased son being heir in clause (a) of sub-section (1) of section15 of Hindu Succession Act of 1956. Stepmother, brother and widow of brother will not get anything according to the rule 1 of section 16 of the Act of 1956. The two sons of the predeceased son would get the share of their father according to the rule 2 of section 16 of the Act 1956. The rule of representation is recognized under Hindu Law. The proportional share of each heir would be-

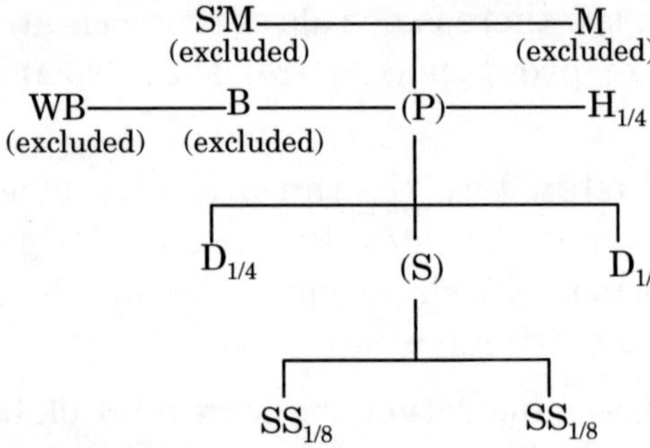

Under Christian Law

According to Indian Succession Act, 1925, which governs the Christian Succession the property of a female Christian intestate shall be devolved upon the husband, two daughters and the sons of the predeceased son. Mother, stepmother, brother and the widow of brother will get nothing. According to section 33 read with section 35 the share of the husband would be 1/3 and other 2/3 be divided among other heirs who are deceased daughters in this case.

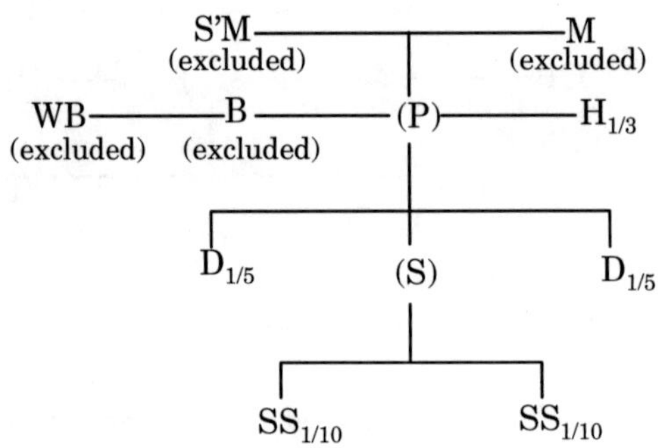

Under Parsi Law

In the given illustration the property of a Parsi female intestate, shall be devolved upon, mother, husband, two daughters and the sons of predeceased son. Stepmother, brother and the widow of the brother will get nothing. According to sub-section (2) of section 51 the share of mother for each surviving parent) would be the half share of each child. Clause (a) of sub-section (1) of section 51 of Indian Succession Act, 1925 says that husband and each child will inherit equal share. In the view of section 53 the children of the predeceased child would get the share of their parents collectively. The proportional share of the husband in this illustration would be 2/9, mother 1/9, each daughter 2/9 and each son of predeceased son 1/9.

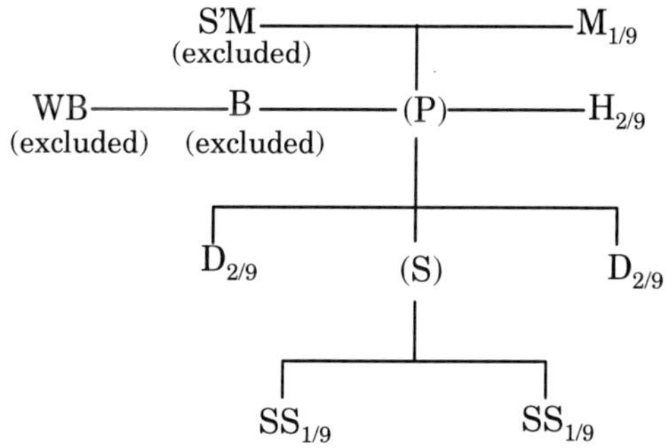

Illustration No. 2

A, a male died in 1987, leaving behind son, daughter, father and widow of a predeceased son. Divide his property among the heirs according to Muslim, Hindu, Christian and Parsi Law of succession.

Under Muslim Law

According to the Muslim law of inheritance the property of Muslim intestate in the given illustration shall be devolved among the son, daughter and father and the widow of the predeceased son will get nothing, as there is no rule of representation is recognized in Islamic Law. The proportional share of the father in the presence of children will be 1/6 and residue of 5/6 will be divided between the daughter and son, according to the rule of that the share of the daughter be the ½ of the son. Here the daughter in the presence of son be residuary and not inherit as a sharer, (where her share is fix according to Holy Quran).

Father	-	1/6
Son	-	2/3 (of 5/6) = 5/9
Daughter	-	1/3 (of 5/6) = 5/18
Widow of Predeceased son	-	excluded.

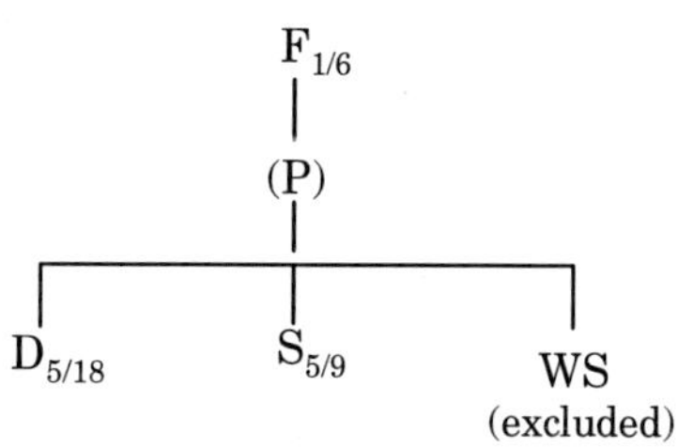

Under Hindu Law

In the given illustration according to Hindu Succession Act of 1956 the property will be devolved among the son, daughter and widow of predeceased son equally and the father will get nothing. Clause (a) of section 8 of the Act of 1956 says that the property of male Hindu dying intestate shall devolved-firstly upon the heirs, being the relatives specified in class I of the schedule. The son, daughter and the widow are the relatives who are specified in class I of the schedule. So they inherit simultaneously and in equal share. If there is no heir in class I then the property shall devolved in the heirs specified in class II. Father being class II heir shall get nothing in presence of class I heir.

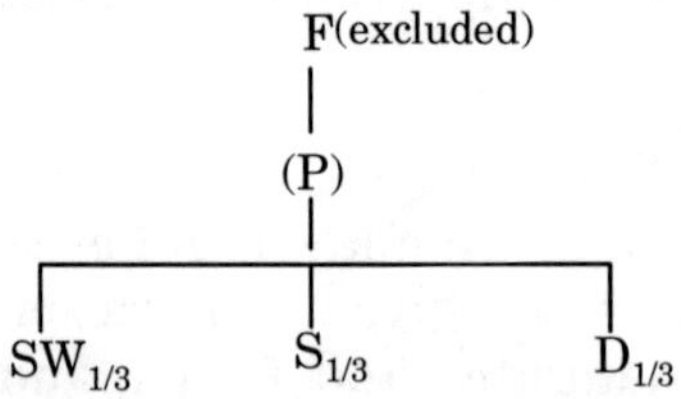

Under Christian Law

According to Indian Succession Act, 1925 in the given illustration the property of a Christian intestate shall be devolved among the son, daughter and the widow of predeceased son and the father in the presence of lineal descendant would get nothing. The heirs will inherit the property in equal share.

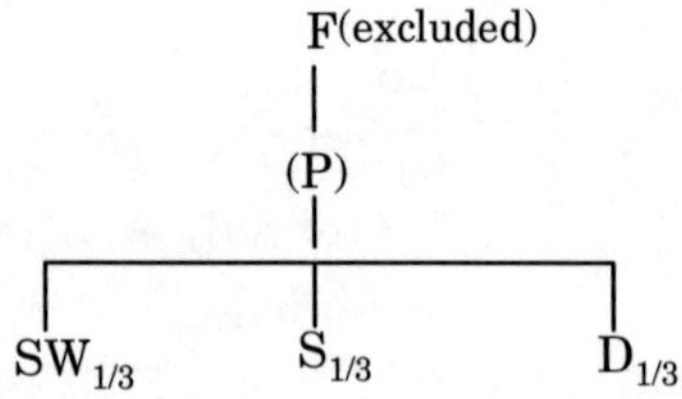

Under Parsi Law

Under the provision of Indian Succession Act, 1925 the property of a Parsi intestate in the given illustration shall be devolved among all the four heirs who survived the intestate. According to sub-clause (a) of section 51 of the Act of 1925, the father's share would be the half of each child. The son and daughter shall inherit equally. The widow of the predeceased son shall receive the share of her husband which he would have if survived the deceased. It means here the share of son, daughter and the widow of predeceased son is equal and the father's share shall be half of each child.

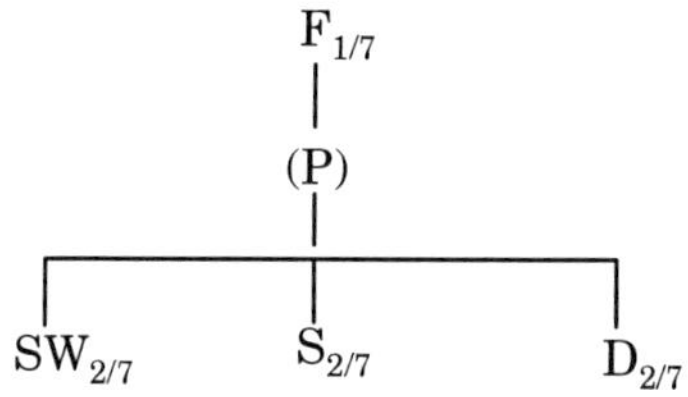

Illustration No. 3

A male intestate died leaving behind a daughter, mother, widow, son's widow and father. Divide the property, supposing the intestate, if he is Muslim, Hindu, Christian and Parsi.

Under Muslim Law

In the given illustration the property of a Muslim intestate be divided according to Islamic Law of inheritance among the daughter, mother, widow and father. The son's widow will get nothing, as the rule of representation is not recognized in Islamic law. The Proportional share of the daughter would be $^1/_2$ as there is no son; the mother's share would be 1-/6 in the presence of child. Father's share also is 1/6 in presence of child. The widow's share would 1/8 in the presence of child.

Daughter	-	1/2
Mother	-	1/6
Father	-	1/6
Wife	-	1/8 (No change in wife's share)

Here the shares does not complete the unity and by applying the doctrine of Return or Radd the residue will be proportionately revert to the heirs. It is a rule that the wife or husband in the presence of child or children not entitle to the return. Therefore in the given illustration the residue will be distributed among daughters, mother and father.

Daughter	1/2	3/6	3/5 (of 7/8)
Mother	1/6	1/6	1/5 (of 7/8)
Father	1/6	1/6	1/5 (of 7/8)
		5/6	5/5

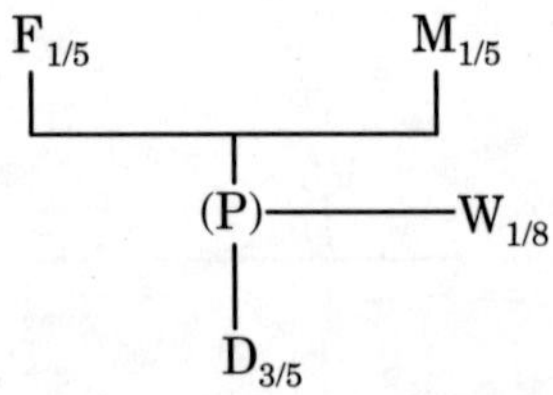

Under Hindu Law

In the given illustration according to Hindu Succession Act, 1956 the daughter, mother, widow and son's widow will inherit the property simultaneously in equal proportion because they all are the heirs specified in class I of schedule. Father being class II heir will be excluded.

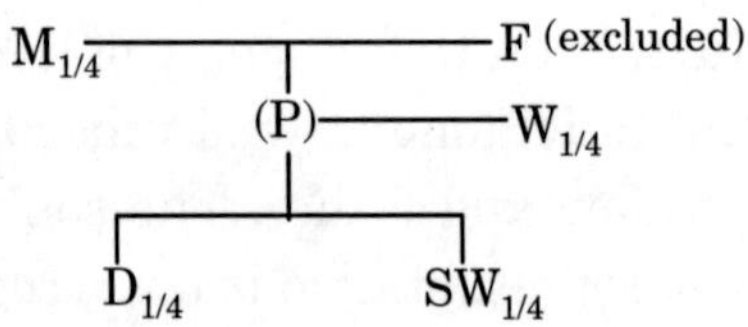

Under Christian Law

In the given illustration the property of a Christian intestate shall be devolved among the widow, daughter and son's widow. Mother and father are not entitled according to the provision of Indian Succession Act, 1925 to inherit the property in the presence of child or children (how low so ever). Section 33 clause (a) says that in the presence of lineal descendant the share of widow shall be 1/3 and the other 2/3 be distributed among the lineal descendants. Here the proportional share of a Christian wife would be 1/3 and the other two third 2/3 be equally divided among the daughter and the widow of son. The widow of son will be entitled to the share of her husband if survived the intestate.

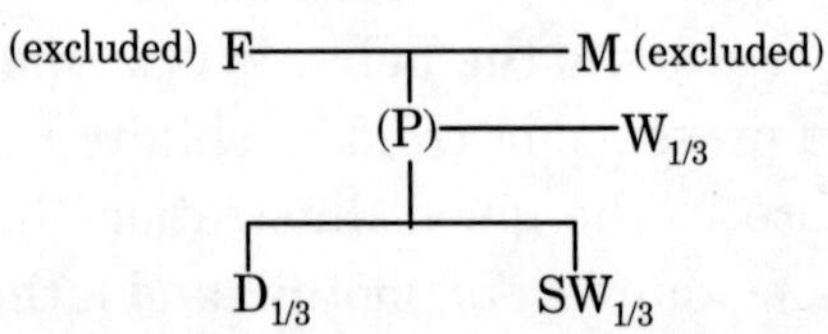

Under Parsi Law

According to Indian Succession Act, 1925 the property of a Parsi intestate in the given illustration shall be divided among the father, mother, widow, daughter and son of widow. All the heirs are entitled to inherit their due share. According to the provision of clause, of sub-section (1) of section 51 the widow and each child would receive his due share equally. Sub-section (2) of section 51 says that the share of parents, if survived the decease would be $^1/2$ of each child.

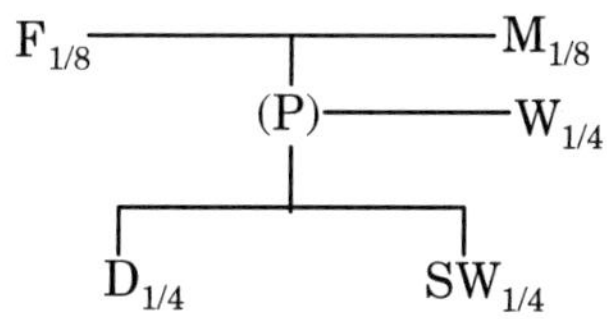

Illustration No. 4

A died leaving behind widow, mother, father and brother. Divide the property according to Muslim, Hindu, Christian and Parsi Law.

Under Muslim Law

In the given illustration under Islamic law the widow's share in the absence of children would be maximum which is 1/4 and the mother's share would also be maximum that is 1/4 of the remaining 3/4. The father will inherit as a residuary.

Widow	-	1/4
Mother	-	1/4 (of 3/4)
Father	-	as residuary

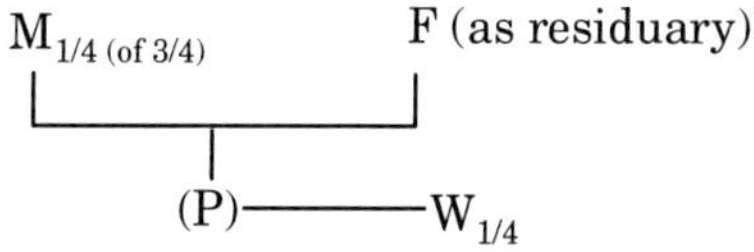

Under Hindu Law

In this given illustration according to the provision of Hindu Law, which is governed by Hindu Succession Act, 1956 the property of deceased will be divided among the widow and mother equally being class I heir. Father being class II heir shall get nothing because in the presence of class I heir the heirs of class II are not entitled to inherit.

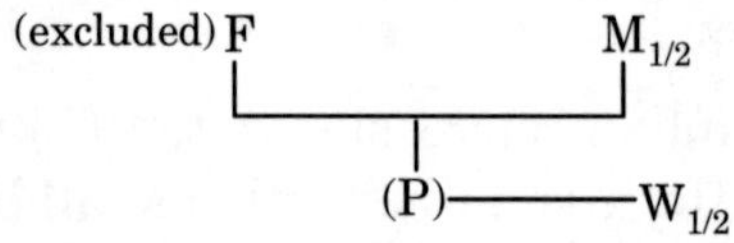

Under Christian Law

In this given illustration the property of a Christian deceased be divided among the father and the widow as under section 42 of Indian Succession Act, 1925, in the presence of father the mother is not entitle to inherit. Under section 33 clause (b) if the deceased has no lineal descendant but left widow and kindered to him the 1/2 property will go to widow and the other 1/2 to kindered. In the given illustration the father excludes the mother so here the 1/2 property will go to father and other 1/2 to widow.

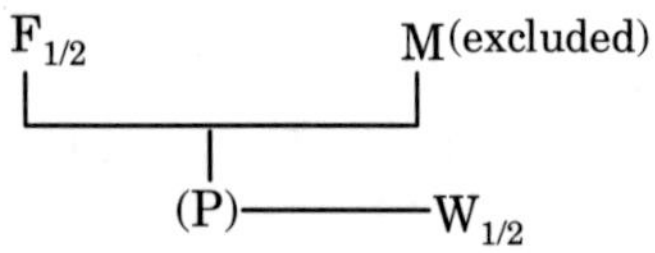

Under Parsi Law

In the given illustration the property of a Parsi be distributed among all the heirs. According to section 51 of Indian Succession Act, 1925 the parent's share shall be half of each child the widow and children will inherit equally. In this given illustration there are no children so all the heirs would inherit equally.

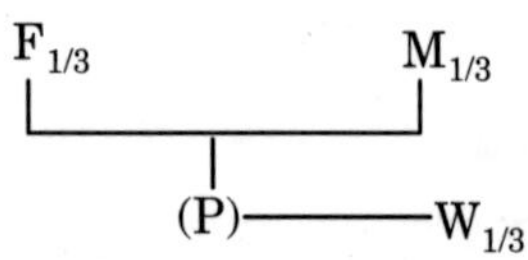

In the above discussion we have seen that how the shares and the sharers fluctuated according to the provisions of different religious laws. In different situations the proportional shares are different within one religion. As in Hindu Law, generally mother is entitled to inherit but in case female intestate the mother is not entitled. In Islamic law the father is always entitled to inherit. In each law there is discrimination among the shares of the heirs.

Recapitulation

On the basis of the above comparison it is evident that the female's property right to inherit is discriminatory in every system in some form or the other. What ever is the reason behind this discrimination, females are not treated equally and therefore suffered a lot. As in Muslim law the share of female is always half of her male counterpart except in the case of uterine brother and sister. In Hindu law there are different set of rules to govern the Hindu female even after amendment of 2005, though the Hindu Succession (amendment) Act, 2005, has brought revolutionary changes in the era of women's property right and abolished near about all the discrimination. It has included four new female heirs in the schedule, which are mainly concerned with the daughters. This Act not only recognizes the share and rights of daughter equally with that of son but also has given the lineal descendants of daughter equal rights, which the lineal descendants of son possess. This Act has gain warm welcome in the women folk lets we wait and watch how much effective it may be proved in practical life and how the old ages social ethos would be changed. In Christian law though it is codified law, the mother is not entitled to inherit the property in the presence of father. It is argued that these discriminations are based because of the prevailing conditions of each society. This cannot be justified and attempt should be made to equalize the female to their male counterparts. As recently under Hindu law the daughter is given an equal share to her brother in the ancestral property also. The other laws must take an inspiration from it.

References

1. Harold Berman J. : The Comparison of Soviet and American Law; cited by Henry W. Ehrman, 'Comparative Legal Cultures', p. 11.
2. Lapaulle: "The Functions of Comparative Law:" 35 Harvward Law Review, 853 (1922).
3. Gulteridge H.C.: Comparative Law, Introduction to the Comparative Method of Legal Study and Research, Cambridge (1946), p. 2.

4. Freund O' Kahn : "Comparative Law as an Academic Subject", 82 Law Quarterly Review 45, (1966).
5. Rheinsteen M. : "Teaching Comparative Law": Law Review 616 (1938).
6. See: David Rene and John E.C. Brierly: 'Major Legal System in the World Today.' (1968) 1st ed., p. 14.
7. *Ibid.*
8. The Encyclopaedia of Religion, Vol. 3, p. 578.
9. Louis H. Jordon: Comparative Religion; Its Genesis and Growth, Edinburg, 1905 p. 11.
10. Derrett J. D.M.: An Introduction to Legal System, Ist, ed. Indian Reprint (1999), p. 54.
11. *Ibid.,* p. 58.
12. See Nickman N.A. and Mckeon R.: The Edicts of Ashoka, (Chicago London), Phoenix, 1966.
13. Derrett, *op cit.,* p. 83.
14. Rene David, *op cit.,* p. 261.
15. *Ibid.*
16. Now the Hindu Succession Act, 1956, is amended by the Hindu Succession (Amendment) Act, 2005.
17. Now the daughter is also made a coparcener.
18. This section 24 is abolished by the Hindu Succession (Amendment) Act of 2005.
19. After the Hindu Succession (Amendment) Act, 2005.

6

Summation and Suggestions

The domestic life, religion and right to property are intimately related to each other. Property always plays a vital role in the life style of individual, family, community and country. In general utility, the property allows of successive improvement in the distress.

The property rights of women have been the subject of repeated controversy till the dawn of civilization and still a talk of the day. The existence and perpetuation of gender discrimination is a blot and slur on the modern welfare states. It generates much heat and passion due to the changing concept of gender equality and the impact of the West. Underlying the laws to ameliorate various forms of social injustice towards women, is an assumption, described by Moore and followed by Roscoe Pound as the *'social engineering.'*

The transition, from the rigorous law of ancient period to the liberal and humane laws of the modern era, took several centuries. A macro-change in the composition of the infrastructure, is the need of the time. The distressing aspect of our Indian legal system is, however, that the women's right to inherit like their other rights, is also observed more often in breach than in practice. Though the legislation is an important medium for imparting the normative values to the society but the mere existence of such mechanism even if it is not frequently restored, may not be proved profitable.

Besides legislative enactments, the resurgence of woman's liberation movement has been accompanied by endeavours at research, opinion polls, social surveys and empirical studies which have helped to analyze the nature and mode of economic discrimination and to suggest remedies for their eradication. As a result of growing awareness of the seriousness of the problem of domestic violence, the legislators, jurists, social scientists, reformers and activist for the women cause have come forward to alleviate the misery of females in their own way. But the women's emancipation is still a distant dream. The reason may be that the laws are not changed sufficiently and radically but only conventionally and superficially. The laws, themselves seemingly neutral, are crypto-partial to men. It is one step forward and two steps backward for the common woman. There are contradictory forces at work. On one hand there is the progressive thinking, which has led to decentralization of powers, which is pro-woman, but on the other there is economic onslaught, which is detriment to woman.

A complex interplay of biological, social, cultural and economic factors put the women and even young girls at greater risk of getting infected with HIV virus. A growing number of women are infected with HIV all over the world. An overwhelming reason for this trend is economic dependence of female over their male counterpart.

In a diverse country like India gender issues and their solutions can never have a set model, what may work for woman in Kerala, may not work for women in Punjab. It is also a matter of regret and surprising that the local legal culture has also not spared the women from divesting her property right and they are still in continuation even after the independence. So many anti-woman customs not only still prevails in different parts of India but they are protected by the judiciary. Throughout the course of discussion there is no reported case from Muslim females relating to the unequal share of inheritance. The cases, which are found, mostly relate to the customs and claims were made to follow the Islamic law.

From the foregoing discussion, it is crystal clear that the Islamic law is not discriminatory towards woman. Islam is the leader of feminist movement. Equality is a comparative concept. The equality can be judged by taking into account all the conditions and circumstances of two different social systems, their setups in which the question of inequality arises. It must be recognized that every difference in treatment between individuals under the law will not necessarily results in inequality and as well that identical treatment may frequently result in serious inequality.

Under Islam equality does not mean literal and mathematical equality. Here equality means a judicious treatment with the males and females keeping in view their social, biological and economic responsibilities. This may be appreciated when we compare the Islamic system with other systems of law.

In Islam, there is a peculiar Islamic attitude towards women, which is based on a characteristic appreciation of values and a full cognizance of the nature of the reality. According to Dr. Alexis Carrol, the noted physiologist, "between the two sexes there are *irrevocable difference, and it is imperative to take them into account in constructing the civilized world.*" The Islamic attitude which is based on the appreciation of difference is only partly reflected in the terms of rights that it accords to women in the society. At the very outset it has been asserted in unequivocal terms that the Quranic evaluation of womanhood can be judged, only by the place assign to woman in the whole scheme of things in the cosmic order as such. First and foremost the Quran emphasizes the '*musawah*' means equality. As biologically, psychologically and metaphysically the role of the two sexes are totally different, so their privileges and liabilities are also different.

The principle of double share for male is, no doubt, extremely equitable since the female heirs receive additionally '*maher*' and maintenance from the husband. The male member is also liable for maintenance of his wife and family. The female heir has no such responsibility. The creation of property rights generates the rights and duties. Such as those, who receive something, make compensation or restitution. The law of property and obligation are categorized of the same kind. They assign one another. Rights are creature of events. Haji Sulaiman Abdullah in a discussion on woman, family and law, spoke of the need, '*to took at the whole system before deciding whether a particular law is discriminatory or not.*' The complexity of interpreting what is discriminatory and the notion perspective, '*looking at the whole system*' and the gender assumptions, that drive it, are tied to the question of how abstract goal of equality may be achieved in practice.

The above principle can be easily understood by the following example - a Muslim dies leaving behind a daughter and a son and property of worth Rs. 60,000/-. Son would take 40,000 and the daughter's share would be Rs. 20,000/-. Suppose the daughter was already married and received 10,000 as her '*mehar*' from her husband. So the total share of the daughter became Rs. 30,000/-. The son got married later and paid Rs. 10,000/- as a '*mehar*' to his wife what left to him was 30,000/ - only with, other responsibility of maintaining the family.

It is just an instance. If one sees the Islam with a deep insight, he will realize that it is the daughter who is ultimate beneficiary though apparently the discrimination is visible.

The son of Abu Ahuja having expressed his ignorance and doubt of the cause why a female the weakest and most helpless of the two, enjoyed only half the portion of inheritance bestowed upon a male. Imam Jafar Sadiq replied that a female is excused from performance of many duties imposed by law upon a male such as service in the holy wars, maintenance and support of relations and payment of expiatory fines and dowers etc., for this reason her share of inheritance has been justly limited to half the portion of male.

Any attempt to assign a woman artificially a legal status, not congruent with her social custom or law, will disturb the equilibrium between the two spheres. It will create tension and usually will not stand the test of reality. To resort to the Islamic law of inheritance if woman were to be given their due share according to Islamic law, there would be no question of a woman becoming destitute. It is a matter of regret that the majority of Muslim women fail to get their due share of inheritance from their deceased father or husband as stipulated by Islamic law. If they could do so, this would be more than enough to meet any type of contingencies.

The traditional Hindu Law conferred rights of inheritance only on sons because it was considered that they saved the parents from hell. Human society has always been kaleidoscopic to meet the ever-changing needs of the time; the law should also be changing with the gradual growth of property law. With the lapse of time some property rights were conferred to women, though they were discriminatory as they were only entitled to hold the Stridhan. The journey of women's property right which started by the Hindu Law of Inheritance Act, 1928, continued till 2005 (the Hindu Succession Amendment Act 2005). By the Act of 1937, significant changes were brought in the law of partition, alienation of property, inheritance and adoption.

The Hindu Succession Act, 1956, has been considered the piecemeal legislation because it gives daughters equal right to the son though only in separate property and self acquired property. During the debate on the Hindu Code Bill the majority of legislators had took a stand against daughter to be a coparcener. Perhaps it was the most shameful moment in the history of parliamentary proceedings. The Act of 1956, too had many drawbacks and created a lot of chaos in the practice. There were plethora of cases in which different courts have different verdicts. Sometimes they leaned towards women, but sometimes the literal interpretation has been given. Section 6 of the Hindu Succession Act, 1956, deals with the devolution of interest of a male Hindu in coparcenary property and recognized the rule of devolution by survivorship among the member of the coparcenary and talked about the notional partition which is the most bewildering provision of the Act. The net result of section 6 was that only male members were entitled to have a share in the coparcenary property, completely excluding daughters. This was a blatant discrimination with daughters caused by the principles of notional partition.

Thus the Act of 1956, though brought considerable changes in the rights of female yet it did not go the whole hog in making daughter, member of the coparcenary with equal rights of partition and survivorship. Section 14, which is the most controversial section and created a great hardship in its implementation, is still prevailed. No changes has been introduced even by the new amendment of 2005. The words used in section 14 always remain in controversy in regard of its interpretation. The decisions given by the courts are, so divergent that instead of resolving the controversies increase it. Generally the court leaned towards the favouring of women.

Sections 23 and 24 were also very discriminatory because under section 23 only qualified right of partition was given to the female heirs in the dwelling house. She was not entitled to claim partition unless the male members choose to partition even there was only one male member, at this situation there was very little chance to choose partition. Sections 23 and 24 are now omitted clearing the way for the daughter to have share in dwelling house, to demand partition and the widow to retain property even after remarriage. The bar imposed upon widow by the section 24 not to inherit the property of her previous husband on remarriage, has now been removed by the new amendment by omitting section 24. Despite of this amendment there are still two sets of rules governing the intestate succession of male and female separately.

By this amendment some new heirs have also been added and most of them are related though female's or females themselves. So it is expected that the recent steps, taken by the Parliament to ameliorate the position of women, will restore the glory of Hinduism and will take the country to a high pedestal, globally.

Christian and Parsi laws, which governed Indian Christian and Parsi, are no more a religious law, in their strict sense. Because there is no spiritual sanctity or religious values behind them. The Christian and Parsi's intestate succession is governed by the pre-independence Act of 1925. Inspite of the policy of non-interference in the matters of personal affairs by Britishers, so many statutes had been passed to govern the Indian Christian and Parsis. The British rule in India began on the legislative front with the Indian Succession Act, 1865 and Parsi Succession Act, 1865, which were based upon English Law in letter and spirit.

The Christian intestate succession is governed till now which did the provisions of the Act of 1925 base on the Act, 1865. The Act of 1925, had been passed through a long list of amendments, which started just after one year of the passing of the Act in 1926 (The Indian Succession Amendment Act 1926, (37 of 1926), (40 of 1926), (18 of 1927), (14 of 1928), (18 of 1929), (17 of 1937), (17 of 1939), (35 of 1949), (34 of 1957), (16 of 1962),(51 of 1991) and latest in 2002 (26 of 2002).

In the Act of 1925, there are two different sets of rules to regulate the movable and immovable property of a intestate Christian. The domicile of the propositus is the main factor to decide the law of which country be applied to govern the succession. Under the provision of the Indian Succession Act, 1925, there is no place for the English concept of marital property. There is no distinction between real and personal property. The heir-ship of a Christian intestate be decided by the consanguinity but husband and wife are the exceptions. The Christian law does not discriminate between the agnate and cognates, half and full blood, posthumous child and the child born in the lifetime of his father. The remarkable feature of Indian Succession Act, 1925, relating to Christian is that the widower has the same right of inheritance as the widow. The only discrimination is with the mother of a Christian intestate who has no right of inheritance if there is any lineal descendant or even father. It means she is not entitled to inherit the property simultaneously with the father. She is only entitled to inherit the property if there is no lineal descendant and father. On the other hand if there is no lineal descendant, the father will inherit the whole property excluding all other heirs even the mother also. It is a gross discrimination with the Christian mother.

The Parsi law of intestate Succession has passed through many revolutionary changes. The Parsis were much exploited in the British period since their succession was governed by the rules of common law. After a long struggle, the Parsi Succession Act of 1856 was passed. That too was much discriminatory towards women. But by this Act the widow and daughter were made the heirs for the first time. Before it they were entitled only for maintenance. Yet the mother and sister were not included in the list of heirs. Before the amendment of 1939, the son's share in agricultural land was four times more than daughter and two times more than widow. After amendment the son's share was made double of the daughter, by this amendment sister and mother were also introduced as heirs. The drastic changes were brought in the law of inheritance of Parsis by the amendment of 1991, which had abolished all sex based discrimination and made the female equal to the male in the field of inheritance. The only discriminatory share is seems to be of the parents which is half of each child but it can not be said as discriminatory because the parents have no responsibilities.

From the foregoing discussion it is obvious that not only the concept of women's property right is different but even the concept of women's property is also different in every legal system. As in Hindu law, it is termed as Stridhana or women's limited estate. In common law it is called the marital property, which is not prevalent in Indian Christian. In Muslims it is just a property whether related to male or female both have equal right to appropriate it. In Hindu and Common law the consequences and rights attached to the property of male and female were not the same.

Succinctly, it is evident that whatever the reason may be, the inheritance rights of females are discriminatory in almost all system. The difference if any is only of the degree or form. Sometime these are justified in the name of religion and sometime to avoid social and economic problem as to restrain from the fragmentation or to escape the chaos in social order. Even the enacted laws also maintained difference or discrimination between male and female heirs. The customary law which are anti-women still allowed to prevail, which totally excluded the women from inheritance.

The comparative study has facilitated in understanding the real position of women, with regards to their succession rights and shares, in different legal system. Though the comparative process is adopted throughout the work, with critical analysis of different ideologies in theory and in practice, which helped in evaluating the status of women with regards to economic and social empowerment and the progress made in 20th century. It has also enabled us to see some principles which are recognized in one system but not in other as the doctrine of covertures is recognized in Hindu and Christian law but not in Muslim law. The change of the status of females from maidenhood to womanhood does not disturb her proprietary right in Islam. By the comparative chart, the real position of woman according to their status is visible even at a glance.

Courts are generally treated as a warning agency, maintainer of legal order and trustee of law. As per record in a federal democracy, the record of Indian Judiciary is also not free from lapses and blemishes. From a number of decisions the revolutionary and surprising attitudes of the court is quite clear. The courts took a liberal and favourable verdict towards the women in the matter of succession. Ambivalence is the most characteristic trait of court's approach to religious and secular laws. It is also stimulating to note that in some cases the judiciary has held that a woman may be a Karta of Hindu joint family. But it is pity to note that few courts still hesitate to go against the written text. Burgeoning case laws, illuminating many dark spots of existing laws have been taken into account and many burning problems have been highlighted by the courts. However one thing can be said with the air of certainty that the courts in India have played an important role in developing equality oriented jurisprudence, which is obvious by the foregoing discussion of the case laws. Inspite of it Muslim's females are not benefited.

More than anything else Muslim women's right is in jeopardy because of the attitudes and practices developed over the years through the customary based laws. Unfortunately the issue got involved in communal politics to such an extent that even public discourse on the subject is suspicious and inhibited. In such a context incremental reform, through judicial process though slow and uncertain, is still welcomed.

However, it is gratifying that the process towards the realization of an egalitarian pattern of man and woman relationship has begun. Hopes have been raised that there will be no discrimination in social, economic and political field in the foreseeable future. The new amendments of 2005 in the law of sucession are an encouraging step to equalize and emancipate the Hindu females. It is a glaring fact and hard truth that the Islamic law as practiced today has taken a course contrary to the letter and spirit of Shariah therefore causing hardship and miseries to the Muslim woman. The sooner it is set right the better will flow to the society. Now the ball is in the court of judiciary and executive to implement the provision of new Hindu

Succession (amendment) Act 2005 and Islamic law in its true spirit to make a gender-just society.

Suggestions

After discussing the available relevant materials on the subject, an earnest and modest attempt has been made to forward some suggestions though not exhaustive but may go a long way to ameliorate the cause of property rights of women.

- In a literary backward country like India, the people (particularly women) are not awarded about their rights and duties. So far as the property rights are concerned the women do even not know their right of inheritance, provided under the Hindu Succession Act, 1956. Moreover the drastic changes brought about by the amending Act of 2005, are not known to females. For this reason there is an immediate and urgent need to educate the woman about their new rights conferred by the above Act. It is hereby submitted that a special programme should, to spread legal awareness among the woman, be run by the state machinery. Various women's organizations, NGOs and law students should take initiative to educate the women particularly those belonging to weaker or submerged groups living in slums and villages. The general legal literacy is a need of time for the females of all communities.
- Some grass root steps should have to be taken to weed out the patriarchal biases. Participation of both men and women is equally important for the upliftment of woman. Today the need is to establish equilibrium between men and women, as regards to social, legal and traditional status in the existing society. It is a genetic reality that any attempt to assign women a low and artificial legal status wills not stand at the test of justice and fair play.
- The law does not exist in vacuum and mere promulgation of legislations cannot provide the proper solution of the social problem unless it is effectively enforced. It is, therefore, suggested that there should be a number of law enforcing agencies and family crisis wings within the

family welfare centers throughout the country. These institutions should be looked after either by the State Government or by the Central Government.

- The feminist movement could be more effective and result oriented if men also came forward and joined hands with them. To make the society a better place to live, the family problems should be solved within the four walls of home. For that there is a change in the attitudes of men towards the women at family, society, and state and at global level. It is very essential towards achieving the goal by changing the stereotype ideas of male domination. The need is to change the infrastructure of the society.
- The proceedings of the courts are required to be expedious and time bound as the best laws would be rendered meaningless, particularly to issues relating to women, by an ineffective justice delivery system. Sometimes the delay in-justice even frustrated the object of seeking of the justice.
- The legislative steps is recently taken are appreciated and welcomed by the females and the right thinking peoples of men folk. But in this regard the women should act sensibly to reach their goal of attaining equality without disturbing the family bond and harmony. The transition of powers should be smooth and without any heart burning.
- With all due respect to judiciary, it is submitted that our lawyers and judges are not very much conversant with the provisions of Islamic law. It is therefore suggested that the government should provide the statutory status to the Qazi Courts and empower them to handle minor cases of property disputes, succession and family strife's of the community etc. This will not only lessen the burden on courts but will also save the valuable time of the court and money of the litigants. These courts should not be considered as an attempt to create a parallel judicial system, but just an agency to help our already overburdened courts. Creation of such courts are not new

in this country, these courts are already working. In Madhya Pradesh, almost every district has a Qazi Court. Such courts are also working in many cities of Maharashtra. Darul Uloom and Nadwatul-Ulema are the glaring examples of the success of such courts.

- In cases of conflict between statutory law and personal law, reference should be made to a jury of experts in personal law as well as unbiased judges who would ensure speedy justice.
- There must be a comprehensive codification of the entire Islamic law it is inevitable. In this the representation of the Ulemas of all schools should be taken. By this way there would be a uniform law for all Muslims throughout the India. Any delay in its exercise will be detrimental for the cause of Muslim women in the country because the applicability is not uniform what is applied to the woman of Kerala, is not applied to the woman in Jammu and Kashmir.
- In case of agricultural land, the Uttar Pradesh Zamindari Abolition and Land Reform Act, 1950, has excluded all females except widow, from having any share in agricultural land. This is a blatant discrimination with the females. No empowerment of women could be possible unless they are made economically sound. Therefore in this era of women empowerment it is ripe time that a suitable amendment should be made in the land laws to entitle the females to have a share in agricultural land also. It should be noted that some States like Andhra Pradesh, Tamil Nadu and Kerala have already taken a positive steps in this direction. It is therefore suggested that certain amendments should be made in the Shariat Application Act, 1937 to extend its application to the agricultural land as in some States these have been taken relating to Hindu females.
- Even after the attaining of 58 years of independence certain anti-women customary laws still prevail in certain part of the Indian sub-continent as in Jammu and Kashmir, the customs like '*Khana-e-damadi*' or '*pisar-e-*

parvarda' etc. In this direction the Government must take some grass root steps to eradicate these customs and ensure the implementation of the pro-women Islamic law of inheritance for Muslims females.

- To avoid the fragmentation the provision may be attached that if the females want to sale the property or their share in the agricultural land the family members should be given preference to buy it, provided that they give the best price.
- The provisions of inheritance under different system of religions and statutory laws should be strictly enforced. In case of non-compliance of the decisions delivered by the court some sanctions must be provided in the law. In this patriarchal and male dominated society it is impossible for female to get justice without the provisions of sanctions/punishments particularly in the field of succession.
- There must be drastic changes in the infrastructure in all the three components of Government judiciary, executive and legislature. Females should be given lion's share in all the above mention organs of the Government. Hundred of Kiran Bedi, who knows the agony of women-hood, should be employed to treat the cases passionately.
- The provisions of Indian Succession Act, 1925 has done great injustice with the peoples of different religion specially within the field of inheritance, for instance, the parties who have contracted their marriage under the Special Marriage Act, 1954, will be subjected by the Indian Succession Act, 1925, in the matter of succession even if both the parties are of same religion and it will extent to their future generation also. But after the Hindu Succession Act, 1956, this provision is not applicable in case of Hindus where both the parties are of same religion. The Hindu Succession Act, 1956, will govern them. The above provision is highly discriminatory, it is, therefore, submitted that a uniform law applicable to all irrespective of their religion, should be enacted and applied.

- Discrimination against women is so pervasive that it sometimes surface on a bare perusal of the law, made by the legislature itself, as in the case of a Christian mother under the provision of section 42 of Indian Succession Act, 1925. So necessary amendment should be made in the above said Act enabling the Christian mother to inherit the property simultaneously with the father. It will be more appropriate and more humanitarian to entitle the parents to inherit the property even in the presence of lineal descendants, to save them from any social distress.

We can conclude the discussion with the words of K.T. Bhashayam Ayenger, "*We must give back their rights and privileges in law of which we have robbed them. The injustices perpetrated on them in the name of law, should be remedied and as we honoured them in life, so must we make equal them to us in law then the law shall be the real reflections of life.*" Desired result can be achieved only when men and women both join hand for the amelioration of economic independence of women. As the fight for gender equality is not a fight against men, it is a fight against traditions that have chained them, a fight against attitudes that are ingrained in the society, a fight against system and a fight against proverbial 'Lakshman Rekha.'

Nothing in the world is perfect and no word is the last word in any branch of knowledge least of all in the study and practice of law.

5

Judicial Responses

An Overview

"If the law be dishonestly administered the salt has lost its flavours... if the lamp of justice goes out in darkness, how great is its darkness,"[1] Lord Bryce.

Justice is supposed to be the key word for every country and for every government. In a democratic set up the importance of judiciary has been multiplied. In the words of Bryce *"there is no better test of excellence of a government than the efficiency of its judicial system."*[2]

Democratic governance over the centuries has emerged as the most successful political experiment in the history of human civilization. Democracy encompasses in its fold the dignified existence of all human beings advocating liberty, equality, and justice as pre-requisites to enable every human being to live and progress with self-respect and dignity. In its onward march democracy has attuned itself to the native realities and emerging situation in individual countries. India has attained freedom after centuries of foreign subjugation. It was a great challenge for independent India to evolve system of governance with diverse language, culture, religion and stages of development in consonance with tradition and values.

A strong independent judiciary, subscribing to the highest ethical values is the greatest strength of the democracy. It is needless to say that in a democracy covered by "the rule of law, judiciary is the sentinel on the qui-vive to protect the rights of the citizens and to hold the scales even between the citizens and the state".

India a sovereign socialist, secular and democratic Republic enumerated the powers and responsibilities of the organs of the state to be the facilitators of national weal. The spirit of the constitution clearly delineates harmonious relations among the various organs.

Judiciary, which is the interpreter of the Constitution and the custodian of the rights of the citizens, must be independent and impartial. Judiciary have the mandate only to interpret the laws not to lay down general norms of behaviour for the government and the people to be considered binding on all as the law of the land. The scope of judicial review, thus, is confined to seeing whether the impugned legislation falls with in the competence of the legislature or is consistent with the fundamental rights guaranteed by the constitution and its other mandatory provisions. Some issues on which differences have crapped up relate to the powers of courts to review the laws.

The debate on judicial activism has gained ground in recent years, eliciting both admiration and criticism from various quarters. There is difference of opinion among the critics, some critics have the views that in 'judicial activism' sometimes the judiciary is transgressing its prescribed jurisdiction and entering in the domain of the legislature and executive. Some others feel that if the other organs of the state are found to have fallen short in the discharge of their constitutional obligations, the judiciary is well within the rights to take the necessary corrective action. In this context, it is most important that every organs of the government have to look judiciously at different perceptions of specific issues and ensure that there is no injustice prevalent in the society.

Inspite of the plethora of progressive and protective legislations, we have failed to up lift the socio-economic and political status of woman and to place them at par with their male counterpart in different walks of life. In such a situation the role of judiciary in providing social justice to woman become decisive. The Indian judiciary has played a creative role in this regard.[3]

Judicial activism has introduced and elaborated the new ideas, notions and conceptions in the process of deciding the case at hand.[4] Because it is the duty of apex court to fashion itself as a forum of not only to deliver a justice and pay merely a lip service but it must become a forum of articulating, remolding and reinventing the mechanism and the rights to deliver justice to millions of starved and shackled women. For the maintenance of purity in administration of the justice, probity and rectitude of conduct of the judiciary should be laudable. "To keep the stream of justice clean and pure the peoples of higher echelons must be endowed with sterling character, integrity and upright behaviour, erosion there of would undermine the efficacy of the rule of law and the working of the constituting itself. These persons must not be mere men of clay with all the frailties and foibles, human failing and weak character that may be found in those in other walks of life. They should be person of fighting faith with tough fiber not susceptible to any pressure, economic, political or of any sort." Before passing through the role of judiciary in improving the socio-economic conditions and the property rights of women, it is necessary to have a glance over the historical background and a very short look over the development of the Indian legal and judicial system.

Historical Background

The roots of the law and legal system are deeply buried in the past. It is the fruit of the endeavours, experiences, thoughtful planning's and patient labour of a large number of people through generation. Law cannot be understood properly when divorced from the history and the spirit of the nation whose law it.

In India, with the beginning of the British period, our tradition of the hoary past perished away. Though the application of the personal laws in the matter of marriage, divorce, adoption, inheritance and succession were kept untouched. The Hindus and Muslims were governed by their own respective personal laws with the help of native officer. But with the passage of time the English judges felt that they must understand the real nature of the law. So many law books were translated into English in the guidance of the experts. The most famous work in the field of Hindu Law is *A Code of Gentoo Laws* published at London in, 1776. In the era of Muslim law, the Hedaya[5] is famous. With the passage of time the English Judges were able to understand the languages, habits and traditions of Indians and administered the laws, without the help of Maulvies and Pandits (the native law officers).

Development of the Indian Legal System

In the 17th century A.D., the Britishers brought their English Common Law and their own traditional system, into its administration. At first, the English judicial system was designed at the Presidency Towns and dealt with the Englishmen. But with the march of time the adjustment had been made to provide the justice to the Indians also. To begin with Madras, which was the first Presidency Town, it extended to the whole India, with the usurping political power in various parts of the country.[6] Under the plan of 1772, by superimposing English administration on the pre-established system of Qazis Courts, Warren Hastings set up, what the legal historian now call, the Adalat System.[7] The civil and criminal high courts set up, under the system, were called Sadar Diwani Adalat and Criminal Court. To function at the district level the Mufasil Diwani Nizamat Adalat was designated. In 1774, Calcutta, Bombay and Madras, each had a Supreme Court under the British Parliament's Regulation's Act of 1773. With their jurisdiction defined by relevant laws often overlapping and give rise to conflicts. These courts of higher jurisdiction Sadar Diwani Adalat, and Sadar Nizamat Adalat were separately set up, for the acquisitions of the British in North India.[8]

Role of Judiciary in Developing the Different Laws

Introducing social reforms, through law, is always problematic because of its acceptability and implementation. Reform law is always imposed law because they are the product of some elite whose value system and culture is different from the masses. These reform law is prevailed for centuries and hollowed by the religion, through its course of maturation, depicts the sentiments of millions and symbolizes as their cultural identity and their very life.

The impact of the changes can be perceived by the role of judiciary in interpreting and implementing the law. The best laws can be rendered meaningless by ineffective implementations by the justice delivery system. As law is always, in a general statement and there are so many cases which cannot be covered within the general terms. At this time the role of judiciary is, to keep its eyes on the whole system and scenario as well as on the particular case. If the court focuses only on the particular people before it, it may do justice in that particular case and yet make, very poor general policy.

So it is often said that hard cases make bad law. Sometimes the judiciary is confronted with very peculiar situation, where it has to correct the Parliament's technical error. It has to give effect to the intention of Parliament. The public expects that the text of a statute be construed literally, but some time the judiciary has to interpret it liberally in the wider interest of public as in *Monika Gounder* v *Arunachala*[9] where it was decided by the full bench of Madras High Court. On the death of sole surviving coparcener, the widow of a predeceased coparcener did not take from him, by survivorship. The result was that she could never have more than half the estate. This decision was given after a long time of the Act of 1937.[10]

Many cases are perfectly and correctly decided on a technical basis but are wrong in principle. A case, which is certainly bad law, when looked as a piece of judicial therapy for an unhealthy society, on the other hand when viewed through telescope of stare-decisis, it may be very sound. The two distinct criteria the technical and social sometimes meet happily and the decision, passes both the test.

After the above discussion, it is evident that how important role, the judiciary or judicial method of any legal system; play in developing and moulding any particular law or legal institution. Now we will see how judiciary has affected the Indian legal system of Hindus, Muslims, Christians, and Parsis since British period till now.

Islamic Law

"O ye who believe, be maintainer of justice, bearer of witnesses for Allah's (SWT) sake though it may be against your ownselves or your parents or near relations, be he rich or poor. Allah (SWT) is most competent to deal with them both, therefore do not follow

your low desires, lest you deviate and if you serve or turn aside then surely Allah is aware of what to do." [11]

"*Be just that is next of piety and fear God, For God is well acquainted with all that ye do.*"[12]

Under Islam the concept of justice is equality. There should be no discrimination and impartiality between the high and low, prince and peasant, white and black, Muslims and non-Muslims, male and female. In equal situation equals should be treated equally.

In Islamic terminology the function of the administration of justice is called '*qada*'. According to Muslim jurist the judicial work is a part of great responsibility, entrusted by Allah (SWT) to human beings. It is one of the foremost duties after the belief in Allah (SWT) and one of the highest forms of worship.[13]

According to Ibn Farhun[14] "*The Qada is to act as an intermediary between the creator and the creature in order to perform and execute among them the orders and commandments of the creator through the Divine Book and the Sunnah.*"

About the importance of the administration of justice, Mohammad Shahir Arsalan reported,[15] "*a complaint of mal-administration and disruption in politics was once made to Sir W. Churchill. He replied that if there was no disruption in the administration of justice there would be no fear upon Britain.*"

The knowledge of the law, for the proper administration, is necessary. In support of it, two cases of Islamic law held in the period of Hazrat Ali, can be cited.

A woman came to Hazrat Ali at the time when he is about to ride his horse. She said, "*Commander of faithful, my brother has died leaving behind him two daughters, mother, wife, twelve brothers and myself and six hundred dinars but my brothers have given me only one.*" Hazrat Ali replied, "*They gave you justly*" and drove his horse away.[16] This landmark judgement shows, the command of Hazrat Ali over the law of inheritance, because it involved an intricate question of law.

The other case is, that two friends sat to have a lunch, one had fives loaves, the other three. On their invitation, a stranger ate with them. He gave eight *dirhams* to them, who have five loaves took five *dirhams* and three *dirhams* gave to other. But the later one demanded half. Hazrat Ali solved the dispute. He said, that according to justice the later one is entitled only one *dirham.*[17]

To understand, the real spirit of Islamic law this brief discussion was necessary. The law and justice cannot be maintained without being fully, conversant of the law. How the Islamic law is administered today and what justification is done with the law, is a question of great importance. Keeping this background in mind, we will see the contribution of Indian judiciary, in the field of the woman's property right in Islamic perspective.

In Pre-Independence Period

The pre-independence period was the period of British rulers in India. Here I will not go in the history of Mughal period or before that. I have to cover from the British period because there is a pragmatic reason to confine, the study to the British period only. As the present judicial system is, what the Britishers had created. It is also necessary to see, whether it has any co-relation, continuity or integral relationship, with the pre-British institutions.

The personal enactment, which the British Indian legislators gave to this country, were legislated by them wholly in English, in letter and spirit, in form and substance, in style and format. They were interpreted by British Indian courts exclusively in accordance with English judicial precedents, and English principle of interpretation of statutes.[18]

Though, the policy of Britishers was, that the Muslims and Hindus would be governed by their own personal laws. The Privy Council, itself warned the courts that they are not free to deduce any rule of law, based on the Quranic text and reported Hadith. In *Abdul Fata Mahammad Ishak* v *Russomoy Dhar Chowdry*[19] and *Baker Ali Khan* v *Anjuman Ara Begum,*[20] the court cautioned, that fundamental principles of Islam and the religion are so intermingled, that it would be extremely dangerous to draw a fresh logical inference from old and undisputed texts. But this role of Privy Council hindered the development of Muslim law. The eminent jurists also criticized the role of judiciary. Fyzee states.[21]

"This attitude, natural enough in India where the majority of Muslims, being orthodox were averse to any change in the 'Holy Quran' Shariat is the result of the combined effects of the doctrine of 'taqlid', as understood by the later jurists and the common law doctrine of precedent, which tells the judge to interpret and followed, rather than create and expand the law. It has had during the two centuries of British rule, the effect of keeping the law stationary and static except for two broadening influences legislation and the healthy introduction of principles of English equity."

In this way, the well-recognized principle of Ijtihad was not prevalent in the British period. Thus, Muslim jurists were denied the right of independent inquiry and were bound by the doctrine of taqlid, which stopped the growth of law. But it does not mean by the above discussion, that there was no application of equity, justice and good conscience, in the case of a Muslim. Actually there was not much distortion of Muslim law in British period. To know, what is the contribution of Britisher to Muslim law, the case study is necessary.

The most important and famous case in the field of Muslim law of inheritance was, the *Patna case,*[22] which tells the misadministration of British judicial system. This case was bitterly criticized and created terror in the heart of the people. Even Warren Hastings commented adversely on the way, the Patna Council had acted. He wrote to the Council, *"I can not but take notice of the great irregularities, in the proceedings of the law officers, whose business was solely to have declared the laws. The Diwani Court was, to be judge of the facts, their takings on themselves to examine witnesses was entirely foreign to their duty. They should have been examined before the adalat."*

Though, the Patna case was decided according to the Muslim law of Inheritance but the afterwards proceedings of the implementation of the decision, was wrong, harsh and out of the jurisdiction of the court. The facts of the case were – Shahbaz Khan had no issue so he expressed his desire to adopt his nephew Bahadur Beg and hand over his property but before it was done, he died. Then, the dispute arose between the widow and the nephew. The widow claimed the whole property, on the basis of a gift and nephew on the basis of adopted son. The proceedings were wholly entrusted to the native law officers. There were many irregularities during the proceedings of the case, as no witness was examined on oath and Begum's claim was rejected. As there is no adoption in Islamic law, the claim of Bahadur Beg was also rejected and according to the law of inheritance of Muslims, the shares were allotted to them $^1/_4$ to the widow and 3/4 to the Shahbaz brother (the father of Bahadur Beg).

The whole proceedings were exparte, without any notice being given to the Begum. The Begum was not satisfied with the decision and approached, to the Supreme Court. By this way the case became more critical.

The action was taken against Bahadur Beg and the law officers, on the basis of the proceedings, which were illegal and unwarrantable. Therefore, the Begum was held, entitled to the whole property on the basis of gift deed. In this case, the Supreme Court had also been criticized, for taking cognizance of the acts done by the law officers, in the discharge of their judicial functions.[23] This case was decided in 1777, 1778 and 1779.

Another important case of law of inheritance was *Rajah Deedar Hussain* v *Ranee Zahurunnisan*[24] In this case the Shia sects of Muslims were, first time made entitled to govern the succession by their own law of inheritance, till then, they were the subject of Sunni law of inheritance. There are outstanding differences in the scheme of inheritance under these two sects of Islamic law. Arnold J lucidly describes the historical origin of these two sects.[25]

The justice, equity and good conscience was applied in the case of *Munshee Buzloor Rahim* v *Shamsunnissan.*[26] By this case the controversy arose whether the Muslim law be overridden by the rule of justice, equity and good conscience and that conflict was resolved by the court in the case of *Mohd Kaden* v *Ludden*[27] that the personal law could not be overridden.

Another controversy, about the adoption of the old and new juristic interpretation of the Holy Quran, arose in the case of *Mohd Jaffer Bindaneem* v *Kulsoom Bi Bi*.[28] The dispute, in this case, was related to the maintenance of widow, in addition of her share in inheritance. The Privy Council has adopted the juristic opinion of Hedaya and Imamia, which condemned any such right of widow and rejected the re-interpretation of Ameer Ali J, which was in support of this widow. This judgement was bitterly criticized by the legal luminaries and jurists of that time and later on. I also agree with the view of Daniel Latiffi[29] that the Quranic verses be interpreted in "*a Wealthy and humane principles for the protection of widows.*"

The views, of Sir Sulaiman J, in this connection are excellent. He opined that, it is the duty of courts in case of divergent opinion, when it seems impossible to ascertain the comparative, merits of the authorities, the view which is more in accordance with equity, justice and good conscience,[30] should be adopted.

In *Mirza Hashim Mishkee* v *Agha Hussain,* the views, on the spirit of Islam, given by Chari J was strongly criticized by Tayyabji and other legal cleric and *fuqahas,* while speaking about the spirit of Islamic law, he had over looked the important consideration, when he put forward the position of Hanafi law in relation to female share. It is one of the fundamental principles that males take twice as much as females. If such was the principle no explanation forthcoming why cognate like uterine brother and uterine sister, grand parents (in circumstances in which the Holy Quran makes them sharers), take equal shares. The real principle, as explained above, is that newly entitled heirs (other things being equal) take half as much as old established heir whether male or female. It is accidental, that all female heirs are newly introduced heirs because before Islam, there was no concept of woman's property right at any place of the world, except in Hindu law where Stridhana prevailed. That is why, it is considered that it is the rule of Islamic law that male take twice of female but where both male and female were newly introduced, there is no such distinction between their share.[31] He further says, that all the newly introduced heirs by Holy Quran encroached the right of male agnates. The spirit of the innovation may be expressed in the formula:

> *"Unto her, that hath not and unto the relations of, shall be given: and from him that hath shall be taken a little (or may be the whole) of what he seemth to retain."*[32]

The distortion of Islamic law was not done consciously or deliberately by Britishers but the fact is that they were ignorant and not conversant of Arabic and Persian. So they have to rely on the translated work of Hedaya or Fatwa-e-Alamgiri. About Hamiltons Hedaya, Maulvi Mohammad Rashid of Burdwan pointed out, some mistakes and notified its to the then, Chief Justice T.H. Harrington, who however chose to keep mum.[33] These distorted principles of Muslim law were gradually compiled in books like W.H. Mc. Naugthan's *Principles and Precedents of Mohammaden Law*, N.E. Baillie's two volume's of *Digest of Islamic law*, Fitzgerald's *Mohammadan law*. An Abridgement and R.K. Wilson's *Anglo-Mohammad law* etc.[34] about the distortion of Islamic law and Hindu law Justice V.R. Krishana Iyer himself admitted, in the case of *Yousuf* v *Sowramma*.[35]

"Marginal distortions are *inevitable when the Judicial Committee in the Downing Street has to interpret Manu and Mohammadan law of India and Arabia,"*

But the contribution of the British judicial system is also adorable. In *Durga Das* v *Mohd Ali*[36] and *Ali Zamin* v *Akbar Ali*[37] a childless widow was held entitled to a share in movable property and in case no other heir to return also in immovable property.[38] In *Gulbaro* v *Akbar Khalid*[39] a lady was authorized to a decree for possession.

In *Hasina Bibi* v *Zubaida Bibi*[40] the reason was given to the rule of reducing share of widow from 1/4 to 1/8 that it was done for the benefit of sons and daughters but where there is only a daughter whose share is also prescribed the court held that no reason to reduce the widows share. At this time we took the spirit of the law rather than the letter of it. The case should be decided on the equity, justice and good conscience. The Privy Council applied—

"The rules of equity and equitable considerations commonly recognized in the court of Chancery in England are not foreign to the Mussalaman system, but are in fact often referred to and invoked in adjudication of cases." By the above discussion it can be deduced that the judiciary have the mixed role in relation to women's property right, some time it held the case, taking the literal meaning of the law of inheritance. But some time it go beyond the limits and not hesitate to bestow the mother's full share instead of the presence of daughter. Actually what distortion of Islamic law was done in the period of Britishers that was not intentional? Instead the steps taken by the judiciary or British rulers were precautionary not to disturb the established law. As there was a system in Common Law, that the courts were bound to follow the precedent established by the superior courts. Though by this step the development of Islamic Law was much affected and some bad precedent, which were established, be continued till now.

In Post Independence Period

After the independence, the law relating to women's property right has passed through different channel of judicial process. Generally, the judiciary, in independent India, has adopted and based its decision upon, what the British judges said and decided in their period. The judiciary hesitated to put its own construction and deduced analogical reasoning from the original sources. There are very few judges, who bother for the real justice and deviate, from the old established authorities. The reason, behind it, is that the personal law is so sacrosanct, that no interference with in be permitted. But it is the matter of regret that the anti-women's customs allowed to prevail, inspite of the pro-women provisions of Islamic law. For example, the custom of excluding the females from inheritance is still prevailing in many parts of India even after the many decades of Independence.

The anti-women customary laws, which disentitle the females from inheritance makes the judiciary confused. Some cases have been decided in favour of females and customary law was not allowed to prevail. But in so many cases the judiciary favours these customary laws. So to understand, why customary laws are so much favoured in independent India we will go little back and begin it with the British period again.

In *Hira Bai v Sonalee*[41] the question before the Privy Council was, whether Khojas, Cutichs, Memons and Bohras who are converted Muslims and still follow their Hindu customs, specially in matter of inheritance, which exclude females from inheritance, be governed by Islamic law or customary law? In this instant case a Khoja girl claimed her share in her father's property under the provision of Islamic law. But her claim was not accepted and the custom got preference over the Islamic law. Commenting on this decision Rankin J, observed.[42]

"This is a very important decision so far as it removed all danger that the law of India should attempt to enforce any standard of Islamic Orthodoxy it must command approval."

In the above-mentioned case Privy Council has given many arguments in support of customary law. This decision was affirmed in the case of *Khatu Bai v Mohd Ataji Abu,*[43] who were the Halai Memons of Porbandar.

Later on the Privy Council itself in Jwala *Buksh* v *Dharma Singh,*[44] was doubtful to admit the custom against Islamic law and in *Jammya v Diwan*,[45] the custom, excluding daughter from inheritance, was not allowed against the women's right of inheritance. But in *Md. Ibrahim* v *Shaik lbrahim,*[46] the position was again reversed and Privy Council clearly stated – that custom would get precedence over the Islamic law, governing the succession in a particular community of Mohammadan as Mappilla community.[47]

In the case of Punjab, Kumaon Hill and Oudh,[48] the custom got preference and the females were allowed to be excluded from inheritance by the Privy Council. Though in *Abdul Hussain* v *Sona Dero*,[49] in absence of a clear proof of a custom the females were allowed to inherit.

Upon this anti-woman attitude of Privy Council, there was chaos and distress amongst Muslim females and the right thinking Muslim males also. Muslim Women Organizations and Jamait-ul-Ulma-e-Hind made much hue and cry. The result of that is, the Act of 1937.[50] It was presumed that all controversies would come to an end. As according to the provision of section 2 of the Act of 1937, Islamic law of inheritance would be compulsorily applicable to all Muslims but the provision of Section 3 of the Act of 1937, allowed the customarily laws application in case, of will if one had not choose for the application of Islamic law. This created confusion and set at naught the general provision of the Shariat Act relating to compulsory application of Islamic law in respect of inheritance.[51]

During First Decade of Independence

With this background we will proceed with the decision of Post Independent judiciary, which also have a mixed reaction. In some cases, the anti-customary laws were allowed to prevail on the other hand in some cases they were not allowed. The same position of British period exists till now after 62 years of independence.

In the case of *Sahul Hamid* v *Sultan,*[52] the question before the court was about the concept of joint family, (in which the coparcenary exists) whether exists in Muslim law or not? The court held, that Muslim law does not recognize the joint family of Hindu Jurisprudence. As a coparcener the Hindu females are not allowed to inherit, but now by the amendment Act of 2005 the daughter is also be a coparcener and allowed to inherit the ancestral property along with the son.

In *Allayar* v *Rambhau*[53] the question, about custom of coparcenary property (in which woman can have no share) was disallowed, which prevail among some Khojas Ismailies from the time immemorial.

Under the provision of Section 43 of Indian Succession Act, 1925 the mother of the deceased is wholly excluded by the lineal descendants of any degree and in their absence by the father. In *Shaik Mehboob Alam* v *Razia Begum,*[54] the court held that Indian Succession Act, 1925, has superseded the Islamic law and accordingly the provisions of the Act would prevail, where they come in conflict with Islamic law.

In *Rahmatullah v Maqsood Ahmed,*[55] an illegitimate child was held not to inherit with legitimate child as, uterine brother. In *Imam* v *Amir,*[56] the Madras High Court rejected the settlement deed of the successive life estate in favour of male descendants, which exclusively excludes the rights of females.

In *Hooriya v Munna,*[57] no custom, to exclude females from inheritance, is allowed, to prevail. On the other hand, in *Bai Asha* v *Biban,*[58] the custom was allowed to prevail. In *Abdul Jabbar* v *Chairman District Council Kucheryl,*[59] because of the absence of clear proof of custom, the anti-woman custom was not allowed to govern the law of inheritance.

In *Mubarak Begum v Sushil Kumar,*[60] it was held that under Islamic law, a sister can inherit in both the capacity, as a sharer and as residuary, along with the widow of the deceased. In *Abdul Kafoor v Abdul Razak,*[61] the court has favoured the female, and held, if the daughter has agreed to leave her share before the succession open, it cannot be called a family arrangement and it would make no effect upon her right to inherit. In *Mohd Sandhukan v Ratnam*[62] the Madras High Court has held that a custom, which excludes only females from inheritance, could not be allowed.

During Second Decade of Independence

The attitude of the judiciary towards females was not at much variance, in this decade also. Like the pre-independence and the first ten years, this second decade also has mixed reaction and in many cases anti-customary laws were got preference over Islamic laws, which are pro-woman. In *Saira Bai v S.S. Joshi,*[63] the grand daughters were held entitled, to inherit as sharer with the widow of the deceased. This judgement is really appreciable. In *Khazir v Ahmad,*[64] the court has rejected to apply the rule of survivorship to the property of Muslim deceased. In *Aziz Dar* v *Mst. Fazil,*[65] the customary law of Kashmir, which excludes the daughter from inheritance, was allowed. In *Noor Bano* v *Deputy Cust. General, E.P.,*[66] the question, once again, came before the court for consideration, about the customary law of Khojas governing succession and this ruling of Supreme Court is really significant. The Supreme Court relied on Mulla's text that :

> *"Effect of the Shariat Act is to abolish, (except as to agricultural land and other matters to which the Act does not apply) the customary law of succession of Khojas."*[67]

Ali Saheb v *Hajra Begum*,[68] in this case the question before the Mysore Court, was about the doctrine of 'Return' according to Islamic law neither wife nor husband, is entitled to return when there are distant kindred and if there is no distant kindred, then the property will go to government, to avoid the government Escheat, the property could be reverted to the husband and wife only, if there is no distant kindred. In this instant case, one Ali Saheb died, leaving behind the widow and two daughters of his predeceased daughter. The widow gives the whole property to her nephew. The grand daughters claimed as distant kindred. The court held, that the wife is only entitled to her share and remainder be divided among distant kindred.

During the Third decade of Independence

Not much improvement can be found in the attitude of judiciary during the third decade of the independence and mixed reaction is evident and no concrete efforts were made by the judiciary to overcome the grievance of Muslim females. On the other hand because of the passing of the Hindu Succession Act, 1956, the Hindu females were in better position than earlier. The judiciary is also inclined towards the improvement of their conditions.

In another case,[69] an interesting question before the court was whether the husband or wife are entitled to inherit each other in dual capacity? It means as a husband or wife and as a distant kindred. This case was wrongly decided by the divisional bench and corrected by the High Court. It was held that they could inherit each other in dual capacity, as sharer and as a distant kindred. As a husband he is sharer and as distant kindred he is entitle as residuary.

In *Mumtaz Begum v S. Amanatullah Khan*[70] the question again related with the exclusion of the Kashmiri girls from inheritance though the case was decided in favour of daughter because of non-proving of the establishment of custom and not because of the contrary, to the text of Holy Quran. It means if it was proved that this custom exist from the time immemorial, it will make no effect that the particular custom is unconstitutional and un-Islamic and hammered upon the genuine rights of females relating to property.

In *Bai Khatija v Kaimbhai,*[71] again the conflict of custom and Islamic law relating to the succession of Sunni Bohra arose. In this case steps taken by Gujarat High Court, are appreciable. It says, that in order to secure "uniformity" which, the Bombay High Court, was so concerned with the Shariat Act should be extended to the whole of India.

During the Fourth Decade of Independence

In this decade the judiciary leaned in the favour of Muslim females and some cases were decided according to Islamic Law which is pro-women in opposition of the customary law which still prevail in India and which totally excluded the females from inheritance.

In the case of *Ghulam Hasan v Mst. Saja*[72] Jammu and Kashmir High Court has admitted the Islamic Law and awarded 1/3 share to daughter in opposition of customary law of inheritance. Jammu and Kashmir High Court has admitted the Islamic law and awarded 1/3 share to daughter.

In *Narunnisa v Shaikh Abdul* Hamid,[73] one, Abdul Ghani died leaving behind five sons and two daughters. One of his son S.K. Abbas claimed his share 2/12 according to the rules of Islamic Law. The defendant contended his share, on the basis of a will, in which Abdul Ghani has bequeathed his whole immovable property to him. The question, before the court, was whether the will is valid which is made without the consent of other heirs and what will be its effect if not valid ?

The court held, that it is an established law, that a bequest to an heir, either in whole or in part is invalid unless consented by the other heirs and if any one is consented, the bequest is valid to that extent only.[74] It means to the share of that particular heir. In this instant case, one sister has given her consent but the other kept mum. Though she has the knowledge of the executing of the will. But it was held; that her silence is not an implied consent, cited Mulla – where a will contained a bequest excluding the females could not be considered. Mere silence cannot be considered as an implied consent, so she is entitled to her share.[75]

In *S.A. Halima Bivi v S.A. Fatima Bivi,*[76] one Abdul Qadir and his wife Zuleka Bibi had executed a settlement deed, in favour of his two daughters, S.A. Fatima Bibi and Halima Bibi. The son of Halima Bibi on behalf of her mother and aunt enjoyed the whole property. The income of the said property was being divided between them. The dispute arises between them when the delivering of the income was stoped. S.A. Fatima Bibi filed the suit for division of property. The court considered so many issues and also various aspects of Islamic law relating to the right of property were discussed. Throwing light over the concept of the property, the court said, *"in Mohammadan family there is a presumption that the cash and household furniture belongs to the husband."* This decision is contrary to letters and spirit of Islam, since Muslim law does not make any distinction between movable or immovable property so far as the question of inheritance is concerned.[77] Though the case was decided in favour of sister.

In the case of *Zulekha Bibi* v *Mst. Sabna Bibi,*[78] it was held that in the absence of son, the daughter is entitled to share the property to the extent of half. This decision was held perfectly applying the Islamic law of inheritance.

In *Abdul Matin* v *Abdul Aziz,*[79] one intestate Muslim Abdul Ghafur died leaving behind only two daughters who took the property in equal share. After some time one sister has sold her share to the other sister who became the absolute owner. Halima died in 1957, leaving behind her son, Abdul Matin, a sole heir. In 1953, Salima also died leaving behind no heir except husband, Kitab Ali and Abdul Matin her nephew. Kitab Ali sold all the property of Salima, which was challenged by Abdul Matin, being the distant kindred. Gauhati High Court held that according to Islamic law, if the heir is husband or wife only, the residue will not revert to them but will go to the distant kindred.

It makes no difference that her mother herself has sold the property to him.

A very peculiar case of eunuch was decided in 1990.[80] There is a custom in the community of eunuch that the heir of eunuch is another eunuch. They follow the system of Guru and Chela and there was a custom that the property of the Guru be inherited by the Chela, if eunuch. In this instant case the will executed by Munnilal (a Muslim) in favour of Abdul Ghafoor (not an eunuch), was challenged by the chela Badshah alias Kamlajan, in whose favour Munnilal previously executed the will but subsequently, he changed his will. As Munnilal was suffering from cancer and in that hot days no service or help was rendered by Badshah, instead Abdul Ghafoor took care of him and also spent money on his treatment. In these circumstances Munnilal revoked the first will. The question before the court was that under Muslim law one cannot bequeath the property more than one third without the consent of his heir. The disputed property was inherited by Munnilal on the basis of above custom from his Guru Nasiban, another eunuch. The case was decided in favour of Badshah. It is submitted that the decision is doubtful as the case must have been decided according to Islamic law and in it there is no provision of Guru and Chela. As in Islamic law there are elaborate provisions about the succession of eunuchs.[81]

During the fifth decade of Independence

Syed Fatehyab Ali Mirza v *Union of India*[82] two important questions were involved in this case, (i) whether the marriage with a Jewish lady be considered as an apostasy? (ii) Whether the spouses of Muta marriage were entitled to inherit each other? On first question the court held that Islamic law permits to marry with a Kitabiyah so it would not amount as an apostasy. This decision is appreciated by Tahir Mehmood.[83] On the second question the court held that generally Muta marriage creates no right of inheritance but if there is a clear stipulation of such type then there is no bar.

In *Mohan Lal* v *Commissioner of Income Tax Bombay,*[84] it was held by the Supreme Court, that in partnership between father and son, after the death of father both widow and son are entitled to equal share. It is very difficult to say that on what bais the widow was held entitle to the equal share with her son. As it is neither an Islamic law nor customary law. It seems that in favouring the females the court has gone a step further.

In *Maqsooda Begum* v *Shanawaz Khan,*[85] two questions were raised before the court.

(i) Whether the full sister has any interest in the deceased property, in the presence of widow and two daughters?

(ii) Whether in the presence of widow and daughters, the sister can be the legal representative of the estate of the deceased brother ?

Answering the first question the court held, that though, the sister is not a sharer but she is entitle to inherit the property as a residuary and after the allotment of the shares of the sharers, the widow and two daughters, the residue would go to the residuary, the sister.

About the second question, the court held, that there is no bar on sister to be a legal representative. In this case the Islamic law of inheritance is discussed in detail. It is very hard to say that in the presence of children and widow the sister may be a representative. Though the court had not any objection to it.

In *Rukmani Bai* v *Bismillah Bai*[86] the deceased Babu, a converted Muslim, had only one daughter as heir. The claim was made by the niece of Babu. Rukmani Bai that she should be considered as heir of Babu, as Babu was a bachelor and never married with the mother of Bismillah Bai. But it was proved that Babu had married with the mother of Bismillah and had two children with this union. The son predeceased him and only daughter survived, so she would be the sole heir of Babu and therefore would inherit the whole property, as there is no distant kindered. The property will revert to the daughter applying the doctrine of Return. There is a rule that a non-Muslim cannot be the heir of a Muslim in Islamic law of inheritance. The Hindu niece of Babu is not entitled.

In *Newanness v Sheikh Mohammad*[87] one Haji Ihsan died leaving behind his widow, two daughters, two sons and the children of predeceased son. The property, in question, was inherited by Haji Ihsan from his predeceased son. In this case the Islamic Law of inheritance was discussed at length. After sometime the widow, the two surviving sons and one of the surviving daughter and one of the children of a predeceased son also died. Now the inheritance had to be divided between the daughter of Haji Ihsan and the children of his predeceased son. This was an appeal case. The Supreme Court's judgement of this case (as reported in AIR) is very confusing as rightly commented by Tahir Mahmood. The court, relying on the authority of Mulla, determined the sharer.[88] Trial court has ascertained the shares, that out of 1/6th share, the widow and two daughters would get equal respective shares under law, 1/3rd remained as residue. According to Mulla where descendant like son, son's son and ascendants like father and grandfather are not present then the descendants of father will take, as firstly full brother then sister, in default a daughter or son's daughter or daughter's son. In this instant case since only two daughters were survived among the five daughters left behind, the full sister takes the entire residue, which is 1/3rd share.[89]

In 1999 the Gujrat High Court also decided the case of a gift deed in favour of the female.[90]

The Current Position

In *Jamil Ahmad* v *Vlth ADJ Moradabad,*[91] the court held, that the provisions of the U.P. Zamindari Abolition and Land Reform Act, 1950, override the rules of the succession of Muslim law. Section 171 of U.P.Z.A. and L.R. Act of, 1950 is quite discriminatory which gives strong preference for male agnates and always got judicial support.

In a very latest case of 2004 Aysha Bibi v Faiza Bibi,[92] the question before the court was whether the widow of predeceased son entitled to inherit her mother-in-law?

The facts of the case were that one, Muslim lady Chotima died in, 1986 and her son, Abdul Samad predeceased her in, 1985, leaving behind two widows and their children. The widows claimed, their share in the property of Chotima, on the basis of a will, which was made by the Chotima in favour of her predeceased son and secondly on the basis of that, the property in question was purchased with the financial help of the predeceased son.

In consideration of will, the court found no evidence but there were suspicious circumstances, so it was not considered as a valid will. On consideration of second question, whether, she is entitled to inherit or not? It is a well-settled rule of Islamic law of inheritance that the right to inherit arises at the death of ancestor,[93] no birthright is recognized[94] and also no theory of representation.[95] It is the clear rule of Islamic law that if any child dies before the opening of the succession his or her heir cannot claim his or her share.[96] On the basis of these judicial decisions and on the authorities of the text of Islamic law, the court held that the widows are not entitled to share any property in this instant case.[97] This decision was very harsh towards females.

HINDU LAW

In Pre Independence Period

The courts rendered a yeoman service to the cause of personal laws especially, relating to the women's right of property. In the period of Britishers, the Hindu law underwent transformation at the hands of British courts. Mr. Derrett a great critic of Hindu Law, has glorified his countrymen for presenting the English ruler in India as 'Patrons of Shastras'. He has given in one of his book a long list of, about fifty Sanskrit legal treaties which he claims, are attributable to British influence or patronage or possibly written in response to British request or encouragement[98] William Jones judge of Supreme Court of Fort Willaim at Calcutta, himself admitted: "*pandits deal out Hindu law as they please and make it at reasonable rates when they can not find it ready made.*[99]

In 1828 Governor Eliphinstones had remarked, "*the Dharmashastras, as it is understood, is a collection of ancient treaties neither clear nor consistent in themselves and now buried under a heap of more modern commentaries, the whole beyond the knowledge of perhaps the most learned Pandits and every part wholly unknown to the people who live under it.*"[100]

The British judges used to consult the Pandits, attached to the courts. In the case of difference of opinion, on the point of law, the courts consulted the other Pandits. Sir Francis Mcnaugthen consulted 51 Pandits on a question of inheritance, in the case of *Gurubullub* v *Person* in 1834. Hindu law came to be administered by the courts, in British India, they have faced with a number of problems, and some cases took very long time to dispose of.[101]

A judge, in order to be able to discharge his duties properly and effectively, has to understand the psychology, the sociology and the climate of the state in which he functions. Administering Hindu Law in India the problem with the Britishers was that they were totally unaware of the surroundings and sociology of the Indian society. There are many sub-schools, by which the Hindus were governed, and they were quite different with each other.

In British period, though the Supreme Court leaned, towards the application of the laws of the particular school, to which the parties belonged. In *Bai Kesarbai* v *Hansraj Morarji*,[102] the question was, whether a co-widow could succeed the property of a widow dying issueless, in preference to her husband's brother and brother's son. The case was decided, according to the harmonious construction between the Mitakshara and Mayukha School.

The earliest, reported case of Dayabhaga, was D.D.R. Dassi.[103] In that case the widow succeeded to the exclusion of mother (father's widow). The conflict was between the father's widow and the widow of the deceased.

In *Perammal* v *Venkatammal*,[104] the court held that the mother stands, next in order of succession on failure of other heirs and can succeed only in the absence of a widow. Once again the judiciary favoured the widow instead of father's widow. In *Huroosundry* v *Rajeshsurrie*,[105] and *Ballamma v Puttaya*,[106] the widow was held, not entitled to inherit that property which was not vested and possessed by the deceased husband at his death. In *Sondaninoy Dassee v T. Chandra*,[107] the restrictions on the right, to partition on issueless widow, was released by the court. In *Suraneni v Suraneni,* the question before the court, was whether according to Mitakshara School, if the agreement of partition has taken place, but actual separation is not carried out, the widow could succeed the husband property in preference to other surviving co-sharer? The court held that the widow was entitled. Though it seems that the Privy Council had perpetuated the traditional system but somewhat soften its rigours.

One of the most serious deviations of the Privy Council from, the Mitakshara view was regarding the status of Hindu women.

The Privy Council took, a much more rigid and narrow view of the women's position, based on the old texts of Manu, Katyayana and Yajnavalkya ignoring the interpretation like Vijnaneswara. By this way the judiciary has narrowed down the concept of Stridhana, the absolute property of the women.[108] Yajnavalkaye had defined, Stridhana restrictively but Vijnaneswara gave it expansive meaning and include in it, every kind of property acquired by a woman from any source which was judicially recognized in India by several courts.[109] On the other hand the Privy Council in a series of pronouncement,[110] refused to accept Vijnaneswara's view of Stridhana. Perhaps the Apex Court found, Vijneshwara's view too radical because, in England, until 1882, the position of married women, in the matter of their rights to property, was very unsatisfactory and the Married Women's Right to Property Act, 1882, alleviated their position.[111]

In the British period though the Hindu Law was much distorted but in respect of widows property right, it always have a soft corner. The problem to administer the Hindu law was that, at the time there was no uniformity among Hindu laws of succession because of many schools and sub-schools which have their own rules relating to succession. In Hindu law very few females are entitle to hold and inherit the property. The rights given by Hindu law to the females were also not absolute and so many impediments were imposed on them. As the policy of Britishers was non-interference in the matter of personal laws, the judiciary found it's difficult to apply justice, equity and good conscience.

In Post Independence Period

After independence the Supreme Court has adopted a liberal attitude towards the women's right to property in comparison of the Privy Council. In independent India much emphasis was given on gender justice and equality. Many legislative steps had also been taken to modernize, unify, democratize and secularize the Hindu family laws and especially to emancipate the Hindu female.[112] Judiciary was also inclined towards the empowerment of women particularly in the sphere of economic era. Several provisions of these reformatory legislations have been challenged but upheld by the courts from time to time.[113]

During the First Decade of Independence

The Judiciary had played a very creative role because the Hindu Succession Act, 1956 which is considered a piecemeal in the field of women's property right, was not passed and female's had very limited property right, but whenever the matter came before the court, it did not hesitate to favour the females. Even in 1951 the Supreme Court held that the female could be a shebait.

On an issue whether the property includes the right of succession to shebaitship or not? In *Angurbala Mullick v Debarata Mullick,*[114] the Apex Court gives its favour to the female. The court said that there is nothing in the Act,[115] under Sec. 3(1) by which an inference can be drawn that a right of succession to shebaitship does not fall with in the definition of property. If there is no legal objection to a woman being a shebait, why she should be excluded from succeeding to the same.

In 1953 on the issue of the inheritance by prostitute, the court held,[116] that though under Hindu law a maiden was a preferential heir to her married sister. But this rule did not apply to a daughter who was admittedly married to an idol and who lead a life of a prostitute.

In 1955, Supreme Court,[117] upheld the validity of customary law prevailed among agriculturist jats in Punjab where daughter succeeded self-acquired property of her father in preference to collaterals.

In 1957, just next year of the passing of the Act[118] of 1956 the question before the court was whether Section 14 of the Act is retrospective in operation? This question arose because generally a substantive law is not retrospective in operation, unless it is specifically made so. But Section 14 appears, on its face, to be retrospective, when it declares, that the property acquired, before or after the commencement of the Act, shall be held by her as an absolute property and not as limited owner. But this retrospectively of the Act, is given to the acquisition' of the property and not to possession,[119] it was held by the court.

In an other case[120] the court had made it clear, that for the application of Section 14 of the Act, it was necessary that the property must be in possession of Hindu female, at the date of the commencement of the Act, whether actual, physical or constructive.

To favour the women's property right in 1959, the Supreme Court held,[121] that even if a custom under which a sister may claim to succeed to the property of her brother in preference of collaterals, has not been established, she was made entitle to claim the inheritance, under section 5 of the Hindu Law of Inheritance (Amendment) Act of, 1929. Under this Act a sister was a preferential heir of her brother against his collaterals.

During the Second decade of Independence

In second decade the judiciary had got the weapon of the Act of 1956 to favour the females and generally the court interpreted the provisions of the Act, to give more and more rights to females. But sometimes-contrary views were also taken. Because in favouring females it cannot go against the express provision of the laws. In 1962 the Supreme Court held,[122] that, where a Hindu holding occupancy right under the Zamindari, died leaving no son behind him, daughter could succeed to him though with limited interest.

Supreme Court was not always bent to favour the woman. In 1966, on the question whether widow is a karta of joint family. The apex court held, since coparcenership is an essential condition for the membership of Hindu joint family and a widow is not a coparcener, so she could not be a karta of joint family.[123] At another occasion, on the question whether widow acquiring property under the Act, could claim partition, Supreme Court[124] did not give full effect to the statutory conferment upon the widow, of the same right of claiming partition as a male owner.

In 1968, the Supreme Court had to consider the question, whether after coming into force of the Hindu Succession Act,

1956 the widow got rights of full ownership and could alienate the properties without the consent of the male member of the family. It was held,[125] that she had become full owner, by virtue of the provision of section 14(1) of the Act of 1956. At another place the Supreme Court had, the task of interpretation of the scope of clause (d) of Section 8 of the Hindu Law of Women's Right Act (Mysore Act No. X of 1933). In this instant case the apex court had widely interpreted the scope of said section. The Supreme Court held that this section cannot be narrowly interpreted as giving a right, to only those females, who happen to be related to one or the other of the last two male coparcener, and the expression, mother, would include a step mother and step grand mother also, where the step grand mother was a sole surviving heir, she was made entitled to share in the joint family property.[126]

On the issue of a possession of a widow as trespasser, in 1970 Supreme Court held, that before any property could be said to be possess by a Hindu female as required in Section 14(1) of the Act two things were necessary to be considered.

(I) She must had a right to the possession of that property.

(II) She must have been in possession of that property either actually or constructively.[127]

In *Vijai Pal v Dal Consolidation,*[128] the Supreme Court interpreted the word 'possession' in wider sense that the term possession is co-extensive with the ownership. But in *Dindayal and other v Raja Ram,*[129] Supreme Court on the issue of trespasser had, held that she could not be held, to acquire any right under the Act, where she had possessed property as a trespasser.

During the Third decade of Independence

The attitude of the judiciary was not much changed in this period and the mix attitude remained constant. Wherever the issue was not in direct conflict with the express provision of the law, the court always had tried to favour the females.

In *Sasanka v Amijia*[130] the question before the court was, whether an apostate widow or daughter-in-law could claim the benefit of the Act of 1937? The answer was in negative because the benefit was only to Hindu female when she converted to another faith, she was not a Hindu, so the benefit of the provisions of the Act, could not be given to such a woman. Section 26 of Hindu Succession Act made the position clear. But in another case of a Christian female who married with a Hindu male under the Special Marriage Act, 1872, was consider to be entitled to a share as a predeceased son's widow, from the property of her father-in-law as an heir. It seemed that the apex court favoured the females where there was a little chance or capacity to interpret the provision to empower the female in economic sphere.

In *Tulassamma* v *Sesha Reddy*,[131] The Supreme Court, had recognized, that Sec. 14(1) must receive '*most expansive interpretation*'. The facts of this most important case, in which the Supreme Court had propounded so many principles which are as follows :

> The husband of Tulassamma, Venkata Sesha Reddy died, leaving behind Tulassamma as his widow in the state of jointness with his stepbrother *V* Sesha Reddy. Tulassamma, filed a petition for maintenance which was passed as an exparte decree. A settlement took place out of the court under which, Tulassamma was allotted the disputed property as a limited interest only. Tulassamma remained in possession of the property till the passing of the Hindu Succession Act of 1956. By two-registered deed, Tulassamma leased out some of the properties, which was challenged, on the basis that her interest would not be enlarged into an absolute interest, under sec. 14(2) of the Act of 1956. The Munsif Court accepted it. Then Tulassamma went to District Court, who reversed the findings of the trial court and held that sub sec (2) of Sec. 14 had no application because the compromise was an instrument in the recognition of a pre-existing right. In second appeal the High Court of Andhra Pradesh upheld the decision of trial court. At last in Supreme Court P. N. Bhagwati, A.C. Gupta and S.M. Fazale Ali JJ reached at the conclusions that –
>
> - Hindu female's right to maintenance is not an empty formality. It is a tangible right against the property which

is recognized by the Shastric Law.

- Sec. 14(1) and the explanation attached with it should be given, widest possible meaning, in favour of female, to achieve the object of the Act of 1956, which is to abridge the stringent provisions, against proprietry rights, which were often regarded as evidence of her perpetual tutelage.
- The nature of the Sub.-Sec.(2) of Sec. 14 is as an exception to Sub-Sec. (1). This proviso should not be construed in a manner so as to destroy the very purpose of the Act.
- Sec. 14(2) applies to instrument, decree, awards, gift etc., which creates a new right, or interest in favour of female, where the instrument only confirm the pre-existing right it has no application.
- The use of express words in the explanation to Scc. 14(1) that 'property acquired by a Hindu female' at partition, or 'in lieu of maintenance' or 'arrears of maintenance' etc. clearly makes Sub.-Sec. (2) inapplicable to these categories of property.
- The expression "possessed by" should be given a broad meaning and wide connotation which includes the actual as well as constructive possession and symbolic possession. Judiciary also leaned towards this attitude from the beginning.[132] But this widest interpretation could not by any way extended to such an extent as to include the trespasser.[133]
- The words "restricted estate" used in Sec. 14(2) are wider than limited as indicated in Sec. 14(1) and they include not only limited interest but also any other kind of limitation that may be placed on transferee (female).

Applying the principles enunciated to the facts of the present case the judges find

- that the properties in suit were allotted to the appellant Tulassamma on July 30, 1949 under a compromise certified by the court.
- that the appellant had taken only a life interest in the properties and there was a clear restriction prohibiting

her from alienating the properties.

- that despite these restrictions she continued to be in possession of the properties till 1956 when the Act of 1956 came into force and
- that the alienations which she had made in 1960 and 1961 were after she had acquired an absolute interest in the properties.

It was therefore, clear that the compromise by which the properties were allotted to the appellant Tulassamma, in lieu of her maintenance, were merely in recognition of her right to maintenance, which was a pre-existing right and therefore, the case of the appellant would be taken out of the ambit of Section 14(2) and would fall squarely with in Section 14(1) read with the explanation there to. It is a landmark judgement of the court.

It is submitted, that the Supreme Court has misconceptualised, sub-section (2) of Section, 14 as a proviso of the first sub-section because both the clauses have different purposes. It is further submitted that the language of the proviso is wide enough and does not bar its application to the preexisting rights of the widow.

Another thing which draw the attention is, that Supreme Court in considering the words '*possessed by*' takes the meaning '*the state of owning*' or '*having in one's hand*' or power which is not relevant because the legislature deliberately avoid to use the words '*owned by*' in place of '*possessed by*' in Section 14(1) of the Act of 1956.

Since the enactment of Hindu Succession Act, 1956, there has been influx of cases each year under Sec. 14 and generally courts are liberal in favour of women, upholding the decision of Tulassamma case.

During the Fourth Decade of Independence

It can not be said that the role of judiciary is not creative and pro-woman. As it can not deviate from the express provisions of the codified law like previous decade there is not much improvement in this decade also and the cases are decided with the mixed reaction, some in favour and some in against but the majority of the cases are decided in favour than against.

In *Dipo* v *Wassan Singh*[134] the property, inherited from paternal ancestor, is an ancestral property, as regards the male issue of the propositus. But if a person inheriting such property has no son, son's son or son's son in existence, at the time when he inherits the property, he holds the property as absolute owner there of. In this instant case, the last male holder of the property had no male issue and no surviving member of a joint family, who could take the property by survivorship. The court held it, that the sister of last male holder has preferential right against collaterals.

In *Shambhu Chandra Shukla v Thakur Ladle R. Chandra,*[135] the question before the court was whether the widow can transfer her shebaitship right by a will? Justice Per Mukharji, said, "*that shebaitship is a property which is heritable.* The right of a female to succeed to the religious office of shebaitship is already recognized by the Act of 1937. Section 14 of Hindu Succession Act, 1956 enlarge the limited right of a Hindu female to the absolute right, and there is no bar against alienation, which was imposed by the founder.

Amar Singh v Asstt. Director of Consolidation[136] in this case the nature of right and interest of a Hindu widow in her deceased husband's estate vesting in her was recognized.

During the Fifth Decade of Independence

In this decade the judiciary had passed some very significant ruling. As to favour female, it has extended the ambit of section 14 even to include the wife of bigamous marriage as wife. In this decade the International provisions were also taken into consideration and tried to implement.

In *Masilamani Mudaliar* v *Idol of Sri Swaminath Swami,*[137] a very significant judgement was given by the court because it had not only recognized the absolute ownership of females, over certain properties but also discussed various International Conventions as, The Protection of Human Rights Act, 1993 and other constitutional provisions to emphasize the concept of equality of gender. In *Raghubir Singh* v *Gulab*

Singh,[138] Supreme Court has reaffirmed and reiterated the females limited estate into absolute one.

In the case of *Beni Bai* v *Raghubir Prasad*,[139] an interesting question came before the apex court whether under Hindu Law the term 'wife' includes the third wife or not? As in Hindu law no bigamy is permitted so the third marriage is void, then the question arose that the benefits given to wife could be given to the third wife also? The facts of the case were that the third wife in favour of her daughter executed a will. The Supreme Court held, that to read a 'female Hindu' as only wife was totally misconceived. It is apparant that the attitude of the judiciary towards females was generally lenient and pro-women.

In *Naresh Kumari v Shashi Lal*,[140] the court held that if the widow had relinquished her right, through the sale deed, her limited interest would not ripen in the absolute ownership or where she herself had surrendered,[141] her share, in favour of her only son, the benefit of section 14 of the Act of 1956, could not be given to her. Here though the decision was not pro-women but according to law.

In *Velamuri Venkata Sevaprasad v Kothuri Venkateshwra*,[142] the Supreme Court, on the point of the remarriage of the widow, gave, another significant judgement. The Act of 1856 says that the widow on remarriage, (Section 2 of Hindu Widows Remarriage Act) would be deemed to be dead. The facts of this case were that a widow remarried in 1953 prior to the Act of 1956 though her marriage was bigamous under the Madras Hindu Bigamy (Prevention and Divorce) Act, 1949 so void. The question before the court, was, whether such widow was entitled to inherit or not. The court held, that voidness of marriage could not be termed, as absolute nullity and also could not be taken into consideration to aid the conferment of right. The court held, that she was not entitled to inherit. Here the judiciary did not allow to take undue advantage of the Act of 1949 of Madras and applied the clear provisions of the Hindu Widow's Remarriage Act.

The Current Position

In *Palchuri Hanumayamma v Tadikamalla Koltingham*[143]

such a situation had emerged which was unforeseen by the legislature. As a result of enlarging the widow's limited estate the original intent of the testator to give equal benefit to the third branch of his family, had been nullified. In this case by a registered will the appellant, maternal grand father provided that his wife R "*shall enjoy all my movable and immovable properties till her death,*" without making allocations. After the death of R each of these three daughters were to be given clearly identified share in the property. In 1944, one of the three daughters, the mother of the appellant, died. The appellant, till her marriage, lived with her grand mother R. In 1955, R with a partition deed had transferred the shares of the two surviving daughters, according to the Will and kept the share of the deceased daughter with her. In 1966, R by a gift deed had transferred that share to one of her surviving daughter and she herself died in 1977.

The appellant challenged the gift deed which was dismissed by the trial court and High Court, when the case had come before the Supreme Court it was held that till 1956 R had no absolute right over the property as this right is given by the Act of 1956 and the partition deed was made in 1955 according to the intention of the testator. After the Act of 1956, the share which was retained by the widow get enlarged into absolute one. So the gift deed was valid. It is submitted that though the case was decided according to the provisions of the Act of 1956, but it was not according to equity, justice and good conscience because the daughter of the pre-deceased daughter had not get the share of her mother.

In *Muthusami* v *Angammal*,[144] the father-in-law of the widow made a settlement deed, with the help of Panchayat for her maintenance, during his lifetime. In 1974, she executed a sale deed, which was challenged. That property was inherited by father-in-law through the husband of the widow. The issue in this case was that the widow's pre-existing right exists in the husband's property and not against the property of her father-in-law and the deed was made by intervention of Panchayat. The Supreme Court held, that the case was covered by Sec.

14(1). Though for time being she was not in actual physical possession of the land, but she was in the legal possession, as she never parted with the right of maintenance. So the sale deed was valid.

In *Gulabrao Balwant Rao Shinde* v *C. Balwant Rao Shinde*,[145] the Supreme Court has corrected, the grave injustice done by the High Court of Bombay. In this case the deceased has contracted two marriages and have children from both the wives. The second marriage was contracted after the death of first wife. The children of the first wife filed a suit, for recovery of their share, in the property left by their father, which was in the possession of second wife. The plea was taken, by the children of the second wife, that the property was in lieu of maintenance of second wife and she also had possession over it, which had ripen into an absolute ownership, by virtue of the provision of Sec. 14(1) of Hindu Succession Act, 1956. The High Court, held in favour of second wife. On appeal Supreme Court saved the interest of the aggrieved, by holding that there was no proof that the deceased has given the property to the second wife in lieu of maintenance and the disputed property was also an ancestral property from which the children of first wife could not be divested, by giving the benefit of Sec. 14(1) to the second wife. The object of Sec. 14(1) is to remove the restrictions, placed by the old Hindu law, on the full enjoyment of the property of a female, but not at all, at the cost of injustice with others.

In *Jose v Ramakrishnan Nair Radhakrishnan*,[146] the Kerala High Court has considered the two expression "*Hindu female*" *and* "*in any other manner whatsoever*" of Sec. 14 of Hindu Succession Act, 1956. The question before the court for consideration was, whether the limited interest of a daughter, would get enlarged to full right after the commencement of the Hindu Succession Act, 1956, when a male Hindu following Mitakashra law died, before the said Act? This question was answered in affirmative a decade ago by K.P.B. Marar J in *Velayudhan v Ithavi*.[147] There could not be any distinction between the rights claimed by the widow and a daughter in respect of self-acquired property of a male Hindu. Section 14 uses the expression "female Hindu" to include daughter as well. To read 'female Hindu' as only 'wife' is totally misconceived.[148] The Apex Court has given, a wider meaning to the expression, '*female Hindu*' which includes not wife alone.[149] The court has given wider interpretation also to the expression *in any other manner whatsoever*. Section 14, has to be read with Section 4, which gives overriding effect of the Act, whatever property in the possession of the female Hindu whether it has been acquired by her self or in any other manner whatsoever shall be regarded, her absolute property.

It is submitted that court has given a wise judgement to give every female Hindu, the benefit of Sec. 14 and thus fulfilled the intention of the legislature. Thus due regard has been given to the role and place of womanhood in the country on the basis of the prevailing socio-economic perspective.

The conditions of the tribal woman after the independence of 62 years is still a forlorn hope to achieve equality before law. The case of *Madhu Kishwar* v *State of Bihar* is a landmark decision in which they asked for loaf of equality, at least to get crumbs of livelihood. In this case sections 7, 8 and 76 of the Chota Nagpur Tenancy Act, 1908, was a challenged, as unconstitutional and discriminatory, against females. Under this Act the tribal woman are excluded from inheritance. Though as unmarried daughter had usufruct right in the property of her father, till marriage and widow has usufruct right till she got an issue. This case was brought before the Supreme Court that had directed the State government to take necessary steps. The State level Tribal Advisory Board suggested, that in case of right to inheritance to the tribal woman would result in elevation of land to non-tribal. On the order of the Supreme Court, the matter was reconsidered by the Bihar Tribal Council, which also gave the same opinion. Thus the discrimination only on the basis of sex still prevails and tribal woman have no right to inherit because the property would pass in the hand of other tribe.

The decision rendered, by a majority of two against one, is regressive in the final analysis. Ramaswami J, was of the view that sections 7 and 8 of the Act,[150] are violative of Art, 14 of the Constitution. He says that in every state, there are legislations prohibiting alienation of tribal lands to non-tribals. But the majority opinion of Punchhi and Kuldip JJ was though conservative, but took a cautious approach by giving limited relief to females. The exclusive right of male succession under the provision of sections 7 and 8 has to remain suspended so long as the right of livelihood of the female descendants of the last male-holder remains valid and in vogue.

In 2005, some very interesting questions were raised before different High Courts of India relating to the issue of inheritance.

In *Brijendra Pratap Singh* v *Prem Lata Singh*,[151] a settlement deed between two brothers was made, that on the death of either of the parties the male lineal descendants of that party alone will succeed how so low ever to the exclusion of all female heirs. It was challenged, on the basis that it will amount legislating new law of inheritance, which was at variance of Hindu Law of Succession Act of 1956. Though, in Hindu law, it is permissible to gift or to will in favour of son or grandson the whole property, excluding all female heirs. But in this instant case, there was no will or gift, they merely laid down an abstract rule of succession, which was against law.

A Hindu cannot create the line of succession qua a settlement, because it will amount to legislating a new law, which is not permissible. The daughters and widow also have the right to inherit the property. This deed cannot be treated as a Will or gift under which the Hindu can make a Will in favour of his son or grandson, to the exclusion of daughter or granddaughter.

In *L.H. Vidyapoornam* v *L.H. Premavathy*,[152] a Hindu male died, leaving behind three daughters, three sons and a widow. The intestate had left self-acquired property, over which the plaintiff had no possession, so it was contended that the plaintiff was not entitled to file the suit. The court held, that it would be presumed that the plaintiff had been, in possession of the said property as notionally partition among them till the actual partition took place. It was very complicated case in which by a fraudulent Will the rights of the daughters in the property of their father was tried to extinguish, but by minute observation the court had prevented the gross injustice to be done.

In another, very latest case of 2005 *Ravi Kirthi Shetty* v *Jagathpata Shetty*,[153] the benefit of section 6-A, which is inserted by Karnataka Amendment Act 1994,[154] was claimed by daughter. The facts of the case were that one Raju Shetty died leaving behind two sons and two daughters. The property was divided among them, according to the provisions of section 6 of Hindu Succession Act, 1956. But one of the daughter claimed that she was unmarried at the time of the death of her father, so she must be given the benefit of section 6-A of Hindu Succession Act of 1956. In absence of any proof that she was unmarried, at that time, the court had not accepted her claim. It is submitted that though judiciary generally bent towards female right but in the absence of material proof it is bound to do justice with males.

Very recently, the Supreme Court has to construe a very different question whether the wife of a murderer be considered as the widow under section 25 of the Hindu Succession Act, 1956 ? There is a provision under section 25 of the Act of 1956 that the murderer be deemed as the predeceased. So whether she is entitled to inherit the property as the widow? It was pleaded by lawyers of the widow. In *Vallikannu v R. Singaperumal,*[155] the above-mentioned question was raised. The facts of the case were as such. His only son murdered one, Ramasami. There was no other survivor of Ramasami as his wife was already divorced and remarried. Under the provision of section 25 read with section 27 of Hindu Succession Act, 1956, the murderer who was the only son should be deemed to have predeceased, so not entitled to succeed the estate of his father. The wife of the son claimed that she was alone entitled to all the properties. Then question was, whether the wife of a disqualified son who succeeds through the husband could be entitled to succeed the property? The answer of this question was given far back before the passing of the Act of 1956, by the Privy Council in negative, on the basis of equity, justice and good conscience in *Kenchava Kon Sanyellappa Hosmani and*

Anr v. Girimallappa Channappa.[156]

The Supreme Court, in the instant case referring the judgement of Privy Council of the above-mentioned case, has explained to the objects and reasons for enacting section 25 as—

> "*A murderer, even if not disqualified under old Hindu law from succeeding to the estate of the person whom he has murdered, is so disqualified upon principles of justice, equity and good conscience. The murderer is not to be regarded, as the stock of a fresh line of descent but should be regarded, as non-existent when the succession opens.*" The Supreme Court held that the wife of the son cannot lay a claim to the property of her father-in-law.

In *Priyamvada Devi Birla* v *Madhu Prasad Birla*,[157] a novel question very recently in 2006 came before the Calcutta High Court for consideration. What is caveatable interest? The second question was, whether the sister of the husband was entitled to inherit, being a class II heir, if there was no class I heir?

In answering the first question that what is caveatable interest? The court has said that the existence of real interest or even bare possibility of real interest in estate of deceased, is said to be the caveatable interest.

Now come to the second question the court held that where a lady dying intestate without having any class I heir of her own or of her husband, the estate would devolve on sisters of her husband who were class II heirs and after them on their heirs, husbands and sons etc.

Implementation of the New (Amendment) Act of 2005

Recently a case has been decided by the Kerala High Court regarding the impact of the amendment in Section 23. In *S. Narayan* v *Meenakshi* (AIR 2006 Ker. 143) the question before the court is – whether omission of section 23 of the Hindu Succession Act by the Hindu Succession Amendment Act, 2005 would have any impact on a suit for partition or appeal there from pending on the date of the commencement of the Hindu

Succession Amendment Act, 2005?

The facts of the present case are one Ramaji died leaving behind her four daughters and a son. After the death of Ramaji one of her daughter who is the plaintiff of the suit, obtained purchase certificate from the Land Tribunal in her name. The other sisters released their fractional shares in favour of the plaintiff. Thus the plaintiff claimed 4/5 shares and contended that the defendant has only 1/5 share.

The defendant contended that the property does not belong to Ramaji but to her husband and before the commencement of the Hindu Succession Act, 1956 all sisters were married, therefore they are not entitled to any share in the property. The lower courts found that the property belonged to Ramaji the mother of plaintiff and defendant. Therefore on her death the property devolved on her children. During the pendency of the suit the son died. Before the case was decided by the court the Hindu Succession Amendment Act, 2005 was passed. The other questions decided by the court in this case are –

- whether a suit for partition at the instance of a daughter could be defeated by invoking Section 23 of Hindu Succession Act, 1956 by the legal representative of a deceased son of the intestate?
- whether section 23 would be applicable in a case where the deceased intestate has left behind him only one male issue and whether it is necessary that there must be more than one male issues to invoke section 23?
- whether the protection in favour of the male heir under section 23 of the Act of 1956 would be available if he inducts a third party in the dwelling house or any portion thereof?

Though all these questions are dealt in this case but after the passing of the Amendment of 2005 these questions have lost their significance because of the omission of section 23 of Hindu Succession Act, 1956. Therefore there is no need to discuss what the answers of these questions are.

Various women's organizations have made a demand to give

equal right of inheritance to the daughter also which is taken into consideration by the Law Commission. In its 174th Report, the Law Commission has recommended such provisions and the Hindu Succession Amendment Act, 2005, has incorporated that recommendations. At the time of the passing of the Hindu Succession Act, 1956, the women's organizations had raised their voices and demanded the solution of their grievances.

Though some commendable improvement were made by that Act of 1956, but much left to be done, which is fulfilled by this Act of 2005. This amendment is considered a great step in the field of women's property right, by making a daughter a coparcener and by deleting sections 23 and 24 of the Old Act. 2005. Instead of this significant progressive legislation the gender discrimination against women was not fully done away by the amendment. As in the opinion of this author the section 14 of Hindu Succession Act of 1956, should also be modified which still creates great amomalies.

In this instant case the son die during the pendency of the case. Now the question arises whether the legal heir of the deceased has any right to resist partition under the provision of section 23 of the Act, 1956 or whether it is a transferable or heritable right? It is a settled law that the right of male heirs to resist the partition is personal to him. It is neither transferable nor heritable therefore it is available only till their death. Thus it can not be said that cessation of such personal right during the pendency of a suit for partition would not entitle the female heir to claim partition taking note of subsequent events, if the contention that the state of affairs as on the date of the suit alone would be relevant, is to accepted, then it would have the effect of indirectly holding that the personal right of the male heir to resist partition could be continued by his legal representatives. Therefore whenever the personal right of a male heir under section 23 comes to an end the right of the female heir to claim partition cannot be defeated. In other words a defeasible right of a male heir would got defeated the moment his personal right ceases. Such personal right of the male heir has been taken away by the omission of section 23 of the Act of

1956 by the Amendment Act of 2005. The effect of such omission would be retrospective.

It is submitted that the Kerala High Court has taken a diligent steps for the implementation of the new Act of 2005 and tries to give flesh and breath to the Act.

LATEST CASES UP TO 2009

Maintenance during the Pendency of Suit for Partition

A Hindu widow has applied for maintenance during the pendency of suit for partition. Karta and the other coparceners were in the possession of Joint family property. The court held that the widow of coparcener has the right of maintenance.[158]

Enlargement of Estate

A Hindu has executed a settlement deed in respect of property. He reserved life interest in himself and created vested remainder in favor of his daughter. There after he has executed a will, creating, life-interest in favor of his wife that included not only the right to maintenance but right to enjoy it during her life time without right to alienate it. After death of father the daughter has claimed to materialize the settlement deed. But court held that by the operation of law under 8.14(1) the widow right has enlarged into an absolute right so the settlement - deed would not be materialized.[159]

If a female receives and possesses any property which she got against her pre-existing right, she become the full owner of that property and not limited owner. She has every right to dispose of the property according to her will.[160] The word possession used under S. I4 means not merely in possession of property without any sort of right in it.[161] Daughter who has not any pre-existing right can not become full owner by virtue of S. I4(1) the death of husband his wife having right of maintenance over the estate of her husband and this right gets enlarged into absolute one. This is a pre-existing right over the property which can never be restricted by virtue of S. I4(2) of Hindu Succession Act.[162]

Property has been transferred to a widow of coparcener for her life in recognition of her pre-existing right to claim maintenance. This limited right would be converted into absolute right if she was alive at the time of coming into force the Hindu succession Act 1956.[163]

Husband has given his second wife right to enjoy rents and profits of a property in implementation of pre-existing right to claim maintenance. The court held[164] the right granted to wife enlarges into full ownerships on account of S.I4(1) A.

Property given to wife by husband for her maintenance would enlarge into absolute one and why gift deed made by her in respect of that property will be valid.[165]

Inheritance of Sebaitship

Whether a female Hindu can inherit sebaitship of Hindu temple whether she can execute a deed for management of such right in favor of her married daughter? Recently the Allahabad High Court[166] has confronted with these questions. The court held that there in nothing in the Act of 1937 that excludes sebaitship from Hindu Law. See 3(1) of Hindu women's Right to property Act 1987 includes all forms or types of interest answering to the description of property in law. Property must be heritable. In the case of Angurbala Mullick,[167] Supreme Court held that property includes both movable and immovable property acquired by female Hindu by inheritance partition, in less of maintenance or gift by any person.

Fomale Intestate: Sec 15,16

A Hindu female died intestate, her husband pre-deceased and they have no issue of their own. According to the rule of preference to succession, her property would go to the heirs of her husband, which include both male and female persons. There is not provision that female heirs did not have any right.[168] But in the case where the father has not surrendered his tenancy right in favor of his daughter in his life-time. On the death of daughter the husband would not be entitled to inherit rather than the heirs of the father would be entitled.[169] Property inherited by mother from her maternal grand father.

Mother died intestate. The property would devolve on her only daughter by virtue of S. I 5(2) (a) of Hindu Succession Act.[170]

Stridhana

A female Hindu died intestate in 1955 before the commencement of Hindu succession Act 1956. Therefore the case would be governed by the old Hindu Law. The property in question was received by a lady from a female member of her paternal side. According to old Hindu Law it is her stridhan. So only her daughters would be entitled to inherit her Stridhan.[171] Female has inherited property from another female as stridhana which is her absolute property according to the provision of sections 11 and 18 of Mysore Hindu Women's Right to Property Act 1933. By this Act the Mitakashara Law was amended. The court held that in case of any inconsistency the provision of Mysore Act would prevail over the Mitakashara law.[172]

Will Executed by a Female

Mother has executed a will deed in favor of her one son that deed fulfilled all the conditions of a valid will such as:

- The document was executed by testator.
- It was signed by the attesting witnesses.
- It was regarding disposition of property. The court held[173] that the will is valid and there is no question of passing of her property to her heirs according to see. 15 of Hindu Succession Act would not arise.

Illegitimate Son

Illegitimate children cannot claim share in ancestral property obtain by father but his or her share in the self-acquired property of the deceased cannot be denied. By see 16(3) it is made clear that an illegitimate son who is admitted to be a legitimate son by virtue of Sec. 16 (1) & (2) will have the rights only in the properties of parents and none else. Sec. 16 contains a legal fiction. It is a rule of 'fictio-jurie' that the legislature has provided that the children though illegitimate shall never the less be treated as legitimate not withstanding that the marriage was void or voidable. But Parliament had no intention of eclipsing the settled concepts of Hindu Law such as coparcenary or coparceners etc. Existence of an antecedent title is a prerequisite for enforcement of night to claim partition. In the life time of father the son can not claim any share in his property. His right accrues only on his father's dying intestate.[174]

Reopening of Partition :

The court held[175] that to confer a better right on daughter as per amended Act the partition cannot be reopened. Amended Act clearly indicates that a daughter can be considered as a coparcener only if her father was a coparcener at the time of coming into force the amended provision. It is of course true that for the purpose of considering whether the father is a coparcener or not, the restricted meaning of the expression 'partition' as given in the explanation is to be attributed . Father died before 1956 hence the case would be governed by old 'shastric law' and not by succession. Daughter would not be entitled to any share.[176] If father has relinquished his all rights in family property accepting certain sum as consideration, he will not be regarded as coparcener. The child conceived after it cannot claim partition after born alive.[177]

Coparcenary Property

Any property inherited by father by way of Will cannot be said as coparcenary property or ancestral property.[41] But it is his self acquired property. It father has made any provision for the devolution of that property it is valid. But gift of entire property by father to his mother was held impermissible by Andhra Pradesh,[178] High Court. The court said that father, who was the sole coparcener of property cannot circumvent law in order to deny the right of wife or children.

On the basis of above discussion, it can be concluded, that in the field of woman's property right, the judiciary has played a very creative role. The rights of Hindu female to property passes through a long channel of judicial activism and now reached at its peak by giving the daughter equal rights of inheritance. The legislature just given a skeleton and judiciary will give the flesh, blood and soul to that enactment. It is not important that how much enactment has been passed for the empowerment of woman but it is more important that how they are implemented.

Christian Law

In some countries, there are special courts for family matters, set up in pursuit of religious, political or social objectives. These include the Christians, Muslims, and Jewish ecclesiastical courts. In some other countries, there is also a fashion, to establish social courts, (another name of family courts) to deal with the legal problems, affecting families. In these courts, it is argued that judges should be given wide discretion in family cases. This seems to have been done in the family codes of Eastern Europe and the Peoples Republic of China, which are loosely constructed with statement of politics, legal principles and leave much leeway to the judges or conciliator. But against this contention, it is argued that such discretion would tend to turn tribunals into courts of morals, in which the personal views of judges could prevail, in the absence of applicable legal rules.[179]

The Supreme Court of India, in *Krishna Singh v Mathura,*[180] opined, that in process of applying the personal law of the parties, the judges of the High Court, should not introduce their own concept of modernity. In view of Supreme Court the constitution maintained the position of personal law status quo. So far as the Christian law in India, is concerned their own laws governed the Christian before the British period, as Muslim rulers did not interfere, in the matter of personal law of any religious community. Similarly Hindus, Muslims, Sikhs, Christians and Parsis were the subject of their own personal laws, especially with the matters relating to the family laws.

In Pre-Independence Period

During the regime of Britishers in India, except Hindus and Muslims, all other classes of persons were made the subject of English Common Law. By the Act of 1781 only Hindus and Muslim's personal laws were reserved. The position of the application of common law to Christians, Parsis etc. was clarified by the Supreme Court[181] in 1844. In *Gradiner v Fell,*[182] it was held by the court of Chancery in England that the descent of lands in the Mofassil of a British subject was governed by the common law.

In fact the early British administrator had no conscious

intention to deprive the people of various religion from the benefit of their own peculiar system of laws, but they have little acquaintance about them till the first judicial plan was introduced.

Later on, the position was changed, and a provision was, therefore, made for applying customs of the country and the 'law of the defendant' to various classes of people. In *Durand* v *Boilard,*[183] the Calcutta Sadar Adalat decided a question of succession amongst the French in accordance with the French law. A question of a succession of the property of a Portuguese was held to be decided by their own customs and usages.[184] In *Aviatick Ter Stephensons v Khaja Michael Aratoon,*[185] it was held that the inheritance of an American was governed by the American law.

In case of Anglo-Indians, no law had been prescribed and their matters were decided on the basis of justice, equity and good conscience.[186] These Anglo Indians were also governed by the principle of English law.

In the leading case of *Abraham v Abraham*[187] Privy Council had made clear the position of native Christians.[188] In this case the question, before the court, was whether the inheritance of these Anglo Indians be governed, by rules of old religion or there would be any other law applicable to these people? The facts of the case were that a Christian died, whose ancestors had been Hindu leaving behind an Anglo Indian wife and children. The question, before the court, was that the separate property of the deceased be the subject of which law? The Madras Adalat held, that Hindu law of coparcenary is applicable but on appeal the Privy Council reversed the decision of Madras Adalat. The Christians were not the subject of single law. The court had to decide the question of law applicable to a particular case in a particular circumstance that prolonged the litigation,[189] and create a great chaos and dissatisfaction among the converts.

On the recommendation of first law commission the English law was held to be applicable to all other than Hindus, Muslims and Parsis. To secure the forfeiture of property on a Hindu or Muslim converts into Christianity, the Caste Disabilities Removal

Act, 1850 was passed. The Indian Succession Act of 1865 was passed amongst much hue and cry, which was the first piece of substantive law enacted for India.[190] Under this Act limited property rights were given to the Christians, Parsis and Jews women to remove the traditional disabilities of married woman under the law of these religion. "The Married Women Right to Property Act, 1874 was passed. After that the Indian Succession Act, 1925 was passed which gave the women equal rights of inheritance as compared to their male counterpart.

In Post Independence Period

In post Independence India the courts were very liberal towards the women's property rights of females and adopted a progressive attitude in matter of gender justice. In *Nepah Bela* v *Sita Kanta*,[191] the court held that a Christian who had converted from Hindu died leaving behind a Christian widow and a Hindu brother and sister. The inheritance, according to the court, between them would be as the half property would go to widow and the other half would be inherited by the Hindu brother and sister collectively. Both of them would be entitled to equal share. This decision seems to be biased against the Christian widow.

But in 1964, in *Siril Christian* v *Mangamura*,[192] the Assam High Court made it clear that the Succession Act, 1925, did not concerned itself with the religion of the claimant. For succession although the religion of the deceased plays an important role and indeed it is almost the determining factor in the matter of applicability or otherwise of the rule of succession laid down in the Act to a particular case. This distinction in the nature of character of the relevant estate depending upon the religion of the deceased owner runs through the Act. But stress was here laid in the matter of its devolution upon the religion of the heir or the inheritor and that the religion of the claimant as disguised from the religion of the deceased owner, was entirely irrelevant for the purpose. A Christian died intestate and his nearest heir being Hindu, inherited the estate of the deceased.

Some times very contradictory opinion were given by the different High Courts as in *Administrator General v Ananda Chari*,[193] the Madras High Court held that where a Hindu married with a Hindu girl and afterwards converted to Christianity, where upon the Hindu wife refuses to live with him and renounces all claims to his estate. She was not entitled to her share as a widow.

On the other hand in *Smt. Shephali Chetterji and others* v *Smt. Kamala Benerji*,[194] the Allahabad High Court interpret, the term 'widow' as 'widows' and said that singular should include the plural. On the death of the husband both the widow and their lineal descendants were, held entitle to inherit the property. In *Rutland v Rutland,*[195] the stepmother was not included with in the meaning of mother and she was also not kindred of the intestate, so she was not held entitled to inherit.

Sometimes in favouring the female the courts unconsciously had done injustice with others for instance, in the case of *Mathew Jacob v Selestine Jacob*[196] The facts of the case were, that a Christian intestate Jacob Massey was survived by his one widow and five children. After the death of his first wife he remarried with another lady, from whom he had two children. He already had three children from his first wife. Selestine's widow claimed the whole property on the basis of an unregistered Will executed by Jacob Massey. The validity of the Will was challenged by the children of both wives on the basis of the exclusion of the natural heirs. But Usha Mehra J, upheld the validity of the Will and stated that there was nothing unnatural in that Will because the wishes of the testator were to protect the interest of his wife. The court relied in this case on the decision of Supreme Court in *Rabindra Nath Mukherji v Pan Chanam Benerji*.[197]

The Indian Succession Act, 1925 did not govern the State of Travancore and Cochin till, 1951, which was extended by the State laws Act of 1951. By this extension the Christian females of the state of Travancore and Cochin has got the right to inherit the property equally with their brother. Before 1951, Travancore Christian Succession Act entitled the daughter's share to Rs. 5000/- only and she was not made entitled to inherit the father's land.

Current Position

In *Land Board* v *Cyriac Thomas*[198] a Christian died leaving behind two sons and four daughters who succeed equally. There was a provision under the Kerala Taluk Land Board that an individual cannot hold the property excess of that the specified limit of the board. If he possessed more than, the specified limit, then he would have to surrender the excess property to the government. One of his sons had cross the specified limit so that board claimed for that. But the son took the plea that the excess land belonged to his sister and she had already executed sale deed of that land. The board argued that the sister was not entitled to inherit the land, under Travancore and Cochin Christian Succession Act. So the sale deed executed by the sister was not valid. The Supreme Court, in this case upheld the decision of the *Mary Roy* v *State of Kerala*,[199] where it was held that the succession would be governed by the provision of Indian Succession Act, 1925, where the daughter has equal right and equal share to inherit and the Christians are no more the subject of Travancore and Cochin Christian Succession Act.

Recently the court in the case of *John Vallamattom* v *Union of India*[200] gives a very landmark judgement, in this case the validity of Section 118, of Indian Succession Act of 1925, was challenged as violative of Article 14 of the Constitution. Under this section 118 a restriction is imposed on a person who has no children or wife or father or other heirs but has heirs of distant kindred, not to bequeath his property to charitable purposes. The court held this provision unconstitutional and against the faith of Christian religious belief. The court further observed that to give property for charitable purposes is an integral part of their religion.

In relation to female generally the courts lean towards the females and in favouring the females, sometime a grave injustice has been caused to other legal heirs. Like all other laws, the laws applied to Indian Christians also passed through a channel of judicial system with some sweet and sore experiences.

PARSI LAW

Pre Independence Period

The process of the development of religious laws started with the Warren Hasting's Plan of 1772. The notable feature of the plan was that the suits regarding inheritance, marriage and other religious institution, would be dealt with their respective personal laws of Hindus and Muslims. But all other categories of persons like Parsis, Christians and Jews would be the subject of English law. This point was clarified by the Calcutta Supreme Court in *J.S. Jebb* v *C. Lefevere and Caroline*,[201] where it applied the English law to the property of a Portuguese descendant situated in Calcutta. The court pointed out that there were only three system of law which were administered English, Hindu and Muslim. In *Jacob Joseph* v *Rowland Rowland,*[202] and *Emin* v *Emin*,[203] by a majority the court held that it had no jurisdiction to administer any other personal law except the Hindu and Muslim laws. Since the parties were not within the exception, the American inhabitant of Calcutta was dealt with English law.

The question was again arisen in case of *Musleah v Musleah*[204] regarding the application of the law with the Jew subject. A cleavage of opinion arose in the court and this was illustrated rather forcefully. In those days of uncertainty, the difficulties of the administration of justice were that of the ascertainment of law. Justice Grant forcefully disagreed with the majority views and held that the Jewish law should be applied to the Jewish subject. But Peel C.J., agreeing with Seton J. held that the lands in question would "*descend according to the course of the English law.*" Detailing the difficulties which the Supreme Court, would have to face if justice Grant's view was accepted, he said—

> "*...that it should decide one law for British subjects another for Europeans not of British origin. One law for American and another for Jews and another for Parsee ...all these must be admitted to be most grave inconveniences*".

The Privy Council ruled out in, 1856 that the English ecclesiastical law was not applicable to non-Christians.[205] The effect of this ruling was that in the Presidency Towns, there was no forum and no law, to give relief to non-Christians (other than

Hindu and Muslims) in personal cases like matrimonial and succession etc.[206]

Prior to 1837, the law applicable to the Parsis and their property was the subject of English Common law but with the passing of the Parsi Chattels Real Act of 1837, the Parsis of Bombay Presidency were relieved from the operation of the English law of primogeniture as regards immovable property but made them subject in all other cases of intestacy to the English Statute of Distribution, by which only 1/3 went to widow and the residue was divided equally amongst the children and their descendants.[207]

In 1838 Parsis made a request to the legislative council "*for embracing the rights of inheritance and succession that are acknowledged by the Parsi Nation.*"[208] But nothing appears to have been done until 1855. In 1859, the Managing committee of Parsi Law Association prepare a 'Draft Code of Inheritance, succession and other matters and presented to the Legislative Council. In 1861, a Commission was appointed who took evidence written and oral, as regards inheritance, and succession of the property between husband and wife, the Mofussil Parsis objected in toto, the right of females to inherit on the death of male Parsi and also objected to the right of married woman during covertures to hold or dispose of their separate property. These objection were overlooked and that the Parsis Intestate Succession Act, 1865, brought these changes that the widow and the daughter of a Parsi dying intestate in Mofussil, first time got a share in the property.[209]

Till 1925, the Parsis were governed by the Parsis Intestate Succession Act of 1865. After the passing of the Act of 1925 all the controversies were resolved regarding the application of law to the Christians, Parsis and Jews subject. All other controversies and objections related to the female's property rights were also come to an end. Now the judiciary had to interpret many provisions of the Acts relating to the right of Parsis females, which came before it from time to time.

In *Mancherji v Mithibai,*[210] the judiciary had interpreted the section 5 of the Indian Succession Act of 1925. In this case an intestate Parsi died leaving behind a widow, sons, daughters, children of predeceased son and widow of another predeceased son, who had died issueless and a posthumous daughter was afterward born, to the intestate. The share, of the widow of the predeceased, son who died issueless, was in question. The court held that the widow in question was entitled to one moiety of the share, which her husband would have taken if he survived the intestate and the other moiety of the share of the predeceased son, developed on the surviving issues of the intestate including the posthumous, daughter and the children of his other predeceased son.

Post Independence Period

A very typical case of *Ersha* v *Jesbai,*[211] came before the court, in which a father Ardeshir completely excluded his daughter, Jerbai and bequeathed whole property to his brother, who predeceased Ardeshir, so the bequest to him was lapsed. It was held that Ardeshir having died intestate, the estate must go according to law and Jerbai was entitled to the property.

Shapoorji v Rustamji,[212] Ratnabai died leaving behind a husband, two sons and two daughters, under the will of the father of Ratnabai, she had a vested remainder after the death of the life tenant of her mother but Ratnabai pre-deceased her mother. The question, in this case, was whether the English law of freehold property in remainder applied to Parsis? It was held that the case would be governed by the Parsi law in which there was no distinction between an estate in possession and an estate in remainder.

In the case of *Hirjibhoy v Barjorji,*[213] a Parsi intestate died leaving behind the lineal descendants in different degrees of predeceased brothers and sisters. The question was whether the estate was to be divided as per capita or per-stripes in equal share subject to the rule that each male is to take double the share of each female of same degree? It was held that the first division should be into three shares, two shares to each of the two brothers and one share to sister and the shares should be sub-divided among their respective lineal descendant.[214]

Current Position

It is quite evident from the above discussion that after the passing of Indian Succession Act, of 1925 the Parsis are governed by the statutory laws which are quite in consonance with their religion. Major changes were brought in the Parsi intestate, succession by the amendments made in 1991, in the provisions of the Indian Succession Act of 1925. These changes are so drastic that there is no need to further change and no apparent discrimination left over. The only discrimination, which one can say, is in the share of parents, which is half of each child, but if we see it in relation to the liabilities it is also not discriminatory.

References

1. Lord Bryce James: Modern Democracies, Vol. II, p. 484, London, Macmillan Co.Ltd. (1923).
2. *Ibid.,* p. 421.
3. Muthamma v Union of India, AIR (1979) SC, 1868 at 1870.
4. Upendra Baxi: 'Democracy, Equality and Freedom,' 1978.
5. Jain M.P. : Indian Legal History, p. 583.
6. *Ibid.,* p. 11.
7. Mehmood Tahir: Islamic Law in Indian Courts since Independence, p. 1.
8. *Ibid.*
9. (1964) 2 MLJ 519 F.B. (cited by Derrett): *op. cit.,* p. 26.
10. Hindu Women's Right to Property Act, 1937.
11. Al Quran IV : 35.
12. Al Quran V : 9.
13. Al Sarakhsi: Al Mabsut, XVI: 59 (Shamsal Din) K. al Mabsut (30 parts) Dar-al-Marifah, Beirut.
14. Ibn Farhun: Tabsirat-al-Hukum fi Usual-al-Aqdiyah wal Manahiji-al-Ahkam, on the margin of Fathal-Ali—al-Malik (Vol. 2) Matbaah Mustafa-al-Bibi-al-Halabi, Egypt; 1356, H : 1937 A.C.
15. Md. Shahir Arsalan; Al Qada wal Qudat, p. 8, Dar-al-Irshad, Beirut 1389 H.
16. Haji Syed Mohsin Amin, Amute; Qadwatha Muhayyir-al-Ugul p. 136. Chapakhanah Islamiyah, Tehran 1333.
17. Al-Muhib-al-Tabari; Al Riyad-al-Nadirah fi Manaqib-al-Asharah, Matboah Dar-al-Tahif 1372 H.
18. Mahmood Tahir: Personal Law in Crisis, p. 103.
19. 22. 1A 76.

20. 30, 1A 94.
21. Fyzee: Outline of Mohammadan Law, 51 (1974).
22. Willson: Anglo Mohammadan Law, p. 102.
23. Jain M.P. : *op cit.,* p. 89-93.
24. 2M l.A. 441 (1841) See Hayatun Nisa v Md. Ali Khan, 71 1A, 73-74.
25. Advocate General of Bombay v Mohd Hussain Hussaini (1866) 12 BH CR 323.
26. 11 M.I.A. 551 Fyzee Cases 281.
27. ILR 14 Cal. 276, 286-7.
28. 24 I.A. 196.
29. Daniel Latiffi: Change and the Muslim Law (ILI) Islamic Law in Modern India 99-102 (1972).
30. Aziz Bano v Md. Ibrahim Hussain II.R (1925) 47 All 823.
31. Tayyabji *op cit.,* p. 805.
32. *Ibid.,* p. 807
33. Mahmood Tahir: *op cit.,* p. 52.
34. *Ibid.,* p. 54.
35. (1970) KLT 477.
36. AIR (1925) All 522.
37. AIR (1928) Pat. 411.
38. AIR (1935) Oudh 78.
39. AIR (1936) Peshawar 178.
40. 43 IA 294.
41. Ind. Dec. (O.S.) IV 100.
42. Rankin; Custom and the Muslim Law in British India. 25; Transaction Grotius Society, 89 (1939).
43. 50 I.A. 108-111.
44. (1866) 10 MIA 511, See also: Surmast Khan v Kadir Dod Khan, IFB Ruling N.W.P. (1866).
45. (1901) ILR 23 All 20.
46. AIR (1922) P.C. 59.
47. Jain M.P.; *op cit.,* p. 619.
48. Roshan Ali Khan v Chowdhry Ashar Ali (1929) 57 IA 29.
49. 45 I.A. 10 (1917) Fyzee cases 94.

50. The Muslim Personal Law (Shariat) Application Act of 1937.
51. See-Mahmood Tahir: Muslim Women in India (Religion and Law Review) VI : 1 (1977).
52. AIR (1947), Mad. 287.
53. AIR (1948) Bom. 162.
54. AIR (1950) Lah. 12.
55. AIR (1952) All 640-41.
56. AIR (1955) Mad. 621.
57. AIR (1956) MB 56.
58. 8 (1956) 59 BLR 470.
59. AIR (1957) Nagpur 84 at p. 85.
60. AIR (1957) Raj. 154 at p. 157.
61. AIR (1959) Mad. 131 at p. 135.
62. AIR (1958) Mad. 144.
63. AIR (I960) M.P. 260 at p. 262.
64. AIR (1960) Jammu and Kashmir. 57.
65. AIR (1960) Jammu and Kashmir. 53
66. AIR (1966) SC 1937.
67. Mulla: Principles of Mohammaden Law 239, (15th ed 1961)
68. AIR (1968) Mys. 351 (1968) 2 Mys LJ 14.
69. AIR (1970) Cal. 387 at pp. 388-89 (D.B.).
70. AIR (1973) Jammu and Kashmir. 28.
71. AIR (1974) Guj. 4, See Mahmood Tahir: *op cit.,* pp. 202-205.
72. AIR (1984) Jammu and Kashmir 27.
73. AIR (1987) Kant. 222.
74. Mehboobi v Kampaiah AIR (1953) Mys. NOC 705.
75. Mulla, *op cit.,* p. 138.
76. AIR (1987) Mad. 129.
77. (1933) 145 Ind.Cas. 461; AIR (1933) Rang 393; (1885) ILR 11 Cal. 597; (1 889) ILR 11 All 456.
78. (1987) 13 All LR 38 (All)
79. AIR (1990) Gau. 70.
80. Illiyas v Badshah AIR (1990) 334 M.P.
81. Hamilton, Hedaya, (1994) 2nd ed. Vol. IV Book LI 11, p. 704.

82. AIR (1991) Cal. 205 at, pp. 222-223.
83. Mahmood Tahir: *op cit.,* p. 146.
84. AIR (1991) SC 479, p. 480.
85. AIR (1991) Jammu and Kashmir 8.
86. AIR (1993) M.P. 45.
87. AIR (1996) SC 702, pp. 702-703.
88. Mulla *op. cit.,* 18th ed.
89. See Shahid's Muslim Law Digest, p. 163.
90. Nooribibi v Ayeshabibi AIR (1999) Guj. 27.
91. (2001) 8 SCC 599.
92. AIR (2004) Knat 476 para 17,18.
93. AIR (1953) SC 298.
94. AIR (1982) Patna 89.
95. AIR (1970) Nad. 200.
96. AIR (1961) Ori. 92.
97. AIR (1951) SC 327.
98. Derrett, J.D.M; Religion, Law and the State in India p. 225 (1968).
99. Jain M.P.; *op. cit.,* p. 583, 3rd Ed. 1972.
100. *Ibid.,* p. 588.
101. Rungama v Acchana 4 M.I.A.
102. 33 IA 176, 187.
103. (1774) Mort Montr 353.
104. (1863) 1 MHCR 223.
105. (1865) 2, W.R. 321.
106. (1894) ILR 18 Mad. 168.
107. (1876) 1LR2 Cal. 262-271. See also D. Nath v Chintamani (1903) ILR 31 Cal. 241.
108. Sastri G. Sarkar : A Treaties on Hindu Law, pp. 58-59.
109. Salema v Lutchmana ILR (1898) 21 Mad. 100, 103, 104.
110. Mst. Thakur Daylee v Rai Balk Ram 11 M.I.A. 139, Bhawandeen Dubey v Maina Bai 11, LA.A. 487 Chotey Lal v Chunnoo Lal 6, I.A. 15.
111. Jain M.P. : *op cit.,* p. 598.

112. 3 Law and Society Review.
113. Kurain Augusty v Devassy Alley AIR (1957), Fran Pauline Lucas v Jersome Pascal AIR (1977) Mad. 270.
114. AIR (1951) SC 293: (1951) 1125; (1951) SCJ, 394.
115. The Hindu Women's Right to Property Act, 1937.
116. Sarawathi Ammal v Jagadabel and another (1953) SCR 939.
117. Gopal Singh and others v Ujagar Singh and others (1955) 1, SCR 86: 1954 SCJ 562.
118. Hindu Succession Act, 1956.
119. Smt. Kamala Devi v Bachulal Gupta AIR (1957) SC 434, (1957) SCR 452.
120. Gummalapura Taggiana Matada Kotterswami v Setra Veerawa and others (1959) Supp. SCR 968 AIR (1959) SC 577.
121. Ujagar Singh v Mdt. Jeo AIR (1959) SC 1041.
122. Sunka Villi Suranna and others v Goli Sarhisajue and others (1962) 3. SCR 653: AIR (1962) SC 342.
123. Commissioner of income Tax, M.P. v Seth Govind Ram Sugar Mills AIR (1966) SC 24.
124. Satrughan Isser v Sabijpari AIR (1967) SC 272.
125. Sukh Ram and another v Gauri Shankar and another AIR (1968) SC 365.
126. Nagindra Prasad and others v Kemponan Jamma AIR (1968) SC 209.
127. Mangal v Ratno (1967) SC: Mahesh v Raj Kumari (1996) SC 869.
128. (1996) SC 146.
129. AIR (1970) SC 1019, See Ram Pakhi v Amar Singh 1983. P&H 156; Sumer Chandra v Sardha Ram (1991) P&H 103.
130. AIR (1974) 78, Cal. W.N. 1011.
131. AIR (1977) SC 194. See also Vajiya v Thakarbhai AIR (1979) SC 993.
132. Kottiruswami v Veeravva AIR (1959) SC 577, Radha Rani v Hanuman Prasad AIR (1966) and 216; Mangal Singh v Ratno AIR (1974); Kuldip Singh v Surain Singh (1968) SC D. 881; Badri Prasad v Kanso Devi AIR (1970) SC 1963 etc.
133. Dindayal and others v Raja Ram AIR (1970) SC 1019.
134. (1983) 3 SCC 376-378; AIR (1983) SC 846.

135. (1985) 2 SCC 524, 533; AIR (1983) SC 905; See also Ram Ratan v Bajrani Lal (1978) 3 SCC 236; K.K. Ganguli v Panna Benerji (1974) 2 SCC 563.
136. (1988) 4 SCC 143, 146, AIR (1988) SC 2020.
137. AIR (1996) SC 1697; See also Nazar Singh v Jagjit Kaur AIR (1996) SC 855; Vijay Singh v Dy. Director Consolidation AIR (1996) SC 146, Laxmappa v Batawa K.T Chavdi AIR (1996) SC 3439.
138. AIR (1998) SC 2401; See also Lachho Devi v Balbhadra Rao (1998) AIHC 3696: Banarshidas v Madhav Rao AIR (1998) P&H 98.
139. AIR (1999) SC 1147.
140. AIR (1999) SC 928.
141. D.V. Jagannathan v P.R. Sriniwasan (1999) AIHC 4444 Mad.
142. AIR (2000) SC 434; See also Ram Sharan v Ujiyari (2000) AIHC 338, M.P.; Lalthachami v Laltha Chungi AIR (2000) Gau. 96.
143. (2001) 8 SCC 552.
144. AIR (2002) SC 1279; See also Yamanappa Dudappa Marve v Yelluba AIR (2003) Kant. 396.
145. AIR (2003) SC 167 (from Bom.) See also Anup Kaur v Anoop Singh Grewal AIR (2003) P&H 241.
146. AIR (2004) Ker. 16.
147. (1994) 1 Ker. L.T. 617: AIR (1994) Ker. 267.
148. Vidya v Nand Ram (2001) 10 SCC (2001) AIR SCW 2251.
149. Velamuri Venkata Sivaprasad v Kathuri Venkata Swaslu (2002) 2 SCC 139; AIR (2000) SC 434.
150. The Chota Nagpur Tennacy Act, 1908.
151. AIR (2005) All 113.
152. AIR (2005) Mad, 193.
153. AIR (2005) Kant. 194.
154. By the provision of the Section 6-A an unmarried daughter be considered as a coparcener and is entitled to equal share to his brother.
155. AIR (2005) SC 2588.
156. AIR (1924) PC 209.
157. AIR (2006) Cal. 6 (Jan).
158. Smt. J. R. Barge V.M.M. Barge AIR (2007) (NOC) 92 (BOM) 2006 (6) AIR BOM R.68

159. Komireddy Ventata Narasamma Kondareddy Narasimha Murthy AIR (206) A.P. 40 See also . AIR (2002) S.C. 3062, AIR (2000) S.C. 1908

160. Vasant Dattatrya Sarade V. Manohar Dutt AIR (2009) (NOC) 273 BOM

161. Smt. Akkayamma V. Statre of Karnatak AIR (2007) NOC 125 Karn, 2006 (6) AIR Karn R. 412. 25*Baktharatsalam V. Alagisiswamy AIR (2008) NOC 733 Mad

162. Sri Harikant Singh v. Shri Ram Krishna Sharma AIR (2007) Pat. 117

163. Ram Krishna Mutt v. Maheshwaran AIR (2007) Mad 180.

164. Smt Laxmi Devi v. Chain Singh HR (2008) NOC 2657 H.P.

165. Shri T.B. Maharaj V. V. Mandir Oasha Barsena AIR 2006 All .34

166. Angurbala Mullick V. Debar ta Mullick AIR (1951) S.C. 293

167. Soumen Kumar Kar V. Swapan Kumar Kar AIR 2008 Cal 213

168. Smt. Akkayamma V. State of Karnataka AIR 2007 (NOC) 125 Karn = 2006 (6) AIR Karn R. 412

169. Radhika V. Aghnu Ram Mahto (1994) 5 SCC 761.

170. Hira Singh Sardari Singh Parmar V. Smt Ram Kumari Bai AIR (2008) (NOC) 2655 (Bom)

171. Thilliammal V. Thandavamurthy AIR 2008 NOC 190 Kar.

172. Vasant Dattatraya Sarade V Manohar Datt car AIR (2009) (NOC) 273 Bom.

173. Kenchegowda V. K..B. Krishnappa AIR (2009) NOC 277 Kar.

174. Smt. Bhagirathi V. Manivaman AIR (2008) Mad. 250.

175. Devidas Udhao Gaurkar V. Smt. Vithabai AIR 2008 Bom. 183

176. Meva Devi V. Omprakash Jagannath Agarwal AIR (2008)

177. Jagdish Kumar V. Parveen Kumar AIR (2009) H.P. 13

178. V.V. Rao V. V.D. Prasad AIR (2007 (NOC) 226 A.P.

179. Encyclopedia Britanica Vol. V, p. 82 (Family Law)

180. AIR (1980) SC 707.

181. Ind. Dec. (O.S.) 1, 92.

182. I.M.I.A. 299.

183. 5Beng. Sad. Rep. 176.

184. Beng. Sad. Rep. 227.

185. Beng. Sad. Rap. 9.

186. Barlow v Orde 13 M.I.A. 227.
187. I.M.I.A. 240.
188. Native Christian are those whose ancestor are either Hindu or Muslim and converted to Christianity.
189. Jain M.P. : *op. cit.,* p. 455.
190. *Ibid.*
191. 15 CWN 158; See also Benoy Kumar v Panchan (1956) Cal. 177.
192. AIR (1964) Assam 59.
193. 9 Mad. 466.
194. AIR (1972) All 531.
195. 2 P. Wms. 216.
196. AIR (1995) SC 1684.
197. AIR (1995) SC 1684.
198. AIR (2002) SC 3161.
199. (1986) 2 SCC 209.
200. AIR (2003) SC 2902.
201. Ind. Dec. (O.S.) 1.92 (Indian Legal History, p. 417 Jain.)
202. Ind. Dec. (O.S.) 1,68 (1818).
203. Ind. Dec. (O.S.) 1, 778; See also Sarkies v Prosonomoye Dossee ILR 6 Cal. 794 (1818).
204. Ind. Dec. (O.S.) 1, 894.
205. Ardaseer Cursetjee v Perozebee 6 MIA 348.
206. Jain M.P. *op. cit.,* p. 419.
207. Indian Succession Act, 1925, p. 72.
208. See Sorabji Bangalies Parsis at, pp. 156-157.
209. *Ibid.*
210. 1 Bom. 349.
211. 4 Bom. 537.
212. 5 Bom. L.R. 252.
213. 22 Bom. 909.
214. See Gibson v Fisher L.R. 5 Eg. 51.

Bibliography

A. Venkataraman (Prof.) : N.R. Raghvachariar's Hindu Law, 8th ed. (1987) Law Journal Office, Mylapore, Madras–4.

Abdullah Yousuf Ali : The Holy Quran (meaning commentary) Medina Shah Fahad Printing Complex 1413 AH.

Ahmad, Aqil : Text Book of Mohammaden Law, 20th ed. edited by Prof. (Haji) Iqbal Ali Khan, Central Law Agency, Law Publication.

Al-Muhib-al-Tabari : Al Riyad-al-Nawadirah-fi Manaqib-al-Asharah, Matbooh Dar-al-Taif 1372H.

Ali Ashraf Thanvi : Bayanul Quran, Delhi Qutub Ashhadul Islam.

Al Hilli Najm-al-Din : Sharai-al-lslam, Beirut and Tehran ed. 1377 AH.

Ali Ameer : Mohummadan Law, 2nd ed. Calcutta Thacker 1892 (Tagore's Law Lecture).

Ali Ameer : The Personal Law of Mohummadans, 1880, London.

Ali Ameer : Islam, New Delhi Kitab Bhawan, 1906, reprint in 1992.

Ali Ameer : Spirit of Islam - A History of Evolution and Ideals of Islam with a life of the Prophet (PBUH), Delhi Islamic Book Trust, 1981.

Ali Ameer : 'Ayan-Al-Hidayah' (Lucknow) 1938 AD.

Ali Ameer : Urdu Translation to Fatwa-e-Alamgeiri (1922) Dr. Nawal Kishore Lucknow (Tagore's Law Lecture) 5th ed. 1926.

Ali, Mohammad Maulana : Mohammad The Prophet (PBUH), Al Madina Press, Lahore.

Alvarez, A. : The Progress of Continental Law in the 19th Century, 1919.

Amin, Mohsin and (Haji Syed) Amute : Qadwatha Mahayyir-al-Usul, Chapakhana Islamiah Tehran 1333H.

Anderson J.N.D : Islamic Law in Modern World, London Stevenson, 1959.

Anderson J.N.D. : Family Law in Asia and Africa, London, Allen and Unwin 1968.

Anand, A.S. : Justice For Women Concerns and expressions, 2nd ed. 2003, reprint 2004, Universal Law Publishing Co. Pvt. Ltd.

Arsalan Shahir Md : Al Qada Wal Qudat, Daral Ishhad Beirut, 1989.

As revealed by Allah : Al–Quran

Azad, Murtuza Ghulam : Judicial System of Islam, 1994. Kitab Bhawan, 1784 Kalan Mahal, Daryaganj, New Delhi.

Bailee : Digest of Moohummadan Law, London (1865) Part I, 2nd ed, 1875 Part II 1869.

Bailee : Moohummadan Law of Inheritance, London 2nd ed., 1874.

Bentham, Jeremy : The Limits of Jurisprudence Defined, (Charles Warren Reverth) Columbia University Press, New York Morning Side Heights Memxlv 1945.

Bentham, Jeremy : Introduction to the Principles of Morals and Legislations, Oxford Clarendon, 1823.

Benerji, Goorudas : The Hindu Law of Marriage and Stridhana, 5th ed., 1923, Calcutta.

Bhattacharji, A.M. : Muslim Law and The Constitution, 2nd ed. Eastern Law Book House, 1994.

Brijbhushan, Jamila : Muslim Woman in Purdah and Out of it, New Delhi, Vikas Bhawan, 1980.

Brierly John E.C. : (1968) English edition, The Free Press Collier Macmillian Ltd. London.

Buxi, Upendra : Democracy Equality and Freedom, 1978.

Buxi, Upendra : Law and Poverty Oriental Essay, Bombay N.M. Tripathi, 1988.

Chakarwarthy, Manas : Judicial Behaviour and Decision Making of Supreme Court of India, Deep and Deep Publication Pvt. Ltd.

Cohen Morris R/o Cohen Felix S/o : Reading in Jurisprudence and Legal Philosophy, Prentice Hall Inc, New York.

Coulson, N.J. : A History of Islamic law in the Islamic Survey, Vol. 2 Edinburg.

Coulson, N.J. : Conflicts and Tension in Islamic Jurisprudence.

David Rene, and David, Lane : Major Legal System in the World Today, the End of Social Inequality, 1982 Allen and Unwin (London).

Das, P.K. : The Right to Information Act 2005, Universal's Handbook,

Universal Law Publishing Co. pvt. Ltd. 2005 ed. Reprint 2006.

Das, P.K. : New Law on Hindu Succession – Property Rights of Woman and Daughters under the Hindu Succession (Amendment) Act (39 of 2005) Effective 9th September 2005. First print 2005, Reprint 2006, Universal Law Publishing Co. Pvt. Ltd.

Desai, Sandar Lal : Mulla's Principles of Hindu Law, 14th ed. (Bombay) N.M. Tripathi Pvt. Ltd. 1982, 19th ed. Vol. II 2005, Lexis Nexis Butter Worths, Email: editorial@lesisnexisco.in

Derrett J.D.M. : An Introduction to Modern Hindu Law, (1963) Oxford University Press.

Derrett, J.D.M. : A Critique of Modern Hindu Law, 1970 N.M. Tripathi Pvt. Ltd. Bombay.

Derrett, J.D.M. : Essay in Classical and Modern Hindu Law Court, (1995) University Book Traders, New Delhi.

Derrett, J.D.M. : Religion, Law and the State in India, 1968.

Derrett, J.D.M. : An Introduction to Legal System, (1999) University Law Publishing Co. Pvt. Ltd., Delhi (1st Indian Reprint).

Devadassan, E.D. : Christian Law in India (1319)

Dhawan, V.K. : Law Relating to Offences Against Woman, 2nd ed. Orient Law House, New Delhi.

Dicey and Morris : Conflict of Laws, 10th ed. Vol. 1, edited by Lawrence Collins London Sweet Maxwell, 1998.

Diwan Paras and Peeyushi Diwan : Modern Hindu Law, Codified and Uncodified 8th ed 1990, Allahabad Law Agency, Allahabad.

Dotton, Yasin : The Origin of Islamic Law, Law Man (India) Pvt. Ltd., New Delhi.

Dutta, Bhupendra : Hindu Law of Inheritance (an anthropological Study), Navbharat Publishers, 72 Harison Road, Calcutta (A.M. Brown Dr. Phil, Hamburg).

Eekelaar John : Family Law and Social Policy, 2nd ed. London, Weidenfeld and Nichlson 1984.

Ely : Property, Contract and Their Relation, To the Distribution of Wealth, Vol. 1 Book-1.

Engineer, Asghar Ali : Rational Approach to Islam, Gyan Publishing House, New Delhi (2001).

Engineer, Asghar Ali : The Status of Woman in Islam, Bombay, Institute of Islamic Studies.

Farhun Ibn : Tabsirat–al-Hukum-fi-Usul-al-Aqidah wal Manahiji-al-Ahkam (on margin of Falhat-Ali-al-Malik Vol. 2, Malbaah Mustafa-al-Bibi-al-Halabi Egypt 1356 H.

Fitzgerald, S.V. : Muslim Law and Abridgement, (1931) London.

Fredrick, Engels : The Origin of Family Property and the States, (selected work 1973) Vol. III Progress Publisher, Moscow.

Fuad, Abdul Md. : Encyclopaedia of Quranic Words, Deoband Maktaba Tayyaba, 1996.

Fyzee, A.A. : Outline of Mohammadan Law 1964 3rd ed., London.

Gonsalves, Lina : Women and Human Rights (2001) APH Publishing Corporation, 5, Ansari Road, Daryaganj, New Delhi.

Gulteridge, H.C. : Comparative Law - An Introduction to Comparative Method of Legal Study and Research, Cambridge 1946.

Hamilton : Hedaya Book IXL V (Gardy's ed) 610.

Hamilton : Hedaya (1994) 2nd ed. Vol. V Book LIII.

Henry W. Ehrmann : Comparative Legal Culture, Engle Wood Cliff, 1976.

Hidayatullah, M. : Mulla's Principles of Mohammadan Law, 19th ed. (1990) N.M. Tripathi Pvt Ltd. Bombay.

Holland, Thomas Erskine : Elements of Jurisprudence, 12th ed. 1916, Oxford, Clarendon.

Ibrahim, I.A. : A Brief Illustrated Guide to Understanding Islam, 2nd ed. (1997) Darrussalam Publishers and Distributors, Houston Texas U.S.A.

Ibn-al-Hajar : Fath-al-Bari, Commentary on Sahih-al-Bukhari, Cairo 1378, A.H. 1959 A.D.

Ilbert, Courtenay : Government of India, 3rd ed. 1898.

Iqbal, Safia : Women and Islamic Law (revised ed 1991) Adam Publishers and Distributors, Shandar Market, Chittle Qadar, Delhi.

James, Bryce, Lord : Modern Democracies, Vol. II, London Macmillion Co. Ltd. (1993).

Jain, M.P. : Outline of Indian Legal History, 3rd ed. (1990), N.M. Tripathi Pvt. Ltd., Bombay.

Jaising, Indira : Law of Domestic Violence, (A User's Mannual for Women), Universal Law Publishing Co. Pvt. Ltd.

Karim, Fazlul-Al-Haj Maulana : Al Hadis–English Translation of Mishkatub Masabih (Book Agency 95, Baitak Khana Road, Calcutta.

Khan, M.M. : Islamic Law of Inheritance, (1989) Kitab Bhawan 1784, Kalan Mahal, Daryaganj, New Delhi.

Khan, Rahmatullah : An Introduction to the Study to Comparative Law, 1971 ed. N.M. Tripathi Ltd., Bombay.

Khan, Badre, Alam : Economic Rights of Women, 1999, Adam Publishers and Distributors (Allahabad).

Khalid, Rashid : Muslim Law, 2nd ed., Eastern Book Co., Lucknow 1973.

Kiralfy A.K.R. : Pottor's Historical Introduction to English Law, 4th ed. 1958, Sweet and Maxwell Ltd., London.

Kidwai, M.H. : Women Under Different Social and Religious Laws, (1975) Semma Publishing House, Delhi.

Layish, Ahron : Women and Islamic Law in Non-Muslim States–A Study based on the decision of the Shariah Court in Isreal, Israel University Press, Jerusalm.

Louis, H. Jordon : Comparative Religion. Its Genesis and Growth, Edinburg 1905.

Macnaghten, (Sir) W.H. : Principles and Precedent of Mohammadan Law, Calcutta 1825 Sloan Madras, 1897.

Madan, T.N. : Sociology of Law, edited by Indra Deva, First Publication 2005, Oxford University Press, New Delhi.

Maududi, S.A.A.A. : The Meaning of Quran, Vol. I and II Delhi Board of Islamic Publications.

Mayne, J.D. and lyengar : Treaties on Hindu Law and Usage, 10th ed. 1938.

Markby, William Sir : An Introduction to Hindu and Mohammaden Law, KCIE, The Clarendon Press, Oxford 1906.

Md. Junagarhi Maulana : Al Quranul Karim-Translation and explanation (Urdu and Arabic), Madina Shah Fahad Printing Complex, 1417 A.H.

Mahmood, Tahir : Islamic Law in Indian Courts Since Independence, (Ist ed. 1997) Qazi Publishers and Distributors, B-35, Basement Nizamuddin West, New Delhi.

Mahmood, Tahir : The Muslims of India, 2nd ed. The Law Book Co. Pvt. Ltd. Sardar Patel Marg, Allahabad.

Mahmood, Tahir : Personal Law in Crises, Ist ed. Dhawan Printing Works A-26 Mayapuri Phase I, New Delhi.

Mahmood, Tahir : Statutes of Personal Law in Islamic Countries, 2nd ed. (India and Islamic Research Council 1995), New Delhi.

Mahmood, Tahir : Indian Civil Code and Islamic Law, Bombay, Tripati, 1976.

Mitra, Ram Charan : The Law of Joint Property, and Partition in British India, (Tagore's Law Lecture) 2nd ed.

Morely : Digest of Indian Cases, 2 Vols, London 1850.

Muhammad bin Ismail bin Al Mughirah : Sahih-al-Bukari Vol. 8 Al Bukhari English Translation by Md. Mohsin Khan 1984.

Murtaza, Malik Ghulam : Socio-Economic System of Islam, Islamic Academy for Science and Technology Peshawar (Pakistan, Malik Son's Publishers Book Seller Gulbargh Colony, Lahore.

Mulla, Dinshaw : Principles of Mohammaden Law (15th ed) 1961, Pakistan edited by M.A. Mannan, Lahore PLD Publisher 1991.

Mulla, Disnshaw : Principles of Mohammaden Law, 19th ed. (1990) reprinted 2000, Bombay N.M. Tripathi Pvt. Ltd. Bombay.

Mulla, Disnshaw : Principles of Hindu Law, 19th ed. Calcutta Eastern Law Book House, (1994).

Nicholas, Barry : An Introduction to Roman Law, 1962 reprinted in 1987.

Patashar, H.V. : Parliamentary Debate, Rajya Sabha (1955) Vol. 9.

Querry : Droit Mussalman, Vol. 2, Paris 1871.

Radhabinod, Pal : The History of Hindu Law, (1958).

Rahim, Abdur : Principles of Mohammaden Jurisprudence, Lahore, All Pakistan Legal Decisions 1963.

Rankin : Custom and The Muslim Law in British India, 25. Transaction Grotus Society, 89 (1939).

Rahman, Tanzil-ur- : A Code of Muslim Personal Law, Vol. II, Ist ed. (1980) Islamic Publishers D-18/J, North Nazimabad, Karachi-33, Pakistan.

Rahim, Abdur : The Principles of Mohammaden Jurisprudence, Allahabad Law Agency (ND), Allahabad.

Rumsey : Moohummudan Law of Inheritance, London, 1880.

Rumsey : Al Sirajiyah Translation of Sir William Jones 1792, Calcutta (IInd ed.) 1890.

Ryan, Edward Sir : Digest of Mohammaden Law.

Salmond : Salmond on Jurisprudence, 9th ed, London, Sweet 1957.

Schacht, J. : Origin of Muhammudan Jurisprudence, Oxford.

Sen, Nath Priya : The General Principles of Hindu Jurisprudence, 1918 (Tagore's Law Lecture) (1909).

Sen, D.N. : Indian Succession Act, 1925, 2nd ed., Kamal Law House, Calcutta 1989.

Sen, Nath Priya : An Introduction to Hindu Jurisprudence Ist ed. Allahabad Law Agency, Allahabad 1984.

Shabbir, Mohd.(Prof.) : Parsi Law in India S.C. Manchanda, Allahabad Law Book Co. 1991 5th ed.

Shahid's Akhtar : Muslim Law Digest, Allahabad, Premier Publishing, 1998.

Shastri, G. Sarkar : A Treaties on Hindu Law, 6th ed., Calcutta, Eastern, 1927.

Singh, Jaspal : Law of Marriage and Divorce in India, (1983) Delhi.

Sirkar, Sharma Churan : Mohammaden Law, Calcutta, Tagore Law Series, 1875.

Smith, R. : Kinship and Marriage in Ancient Arab, (1907) cited by Tayyabji in Muslim Law.

Srivastava, V.P. : Commentaries on Uttar Pradesh Zamindari and Land Reform Act 1950, Vol. 1, Eastern Book Co.

Tayyabji, F.B. : Mohammadan Law, 3rd ed., Bombay, Tripathi, 1940.

Tayyabji : Muslim Law, 4th ed. N.M. Tripathi Pvt. Ltd., Bombay, 1968.

Tripathi, B.N. : An introduction to Jurisprudence-Legal Theory, 14th ed., Allahabad Law Agency, 2003.

Ullah, Mohammad Al Haj : The Muslim Law of Inheritance.

Verma, B.R. : Walliullah's Mohammaden Law, 5th ed. (1978).

Vernier : American Family Laws, (1931-38).

V.R. Krishna Iyer (Justice): Justice at Cross Road, Deep and Deep Publications, 1992, Delhi.

Wilson, Ronald Knyvet : Anglo Mohammaden Law, (digest) VI ed. 1930.

Walsh, W.F. : Outlines of The History of English and American Law (1626).

Wall, Bhai Merchant : A Book of Quranic Laws, New Delhi, Kitab Bhawan, 1981.

Werner F. Menski : Hindu Law-Beyond Tradition and Modernity, Oxford University Press.

Webber, Max : Essay in Sociology (Translated and edited by H.H. Gerth and C.W. Wills, New York (1946).

Yousuf, S.M. : Economic Justice in Islam, (1988), Nusrat Ali Nasri for Kitab Bhawan, 1784 Kalan Mahal, Daryaganj, New Delhi.

Encyclopedias

1. Encyclopedia Britannica : Vol. 3
2. Encyclopedia Britannica : Vol. 5
3. Encyclopedia Britannica : Vol. 6
4. Encyclopedia Britannica : Vol. 12
5. Encyclopedia Britannica : Vol. 19
6. The New Encyclopedia Britannica : Vol. 16 15th ed. (1993)
7. Encyclopedia Religion : Vol. 3
8. Encyclopedia Religion : Vol. 15
9. Encyclopedia lslam (New ed. 2000) : Vol. 1
10. Encyclopedia lslam (New ed. 2000) : Vol. IX (Glossary and Index of Terms)
11. Encyclopedia of Supreme Court : Vol. 3

REPORTS

- 174 Law Commission Report on "Property Rights of Women: Proposed Reform Under the Hindu Law."
- Halsburry's Laws of England 4th ed. Vol. 8.
- I.O.S. Seminar Report: "Women's Right to Property: Comparative View of Contemporary Laws as Practice in India." R & L.R, Vol. VI, No. 1, 1997.
- National Convention Report on the Status of Women 1975.
- Parliamentary Debate Rajya Sabha (1955) Vol. 9.
- Rao Committee Report.
- Report of Collegian On Justice for Woman. Empowerment through law, Lawyers Collective Women's Right Initiative. Butter Worth, New Delhi, India.
- Report on Status of Women, 1975
- United Nation's Report 1980.

LIST OF JOURNALS

- Annual Survey of Indian Law (2002) Vol. XXXVIII
- Aligarh Law Journal Vol. XII 1997
- All India Reporter (1937) Journal 26
- All India Reporter (1937) Journal 104
- All India Reporter (1937) Journal 106
- All India Reporter (2001)
- All India Reporter (2004)
- All India Reporter (2004)
- All India Reporter (2005) Journal 42
- All India Reporter (2005) Journal 215
- All India Reporter (2006)
- All India Reporter (2007)
- All India Reporter (2008)
- All India Reporter (2009)
- Cambridge Law Journal Vol. 62 part (3) November (2003)
- Cambridge Law Journal Vol. 46 part (2) July (1987)
- Cambridge Law Journal Vol. 56 part (1) July (1997)
- Cambridge Law Journal Vol. 60 part (1) July (2001)
- Civil and Military Law Journal Vol. 37, No. 4-148
- Civil and Military Law Journal Vol. 36, No. 2 -142
- Cochin Law Review Vol. XXII March and June 1998
- Islamic and Comparative Law Quarterly, Vol. 1, No.1
- Islam Culture (An English Quarterly) January-March 1981 Vol. XIX, No. 4 (Winter) 1980.
- Islamic Culture Vol. LX, No. 1, January 1986
- Islamic Culture Vol. LXVlll, No. 3, July 1994
- Islamic Culture Vol. LV, No. 1, January 1981
- Islamic Culture Vol. LXVlll, No. 1, January 1994
- Islamic Culture Vol. LXIX, No. 1, January 1995
- Islamic Culture Vol. LXIX, No. 3, July 1995
- Islamic Culture Vol. LXIX, No. 4, October 1995
- Islamic Studies Quarterly Journal of the Islamic Research Institute Islamabad Vol. XX, No. 1, 1986 (Winter).
- Harward Law Review 853 (1922)

- Harward Law Review Vol. 107:181, No. 6 April 1994
- Journal of Constitutional and Parliamentary Studies, Vol. XXXIII, No. 1- 4, December-January 1999
- Journal of Indian Law Institute Vol. 32, No. 3, July-September 1990.
- Journal of Indian Law Institute Vol. 45-384, 2003
- Law Quarterly Review (1938) 616
- Law Quarterly Review (1966) 45
- Law and Society Review Vol. 28, No. 3, 1994
- Religion and Law Review Vol. IV, No. 1, 1995
- Religion and Law Review Vol. VI, No. 1, 1997
- Supreme Court Journal Vol. 2 (2002)
- Supreme Court Cases

ARTICLES

Ahmad, Akhlaq : "Impact of West on Muslim Education", ISQJ Vol. XX, No. 1, 1986 (winter)

Anees, Munawar : "Survival of the Sexiest", IC Vol. LXVIII, No. 3, July 1994.

Chadha, Purva : "Hindu Property Law in India and Gender Inequality : An Analysis of Hindu Succession Act 1956", SCJ, Vol. 2, (2002).

Chauhan J.K. and Singh, Divendra : "Human Rights of Woman", C and MLJ Vol. 36, No. 2-142.

Charles, Harpum : "Case and Comment," CLJ part (2) July 1987, Vol. 46.

Deborah, L Rhode : "Faminism and State", HLR April (1994) (Prof. of Law Stand- Vol. 107: 181, No. 6 Ford University)

Dr. Misra, Jitendra : "Right to Equality and Gender Justice," AIR 2004.

(Dr.) Qadri, S.M. : "The Quranic Approach to the Problem of Interest in the Context of Islamic Social System", IC, Vol. LV, No. 1, January 1981.

Freund, O' Kauhn : "Comparative Law as an Academic Subject", LQR 45 (1966).

Ganai, Nisar Ahmad : "Interaction of Custom, Personal Law and Economic Necessity, Relating to Marriage and Succession: A grotesque Situation among Muslim in Jammu and Kashmir", JILI, Vol. 32, 1990, No. 3 July-September.

Grantham, R.B. and Richalt CEF : "Period in Great Britain, Property Rights as a Legally Significant Event", CLJ 62 (3), (November 2003).

Hasan, Ahmad : "The Legal Cause in Islamic Jurisprudence", IC Vol. XIX, No. 4 to 1980 (winter).

Hon'ble Mr. Justice Kkatju Markandy : "The Importance of Mitakshara in the 21st Century," AIR (2005) Journal 215.

Irhami, T. Omas : "Inheritance and Equal Right for Toba Batak Daughter", L&SR, Vol. 28, No. 3, 1994.

Jain Prakash Chand : "Women's Property Rights. under Traditional Hindu Law and Hindu Succession Act 1956 some observations", JILI Vol. 45-384 (2003).

J. Ali, Aigbuloko O'Yakhirome : "The Widow's Burden Under Customary Law. Nigeria", JC and PS Vol. XXXIII, Nos. 1-4, January-December 1999.

Jurce, Vichit Vadakan : Special Issue (Southern Asia) "Women and the Family in Thailand in the Midst of Social Change", L and SR Vol. 28, No. 3 1994.

Khalid, Bin Syed : "Islamic, Resurgence and Societal Change", IC Vol. LX, No. 1, January 1986.

Khundmiri, S. Alam : "God the Contemporary Debate Islamic Perspective", IC, Vol. LXIX, No. 3, July 1995.

Kilane, Abdul Razzaq : "Martyrdom in Islamic Traditions and its Relevance in Islamic System", IC Vol. LXIX, No. 4, October 1995.

Lal, Krishna and Joshi, Ambalal : "Sir D.R. Mulla: On Rights of Widow of Gotraja Sapindas under Mayukha," AIR, (1937) Journal 104.

Lapaulle : "The functions of Comparative Law," HLR 853 (1992).

Malika, B. Mistry : "Women's Educationn and Exposure to Mass Media-A comparison of Muslim and Hindu Situation", R and L R Vol. VI, No. 1, 1997.

Masoodi, G. Saqlain and Dhar, Lalita : "Women's Right in Christianity: Some Reflections on Divorce Law", CLR Vol. XXII. March and June 1998 No. 1-2.

Md. Said, Md. Al-Ashmawy : "Religion and Politics", IC Vol. LXIX, No. 1, January 1995.

Mahmood, Tahir : "Role and Working of the Central Minorities Commission", C and MLJ, Vol. 37, No. 4-148.

Mahmood, Tahir : "A Recent Supreme Court Ruling on Christian, Hindu, Muslim Personal Law", R&LR, Vol. VI, No. 1, 1997.

Mahmood, Tahir : "Islamic Laws & Muslim Women in Modern India–Matrimony–Property Evidence and Crimes", R. & L.R. Vol.-VI, No. 1 1997

Misra, Preeti : "Gender Justice: Some Issues," AIR (2001).

Misbahuddin, M.A. : "Ideal Moral and Spiritual Guidance in Multi – Religion State (Nigeria) An Islamic Approach", IC, Vol. LXCIII, No. January, 1994.

Muhib, O' Opleye : "The Theology of God's Word from The Quranic Perspective", IC Vol. LXIX, No. 1, January 1995.

Natrajan, Saryu : "Right of the Women to Claim Partition of Dwelling House: Raw deal at the hand of Supreme Court," AIR (2005) Journal 42.

Prof. Md. Shabbir : "Muslim Personal Law, Uniform Civil Code and Judical Activism: A Critique", ALJ, Vol. XII, 1997.

Poonam, Pradhan Saxena : The Hindu Succession Amendment Act, 2005 Primary Changes Introduced by the Act.

Qidwai, Abdus Salam (Nadwi) : "The Shariah and the Exegencies of the Time," I and CLQ, Vol. 1, January-March 1981.

Rattan Joyti : "Uniform Civil Code in India : A Binding Obligations under International & Domestic Law", JILI, Vol. 32, 1990 No. 3 July & Sept.

Rheinsteem, M. : "Teaching Comparative Law", LQR (1938) 616

Singh, Raghunath : "The Hindu Women's Right to Property Act 1937, A short glance" AIR 1937 Journal 106.

Singh, Subhash Chandra : "Women's Rights Versus Minority Rights", SCJ, Vol. 2 (2002).

Sircar, Raj Kishore : "Does the Hindu Law of Inheritance (Amendment) Act 1929, Apply only to the Madras and Bombay Schools of Mitakshara Law?", AIR, (1937) Journal 26.

Siraj, Mehrun : "Women and the Law significant Development in Malaysia", L and SR

Sherani, Raisuddin : "Human Rights, Justice and Fairplay in Islamic Religious Precepts Relevance in the Modern Society", R and LR, Vol. IV, No. 1, 1995.

Shouree, H.D. : "Religious Fantacism is a curse for Humanity," C and MLJ, Vol. 37-148, November.

Wahiduddin : 'The Quranic Vision of God Man and His Destiny", IC, Vol. LX, No. 1, January, 1986.

PERIODICALS AND DAILIES

1. Law Teller
2. Lawz
3. Political Law Times
4. The Edict
5. The Indian Express
6. The Statesman
7. The Hindu
8. The Times of India
9. The IIindustan Times

ACTS AND STATUTES

- The Caste Disabilities Removal Act, 1850.
- The Hindu Widow's Remarriage Act, 1856.
- The Indian Succession Act, 1865.
- The Parsi Succession Act, 1865.
- The Hindu Wills Act, 1870.
- The Married Women's Right to Property Act, 1874.
- The General Clauses Act of 1897.
- The Coach-Behar's Mohammaden Inheritance Act, 1897.
- The Native Christian Act, 1901.
- The Hindu Transfer and Bequest Act, 1914.
- The Hindu Disposition of Property Act, 1916.
- The Moplah Succession and Will Acts of 1918-1928.
- The Cutchi Memon Succession Acts of 1920-1938.
- The Indian Succession Act, 1925.

- The Hindu Inheritance (Removal of Disabilities) Act, 1928.
- The Hindu Law of Inheritance (Amendment) Act, 1929.
- The Mysore Hindu Women's Right to Property Act, 1933.
- The NWEP Shariat Application Act, 1935.
- The Muslim Personal Law Shariat Application Act 1937.
- The Shariat Application Act, 1939.
- The Dissolution of Muslim Marriage Act,1939.
- The Hindu Women's Right to Property Act (Andhra Pradesh extention to Agricultural Land) Act, 1947
- The Uttar Pradesh Zamindari Abolition and Land Reform Act, 1950.
- The Hindu Women's, Right to Property Act, 1952.
- The Hyderabad Hindu Women's Right to Property (extention to Agricultural Land) Act, 1954.
- The Special Marriage Act, 1954.
- The Hindu Marriage Act, 1955.
- The Hindu Succession Act, 1956.
- The Indian Limitation Act.
- The Kerala Joint Hindu Family System (Abolition) Act, 1975.
- The Hindu Succession (Andhra Pradesh Amendment) Act, 1986.
- The Benami Transaction (Prohibition) Act, 1988.
- The Hindu Succession (Tamil Nadu Amendment) Act, 1989.
- The Hindu Seccession (Karnataka Amendment) Act, 1994.
- The Hindu Seccession (Maharashtra Amendment) Act, 1994.
- The Protection of Women from Domestic Violence Act, 2005.
- The Hindu Succession (Amendment) Act, 2005.

INTERNATIONAL CONVENTIONS AND DECLARATIONS

- Declaration of Human Rights, 1945.
- Universal Declaration of Human Rights, 1948.
- American Declaration of the Rights and Duties of Man, 1948.
- Rome Convention for the Protection of Human Rights and Fundamental Freedoms, 1950.
- European Social Charter, 1961.
- International Convention on Civil and Political Rights 1966.
- International Convention on Economic, Social and Cultural Rights, 1966.
- American Convention on Human Rights, 1969.
- Convention on Elimination of all Forms of Discrimination Against Women, 1979.
- African Charter on Human and People's Rights, 1981.
- Vienna Declaration and Programme of Action, 1993.
- United Nations Millenium Declaration, 2000.

WEB SITES

1. www.unilawbook.corn
2. www.islam-guide.com

Index

J

K

L

M